In the years between 1860 and 1880, dozens of bushrangers, some bold and famous, some little more than petty thieves, rampaged across the New South Wales and Victorian countryside — looting and murdering, 'bailing up' travellers, harassing police, terrorizing settlers.

Perhaps the most famous of these in the 1860s was a handsome young man named Ben Hall, the first official 'outlaw' under a new Act, shot dead by police in 1865. Other members of his gang, 'Flash' Johnny Gilbert, Johnny Vane, O'Meally and Dunn, were all captured or shot by their pursuers. Also outlawed were Frederick Lowry, the ferocious Daniel Morgan and Fred Ward, better known throughout New South Wales as 'Thunderbolt'.

Finally, in this second volume of his *History of Australian Bushranging*, Charles White examines at length the incredible story of the Kelly Gang — Ned, Dan, Steve Hart and Joe Byrne.

HISTORY OF AUSTRALIAN BUSHRANGING

Volume 2
Charles White

Rigby
in association with Golden Press and Lloyd O'Neil

First published in this edition 1975
by Rigby Limited
Adelaide Sydney Melbourne Brisbane Perth
Printed in Hong Kong
ISBN 0 85179 9655

The cover is taken from the painting 'Bushrangers' by G. Lacy
(With the permission of the National Library, Canberra)

CONTENTS

ILLUSTRATIONS

CHAPTER X.

BEN HALL'S GANG.

BRIEF SKETCH OF ITS MEMBERS.

For some time after the robbery of the Escort at Eugowra Rocks, Hall, Gilbert, and O'Meally kept away from their usual haunts; but were by no means idle during their temporary seclusion, and not a few cases of "sticking-up" in lonely parts of the bush roads in the Lachlan district were, not without reason, charged against one or other of them by the authorities and the public.

While the fate of their late companions—Mann, Bow, and Fordyce—was hanging in the balance they were arranging fresh plots under the very noses of the police. As in the case of Gardiner, a perfect system of "bush telegraphy" had been established in every locality where their friends resided; and as they invariably moved with a given object from their hiding places, and either returned direct to the place from which they had started or made for some other friendly shelter in another direction, they were always in touch with their "telegraphs," and were thus kept posted in every movement made by the force whose aim it was to capture them.

Upon these "telegraphs" the bushrangers depended as absolutely as did the officers of an army upon their scouts when in the territory of an enemy. Flitting on fast-footed horses from station to station in the disturbed districts, or mixing with the people in the nearest town, generally the head-quarters of the police, the "telegraphs" would pick up every scrap of information likely to be of interest to the hunted men, sometimes coming into contact with the police, and learning directly all they desired to know. And having satisfied themselves concerning police intentions, they would suddenly disappear and convey or send their news to the camp where the bushrangers were located. Occasionally one of these "telegraphs" would be arrested, but as nothing could be proved against him, a few days' confinement between the time of his arrest and his discharge by the magistrate formed the worst of his sufferings. And should a suspected "telegraph" find himself too closely watched or be arrested, others were always ready to take up the work. They were invariably young men, some of them mere boys, intimately acquainted with the bush, who could cover miles of the roughest country more speedily than the badly-mounted troopers could ride along good roads. Ben Hall, Gilbert, and O'Meally had hosts of such friends in the Lachlan district, where they had lived for years, and amongst whom their bushranging instincts had been developed.

A brief sketch of the three men just mentioned will form a suitable prelude to the account of their outrages.

Ben Hall was born at Breeza, Liverpool Plains,

in February, 1837, and was consequently but a young man—about twenty-five years of age—when he assumed the command which Gardiner had renounced. While the colony was ringing with the account of his exploits his parents were living at Murrurundi, where his father was a freeholder, and well-to-do farmer. It was at Breeza and Murrurundi that young Hall lived until he was ten years old. While at Murrurundi he attended school for about two years and a half, learned to read and write, and obtained sufficient knowledge of arithmetic to enable him to conduct his own business. Thus early in life, and while assisting his father upon the station, it is related that he evinced a remarkable degree of perception and aptness in regard to stock. If he saw a calf dropped, he could, in a year afterwards, identify the cow and the calf and locate them. When this lad was about ten years old, his father removed to the Lachlan district and took charge of a station belonging to Mr. Hamilton, about fifteen miles from Forbes, on the road to the Pinnacle. The son resided with his father upon this station until he was about eighteen years old, and was almost exclusively engaged in stock-keeping, looking after the stock of Mr. Hamilton as well as that belonging to himself and father. About the year 1852, the elder Hall returned to Murrurundi and commenced farming on his own account, leaving Ben on the Lachlan. Father and son never again saw each other. It was much against the old man's desire that his son remained behind; but the young man had formed an intimacy with Miss Bridget Walsh, the second daughter of Mr. John Walsh, of Wheogo, and nothing could induce him to leave the locality. The father, intent on separating his son from this connection, also removed, not only his own but his son's cattle to the other side of the country. A short time before his father's departure, Ben surreptiously left home and went into the employment of Mr. Walsh, at Wheogo, as stock-keeper. A year after he married Miss Walsh. Two children were born to him by this marriage, but the youngest was only about twelve months old, and still in arms, when Mrs. Hall eloped with a man named Taylor, and went to reside with him somewhere on the Fish River. Shortly after his marriage, Ben Hall, in company with John McGuire, obtained the lease of a run adjoining Wheogo, called Sandy Creek, which they stocked with cattle and horses. Up to this period Ben Hall was held in high esteem by the settlers throughout the district, not only for his generous, open-hearted qualities, always showing a disposition to assist his neighbours, but for the enterprise and energy he displayed in conducting his business affairs.

Very shortly after the elopement of his wife with Taylor, which occurred while he was absent attending a muster at the Bland, and after he had taken a most affectionate leave of her, without for one moment entertaining the slightest suspicion of her infidelity, he was arrested by Sir Frederick Pottinger at the Wowingragong racecourse, charged with highway robbery under arms.

The residents of the district were greatly surprised that a charge of this nature should be brought against a man who was held in such good repute. After lying in the lock-up for four or five weeks he was taken to

BEN HALL

FROM A PHOTO BY DAVIES & Cº MELBOURNE

FROM A PHOTO BY FREEMAN Bᵗˢ SYDNEY

SHORTLY BEFORE HE WAS SHOT

Orange and tried, but the jury acquitted him without leaving their seats. This was towards the end of May, 1862, and immediately upon his release he returned to Sandy Creek station and commenced mustering his horses. He had been engaged several weeks in this work, and the business was still progressing, when Sir Frederick Pottinger and Sub-Inspector Sanderson appeared upon the scene. They had good grounds for suspecting that Hall had been doing something besides mustering horses. The Eugowra escort had been robbed; and instinct and information had led the officers to Sandy Creek station. Hall was arrested on a charge of being in some way implicated in that robbery, and was straightway removed to Forbes. He remained in the Forbes lock-up some six or seven weeks, being brought before the Bench of Magistrates from time to time and remanded, at the instance of the police, for the production of further evidence. He was ultimately admitted to bail, himself in £500, and two sureties of £250 each, to appear when called upon. He was not committed. When he returned to Wheogo and Sandy Creek he found that all the labour of mustering his horses had been in vain, some of them having perished in the yards, and the greater portion having dispersed. After looking about to see if he could recover them he found they were hopelessly scattered, and gave up the idea of collecting them that season.

About this time the Police Station at the Pinnacle was stuck up and robbed of firearms and other things by Patsy Daley. The same night this was done, Ben Hall (unfortunately for himself, and by mere chance, he declared), happened to be stopping at the house of a Mr. Allport, on the Lambing Flat road.   To this house Patsy Daley went after robbing the Police Station.   The police tracked one horseman to Allport's, and from that point they tracked two horsemen, Daley and Hall.   Hall knew at this time that Daley was compromised with Gardiner, but subsequently declared that he did not know Daley had just robbed the Police Station. When he discovered that he and Daley were being pursued by the police, knowing that he was in company with one of Gardiner's gang, he fled. The police pursued and fired upon them, but they escaped, and from that time both openly took to the roads, and Hall joined Gilbert and O'Meally. Some two or three months afterwards Patsy Daley was captured when secreted in a digger's shaft at the Pinnacle.   Upon being tried he was convicted at Bathurst and sentenced to fifteen years on the roads.

Johnny Gilbert, who was the right-hand man of Gardiner, before Hall's troubles commenced, was a Canadian by birth, and came out as a boy to Australia with his family in the "Revenue," from New York, landing in Melbourne in October, 1852. Soon after his arrival young Gilbert commenced a fast career, and bolted from the paternal roof. Shortly after the first rush to the Ovens diggings he was located in Kilmore, where he associated with gamesters; and as he was generally "flush" of money, derived from no one knew where, he became an object of suspicion to the authorities.   Subsequently he crossed over to New South Wales, and next came into notice as a stockman in the neighbourhood of Marengo.   Here he made himself a general favourite by a display of good temper and fairly correct living; but towards the end of 1861 he suddenly left the district, and about three months afterwards re-appeared in company with Johnny O'Meally, flashly dressed and flush of money. It then transpired that he had fallen in with Gardiner, and joined his gang.

John O'Meally was little more than a boy when Gardiner commenced operations on the road. His father kept a shanty at the Weddin Mountains. Here he fell in with Gardiner. From being a sympathiser he soon became an active ally, and having joined in the bold exploit at Eugowra, he threw off all restraint, and plunged into the robber business with an energy and daring that would have been meritorious in a better cause.

There was another member of the gang who should be referred to here, for he became a member very shortly after Hall had assumed the command. His name was John Dunn, and he also was a young man. Born in December, 1846, at Yass, he was but 17 years of age when he broke away from the home circle, and chose the life of a bushranger, Gilbert and another member of the gang, yet to be mentioned, having persuaded him to that course. His father was a respectable settler in the district, and, it is said, rode many miles in the effort to find and reclaim his erring son when he was made aware of the ruinous course upon which he had entered. His fall was certainly not the result of bad up-bringing. He outlived all the rest of the gang, but after narrowly escaping death from a policeman's bullet he was captured and ended his life on the gallows, having been convicted of shooting down a policeman in cold blood.

In June, 1863, exactly twelve months from the date of Eugowra Escort Robbery, six highway robberies were committed in one day near Lambing Flat, and every succeeding day brought forth its "report" of travellers being "stuck up," by either two or three bushrangers. Now it would be of a solitary traveller "bailed" up and stripped of his possessions; now it would be of her Majesty's mail stopped on the road and the letters sorted by hands not legally appointed to the work; now it would be of a store invaded and ransacked, provisions and clothing being carried off in cornsacks and by the hundredweight. It was a serious time, a time of tremulous anxiety to every traveller, every householder, every storekeeper in the Lachlan district; and a time of ceaseless worry, hard riding and fruitless chasing for the police.

Let me give a few illustrations culled from letters and papers of the period:—

I was stuck-up about eighteen miles from here (on my way from Tumut) by two armed bushrangers (writes a resident storekeeper of Young, Lambing Flat, under date 30th June, 1863). They took my watch and chain, a gold pin, and £2 in money, and a railway wrapper. They did not attempt to molest me, and appeared very jolly and well up to their business. I had a little conversation with them and asked them their names. One told me his name was Gilbert, but from the description I gave of him I very much doubt whether it was him. The other would not give his name. They ransacked my buggy, not being exactly satisfied with the amount of money they got. and came across a little box containing some cakes and candy, to which they helped themselves, and then rode off, politely telling me they did not want to delay me any longer. One of them asked me my name, which I told him. "O," says he, "I know vou; I had some of your lobsters." So I told him he forgot to mention that he also had some gin and tobacco. He was one of the men that stuck up my drays some time back, and took those articles from the dray. There were no less than six persons stuck up that day, some within a mile of the township, and others on different parts of the diggings. This place is really in a frightful state, and it is dangerous to ride out of the town. They don't care about the police, and only laugh at them; they always have good horses, and can ride away from the police with the greatest ease.

There was no small amount of excitement here yesterday (says a letter of the same date, and from the same place). Yesterday Coupland was stuck up by two bushrangers, about two miles down the creek. The same two stuck up Howard, Murphy's bookkeeper, and robbed him of five or six pounds, in the afternoon. Emanuel was stuck-up the other side of Wombat, and robbed of his watch and two pounds, and so on.

About the same time the local paper contained the following paragraph :—

On Sunday last a travelling German saddler called on our reporter to state that on the previous Wednesday he was stuck-up on the Bathurst-road, near the Gap, by three armed bushrangers, and robbed of a packhorse and property to the amount of £60; likewise 15s, which was all the money he had about him. He describes one of the bushrangers as a young man, apparently not more than 18 years of age, light hair and fair complexion, riding a dark bay horse; another a tall man, with bushy black whiskers; and the third as a full faced man with foxy whiskers. When about to leave, the youngest of the three robbers turned to the German and handed him 5s of his own money to help him on the road, observing that he was not so badly off, as he had the horse he rode to sell, if he liked. About four miles from where the robbery took place, the German called at a settler's hut, and on making the people there acquainted with the loss, he was told that Gilbert and O'Meally had been there two days before. In answer to a question from our reporter, he said he gave no information to the police, nor did he intend to do so, as he, in common with everybody else, considered it useless. How long is society to continue thus disorganised, and its present state of insecurity to life and property to exist, and how long will the country bear with the reign of terror before it hurls the present imbecile police before the winds?

The fact is that popular conversation was divided between the daring of the bushrangers and the inefficiency of the force empowered to catch them. And it was about this time that "Bell's Life in Sydney," in a jocular sketch of the state of the bushranging news market, published the following *soi disant* telegram :—

Narrow Escape of the Police ! ! !   Last evening three bushrangers espied a large body of troopers, and immediately gave chase.   The darkness of the evening favoured the escape of the troopers, and baffled the bushrangers.   The appetites of Captain McLerie and Sir F. Pottinger continue in undiminished vigour.

The following letter, written by a traveller about this time, will enable the reader to understand the delights of travelling in the disturbed district while the bushrangers held the road, and also the indifference to the presence of the police displayed by Hall and his gang :—

I relate the following incident (wrote this gentleman) to show how very little Hall, Gilbert, and O'Meally cared for the police, and how they kept on good terms with the residents of the parts they frequented.   I left Lambing Flat diggings by Greig's coach, which started at four in the morning, to go to the Lachlan goldfield, about 90 miles distant.   The coach being full, the agent allowed me to ride on the rack with the mail-bags, with strict injunctions to hold well on to the ropes.   It was well he did, for some portions of the road were laid down with logs from 12 to 18 inches thick, and when the coach came on to these the effect was anything but exhilarating.   First a terrible shock, and then a continued bump, bump, bump for perhaps hundreds of yards. These parts were called "corduroys," and were a rough-and-ready way of making a road passable over bogs and swamps, until other improvements could be effected.   The stages were from 12 to 15 miles apart, and in the afternoon we reached the last but one before we came to the township, and it being a public house, most of the passengers got down, and so did I, to stretch my legs.   And when I did I noticed something unusual going on in the yard adjoining the inn.   There were four men on horseback, two standing, seemingly stable men or rouseabouts, and a woman, who I heard was the landlady.   I did not know them, but heard after we started that the four men were Ben Hall and his mates, and the reason of their visitation at the time was the following:—The landlady, who was a widow, had a week or so before gone to Forbes to settle some business affairs, and was away for two or three days, during which period it appears that the man she left in charge of the bar had started drinking, with the result that the yardman and groom and neighbours, and in fact all hands who came along, had joined in the spree, and the quantity of liquor consumed as well as provisions was something enormous, especially as there was very little money to show that any had been paid for. So, at their wits' end for an excuse, the two principals agreed to swear to the landlady on her return that it was the bushrangers who had come and helped themselves. She, who was always friendly to them, happened to tell this to one who informed Ben Hall, who came over and made the real culprits confess their guilt. At that time they stuck up no one on the coach nor any one in the house. But it was a well-known fact that they never did stick up many of the places on this line of road, and it was the general opinion that they were afforded valuable information as to the movements of the police by a very large proportion of the residents in these localities in consequence. As I looked at them over the gate I noticed that the spokesman was a rather tall, robust-looking man, with a fine frank-looking face, and wore a high felt hat and cord breeches and top boots—that was Ben Hall. A slight, fair man, looking like a horse trainer, had a slight, fair moustache and cabbage tree hat, breeches and boots, and had one leg crossed over the pummel of the saddle, listening to what was said—that was Gilbert. A flash, rowdy-looking young fellow, with keen flashing eyes, who was looking at the two men standing with no pleasant countenance, was O'Meally. At this time there were between 30 and 40 mounted police at Forbes, only a few miles distant, under Sir Frederick Pottinger.

But it was time for the gang to change quarters, and as a few days passed without report of fresh outrages in the Young district people began to look for reports from some other direction. And what everybody anticipated shortly came to pass. The gang had taken across country and quietly entered Carcoar, where instead of blackmailing travellers on the road or calling upon the driver of the mail to "chuck out the bags," they proceeded to "stick-up" the bank. This was no midnight descent, after the manner of the ordinary burglar, but a bold and open onslaught in the broad light of day, and it was quite by an accident that the designs of the robbers were frustrated.

Under ordinary circumstances the mere fact of two horsemen riding up to the Commercial Bank (which was situated in the main thoroughfare of the town), alighting, and entering the bank, would not have excited suspicion; but there was something extraordinary in the appearance of both men and horses on this occasion. The former were dressed, not like ordinary customers of the bank, but as "flash" bushmen, and the latter were animals of a superior class, with suspicious-looking pouches attached to their saddles. The door of the bank was invitingly open. There were no customers on the public side of the counter, and only one of the bank officials was in his place on the business side. That official was Mr. J. Parker, who, in his capacity as chief clerk, had full control of the institution for the time being. The manager, Mr. McDonald, was not far away, however. He had crossed the street to "see a friend," and happened to look towards the bank just as the two men entered the door. A suspicion at once crossed his mind that his presence at the bank might be required.

Having entered the bank Hall and Gilbert strode up to the counter and one of them handed to Mr. Parker a rather dirty-looking piece of paper, in form like a cheque, at the same time asking him to cash it. Mr. Parker took the document, but had no sooner begun to inspect it than he was startled by having a revolver presented at each side of his head, the action being accompanied by an assurance from the bushrangers that if he made the least noise or resistance he would find his brains on the floor. It was at this moment that McDonald, the manager, made his appearance at the door, and the noise of his approach caused both the bushrangers to turn their heads, although they kept their revolvers presented at Parker's head. One of the men, no doubt thinking that the visitor was one of the customers of the bank, at once called out "Come in, mate;" but McDonald had taken in the situation at a glance, turned on his heels, and sped down the street to give the alarm at the police station.

The momentary distraction of the would-be robbers was not lost upon Parker, who, although much alarmed at the situation, had not lost his presence of mind. In anticipation of a visit of this kind the bank authorities had sought to make provision for defending their treasures, and loaded revolvers became part of the bank furniture in every country branch. There was a revolver beneath the counter within reach of the startled clerk on this occasion, and as the bushrangers turned their heads to the door Parker dropped behind the counter, seized the revolver, and fired—not at the intruders, for the counter intervened, but into the air, for the purpose of at once creating an alarm and scaring the robbers. Both ends were accomplished. A Mr. Harrison and his daughter, living on the opposite side of the street, at once ran over, the latter calling loudly for assistance and attracting the attention of a number of the townspeople, who also began running towards the bank. At the same time Miss Harrison attempted to let the horses loose from the post to which they were hitched, but the bushrangers rushed from the bank, having realised the danger of remaining longer on the spot, and warning those who displayed an inclination to intercept them that if they did not keep back they would be shot, hurriedly remounted and galloped away.

Suddenly there came a report from another quarter. The gang had gone east, along the old Lachlan Road*, and had made a raid upon Caloola, quietly robbing the local store, kept by Mr. S. Hosie. Here also two members of the gang only presented themselves, Gilbert and O'Meally doing the business. They made their appearance in the afternoon, and going to the counter presented revolvers at the heads of Mr. Hosie and his assistant, ordering them to stand in one corner of the shop while they proceeded to ransack the place. It wasn't money they wanted so much as provisions, and of these they found abundance. Nevertheless they were not prepared to overlook money in their search. One of the intruders found £20 in notes and £5 in silver in the till, and this he appropriated with the remark that it might "come in useful." The other bushranger chiefly acted as sentry, keeping one watchful eye upon the "bailed up" proprietor, and the other upon the road; and while thus engaged he passed the most jocular remarks, and issued directions to his mate concerning the best things to take. Each of the robbers wore a belt in which four revolvers found a resting place. Having gathered together all they required, the booty was placed upon two of Mr. Hosie's horses, brought from the stable for that purpose, and then the unwelcome customers said "Good day!" to the proprietor of the store and rode off. Shortly after their departure a messenger was

---

* This road passed Carcoar a little south of the town, towards Cowra, and crossed the old Bathurst-Trunkey Road near Caloola.

dispatched to Bathurst with information for the police, and before midnight four mounted troopers were clattering along the highway in the direction of Caloola; but before they reached the scene of the robbery the bushrangers had disappeared, and no person in the locality could give information concerning the direction they had taken. Subsequent events proved that they had made back for the Carcoar district.

Hosie's store had been "stuck up" on the Thursday. On the Sunday the bushrangers paid a visit to Mr. Icely's homestead at Coombing; but in the interval between those dates the gang had been strengthened in numbers, a young man named Johnny Vane having cast in his lot with them. This young man had been living with his parents, most respectable people and reputed to be very well-to-do, in the eastern portion of the Carcoar district. He was a typical Australian youth—well-built, active and fearless, a splendid horseman, and fairly intelligent, having an intimate knowledge of the bush. That he had previously come into contact with one or other of the gang there can be no doubt, and Hall was no doubt pleased enough to receive him into the ranks. Little wonder, therefore that he should appear as a prominent figure in the gang within a short time after joining.

The attack upon Coombing was made at night, and all the members of the gang appear to have taken part in it. Mr. Icely was a magistrate and one of the wealthiest men in the district. It was one of the most natural things in the world that he should keep a good stable and that in that stable there should be exceptionally good horses. Now, good horses were in their way more valuable to the bushrangers of the sixties than firearms; hence they were always on the look-out for fresh mounts, and those of the swiftest foot and soundest wind. It was not a strange thing, therefore, that they should set longing eyes upon Mr. Icely's possessions, neither was it a strange thing that having the longing they should seize the first favourable opportunity of gratifying it.

Shortly after dark on Sunday the venturesome quartette stole quietly to the stables, and while two entered two kept guard outside.

On the night of the attack Mr. Icely had a distinguished visitor, in the person of Inspector Morrissett, who had turned in at Coombing for the night, after a day's weary ride through the bush after the bushrangers. It appears that the inspector and his men had come across the tracks of Hall and his mates heading towards Caloola, and they had followed these until they came across fresher tracks of the same horses making back towards Carcoar. These they followed until within three miles of the town, when darkness set in, and the inspector sent his men back to the barracks at Carcoar, himself deciding to accept shelter under the hospitable roof of Squire Icely. Sub-Inspector Davidson had previously called in at Coombing and left his horse for a rest at the homestead, the animal having been well-ridden about the bush in the previous search for the bushrangers. The stables were about a hundred and fifty yards from the house and were in charge of a man named Charley the German, one of Mr. Icely's employees. This man happened to observe some movement at the stables while the host was entertaining the inspector and other visitors in the house, and suspecting that something was wrong he went towards the stables, carrying a gun with him. As he neared the building he saw two of the horses being led out and at once discharged his piece, but without doing any damage. The fire was returned by one of the bushrangers, and with truer aim, for Charley was struck in the mouth. The alarm having been raised Mr. Icely and his visitors rushed out, but only in time to see the robbers making off. A glance at the stalls showed that a favourite grey horse of Mr. Icely's had been taken and also Sub-Inspector Davidson's animal, which happened to be one of the few good horses bearing the Crown brand. Morrissett then proceeded with others to Carcoar, and set the town in a ferment of excitement by the news of the robbery and shooting. The townsfolk did not know what next to expect, and they determined to make provision for the worst that might happen. It was clearly the duty of the police to follow the bushrangers, and if the town were left unprotected the gang might at any moment suddenly swoop down upon it and make a clean sweep of all its portable treasure. To guard against a surprise, therefore, twenty-two of the residents presented themselves before a Justice of the Peace and were sworn in to serve as special constables to protect the town, taking two hours' watch about in small companies. This arrangement having been perfected, the police were free to take saddle and scour the bush, which they did without delay—and, as usual, without success.

The wounded man was taken into Carcoar and

placed under the care of the local surgeon, Dr. Rowland. It was found that the revolver bullet had lodged in Charley's neck, and some days elapsed before it was considered safe to operate for its extraction. The wounded man slowly recovered, and thus for the present the bushrangers were free from any charge of actual murder.

As a spur to the police and a temptation to any of the friends of the bushrangers who might not have any scruples concerning the taking of what was called "blood money," Mr. Icely caused the following notice to be published in the district newspapers and posted in conspicuous positions :—

£100 REWARD.

Whereas the stables at Coombing Park, Carcoar, were robbed on the night of the 2nd August, instant, by two or more men, unknown, and the man in charge was fired at, and dangerously wounded; I hereby offer a

REWARD OF £100

to any person who will give such information as will lead to the conviction of the guilty parties.

T. R. ICELY,

August 6th, 1863. Coombing Park.

Finding that they could not catch the bushrangers while the telegraphs were allowed to watch them and report, the police decided that the next best thing open for them to do was to catch the telegraphs; but in carrying this decision into effect they brought themselves into very serious trouble, which very nearly cost at least one of them his life. After spending a week in the bush, riding hard by day and not infrequently camping out under a tree, almost perished with hunger and cold—for it was winter, and large quantities of snow had fallen on the ranges among which the chase had been pursued—they succeeded one morning before daylight in arresting three men who, they had good reason to believe, had been aiding and abetting the bushrangers. These three men were taken at once into Carcoar, and about noon were despatched in the mail coach *en route* to Bathurst. Fearing an attempt

CONSTABLE SUTTON.

might be made to rescue the prisoners, Superintendent Morrissett, Sergeant Grainger and Senior-Constable Merrin accompanied them in the coach, while Trooper Sutton rode the Superintendent's horse behind the coach.

That the Superintendent's fears were not groundless was proved before the escort had proceeded far on the road. When about four miles on the Bathurst side of Carcoar, three mounted men galloped up to the coach calling upon the driver to "pull up." This he immediately did, and the police who were inside the vehicle at once jumped out on to the road prepared to fight, for they knew that fight was intended, and that they would for the time being have to act upon the defensive. No sooner had Morrissett and his companions alighted than the bushrangers fired upon them, although in their haste they did not take good aim, and no damage was done. The police at once returned the fire, and the bushrangers fired again, this time also without doing damage—it is probable they hesitated in their aim from fear of wounding their friends who were still in the coach—and then drew back. At this moment Constable Sutton, who was the only member of the force on horseback, came up and charged at the attacking party, firing two shots from his revolver as he did so; but as he raised his hand to fire a third, one of the men shot him through the arm, which fell to his side powerless, and being unable to do anything further he turned his horse and rode back to the coach, the bushrangers firing at him as he went, evidently with deadly intent, for one of the bullets passed through his hat and knocked it off. Emboldened by this success the bushrangers rode forward an commenced to fire again, the fire being returned by the police, but without other effect than that of causing the bushrangers to again retreat. The firing was kept up on both sides with considerable spirit, the bushrangers being well equipped and armed with double barrelled guns and revolvers, and having discharged the former they continued to fire with the latter, until they found they had no chance of success, and as the police advanced upon them they gradually backed their horses out of reach and then galloped off.

The three men were very stylishly dressed and looked like gentlemen; but they were soon discovered to be no other than Gilbert, O'Meally, and Johnny Vane. O'Meally was riding Mr. Icely's horse, and Vane was mounted on Mr. Davidson's—the two horses which were on the previous Sunday night stolen from Mr. Icely's stables at Coombing, when the German was shot in the mouth.

The wounded trooper Sutton, who certainly deserved praise for his plucky attempt, proceeded with the coach to King's Plains; but as he was weak from loss of blood, the Superintendent arranged for him to stay at McNamara's inn, while the coach with the prisoners and their escort proceeded on the journey to Bathurst, which town they reached without further molestation or mishap, and the prisoners were safely lodged in gaol.

On the following morning Dr. Machattie proceeded to King's Plains by the mail coach for the purpose of attending to Sutton's wounds, which he found to be of a serious nature, the ball having entered his arm between the elbow and the shoulder and passing upwards crossed into the body and came out about the centre of the right breast. It will thus be seen that his escape from death at the hands of the bushrangers had been a remarkably narrow one. The same day he was driven into Bathurst by Mr. Major West, jun., and thereafter suffered a tedious recovery. It may interest the reader to know that Sutton was until lately an active member of the police force in the western districts, being stationed in Orange, and during the thirty years that have elapsed since this memorable brush with Ben Hall's gang his name has been constantly before the public as a steady, painstaking, zealous, and efficient officer.

The following letter written by a gentleman in Carcoar to a friend in Bathurst shortly after the occurrence here related will indicate how completely the bushrangers were masters of the situation:—

Carcoar, 9th August, 1863.

. . . . We are all here upon our mettle, and in a considerable state of excitement. The attempt to rescue the prisoners from Edric (Morrissett) and the three troopers shows that there are men not many miles from us prepared to do almost anything. You will know full particulars of the affray long before you get this. . . . . Sutton was the only man wounded, and he was shot by O'Meally. O'Meally rode Comus, John Vane Davidson's grey, and Gilbert a racehorse called Matheroo, stolen some ten days since from Grant —three first-rate horses, and Edric says all in splendid condition. Comus seemed to have been taken great care of and he said looked as well as he ever saw him, but became unmanageable, and almost brought his rider to grief. The attack doubtless was daring, but I don't think the bushrangers showed much pluck. They each had a double-barrelled gun and a brace of revolvers, but they seem only to have used their guns—the only shot fired from a pistol was the one that wounded Sutton. Pottinger and Morrissett are here with six troopers and a black tracker and are just starting out again. This part of the country really is in a fearful state and will, I am sure, get worse and worse. I am satisfied from what I have seen during the past week when in company with the police that it will be impossible to put bushranging down unless the harbourers are punished with the greatest severity. I believe there is scarcely a house between Mount Macquarie and the Abercrombie River that will not afford any criminal shelter when required, and I am satisfied that there are hundreds of lads in that neighbourhood under twenty that would give one of their eyes to have the same notoriety as Gilbert and Gardiner. They never work, never have worked, and are without exception the flashest lot I ever did see. Something must be done by the Government or things will become worse and worse, and what will be the end of it no one can tell. At present the police can get no reliable information. Morrissett, as you may fancy, is most anxious and would give anything to take these fellows, but he works as it were with a blindfold, and you may depend on it if the Government do not take the most stringent measures to punish most severely all harbourers, bushranging and its accompanying evils not only never will be suppressed but will get worse and worse, until consequences will follow which, I believe, it would be difficult to overrate.

Some time after the mail and its occupants had left the scene of the encounter, Gilbert and his companions —Hall appears to have been otherwise engaged when this attempted rescue was made—returned and found the revolver that had dropped from Sutton's hand when he received his wounds. About seven o'clock the same evening Chesher's Inn at Teasdale Park was "stuck up," and about £40 in money and property taken away. Amongst the property that was taken there was a good deal of spirits, on which, it was supposed the bushrangers intended to regale themselves for a few days. Before leaving Chesher's they insisted upon having some hot punch made, and compelled the landlord to partake of it before they touched it themselves.

The three prisoners were remanded from time to time by the Bathurst Bench, but no definite charge could be brought home to them, and they were eventually discharged. Shortly afterwards one of the three became one of Ben Hall's most active allies.

The bushrangers were next heard of at Trunkey Creek, where in one day they stuck up three stores, kept respectively by Messrs. Jamieson, Dominique and "Alick the Greek," and one hotel, kept by Mr. Stapleton. They plundered each of these places, removed a large quantity of provisions, ammunition and clothing, and then disappeared as suddenly as they came. The police appeared on the scene shortly after they had gone, and when out in the bush searching for them Sub-Inspector Davidson managed to shoot himself through the foot.

And it was just here that the *canard* of "Bell's Life" resolved itself into utterance truly prophetic. The bushrangers did actually chase the police. Among other detachments sent out into the bush near Carcoar was one of three, consisting of Sergeant T—— and two ordinary troopers. Fatigued with riding through the bush and not getting sight or information of those for whom they were supposed to be searching, T—— and his companions turned into a hut occupied by a man named Marsh, who had told them that there was a horse with saddle and bridle on running near his place. After dinner one of the policemen went out with Marsh for the purpose of catching the horse. The bushrangers, who had followed them to the hut, suddenly swooped down upon the two, and before any resistance could be offered they found their hands fastened behind them, their arms round a sapling, and their horses tied up at some distance from them. The bushrangers next went to the hut, and before the other troopers had realised the position they too were prisoners. Marsh and his companion were then released and brought down to the hut, and the bushrangers proceeded to appropriate the carbines, revolvers, ammunition, and even the handcuffs which had been intended for use against themselves; and having released the other two police horses—they were not worth taking, for police horses in those days were "queer cattle" at the best—they laughingly took leave of their victims, advising them to furnish a true and faithful report of the occurrence when they returned to police quarters at Carcoar.

About this time the Inspector-General of Police, Captain McLerie, made his appearance in the Carcoar district. So much had been and was being said, both in the press and in Parliament, about the failure of the police to capture the gang or any of its members, that the head of the force found it wise himself to pay a visit to the disturbed districts. But he had no opportunity to distinguish himself as a bushranger catcher, and the most he did was to visit the police stations at Cowra and Carcoar and make reports upon their condition.

The frequent outrages and prolonged stay of the bushrangers in this part of the country had the effect of attracting thereto Sir Frederick Pottinger, with all the men under him from the Lachlan district. On the day that the attack was made upon the Carcoar coach, when trooper Sutton was shot, Sir Frederick was swimming his horse and men—ten or a dozen in number—across the swollen Lachlan river at Cowra, a feat not by any means safe or pleasant; and under his direction the bush was shortly afterwards kept alive by the constant forward and backward—generally the latter—movements of small bodies of police.

But still the robberies continued, and every other

day cases of "sticking up" would be reported. One rather sensational piece of news was circulated shortly after Sir Frederick's arrival. He had been joined by the Superintendent of the Bathurst police, Mr. Morrissett, and it was said that these two officers at the head of a number of their men had actually chased, and lost, several members of the gang. The story ran that they sighted Gilbert, O'Meally, and Vane and immediately gave chase; after some miles Vane's horse fell with him, when Gilbert, who was riding Mr. Icely's stolen grey, immediately pulled up and Vane vaulted on to the horse behind him, the grey bearing them away in gallant style; the police still pushed on, and were gradually creeping up to the overburdened animal, when the two bushrangers jumped off and plunged on foot into a dense scrub, through which the mounted pursuers could not follow them. But the abandoned horses were not forthcoming, nor did the story account for their absence. Closely following this a report was circulated that the bushrangers had left the district and crossed the Lachlan for their old haunts; but if anyone experienced satisfaction at this intelligence that satisfaction was very short-lived. While the story was passing round, the members of the gang, whose numbers had been increased by the addition of at least one other district-bred youngster named Burke, formerly a "mate" of Vane's when the latter was engaged in "lifting" cattle, were busy carrying out schemes of plunder under the noses of the police.

It was soon evident that the plans formulated by them were on a somewhat larger scale than formerly.

One of the first was carried out between Bathurst and Blayney, when, during one afternoon the gang "bailed up" the Bathurst-Carcoar mail and six or seven individual travellers, chiefly horsemen, amongst whom was an ex-police magistrate and a constable. They had chosen a spot convenient for their purpose, on the top of a rather steep hill, and there, as the travellers one by one began to give their horses breathing-space after toiling up the height, they were suddenly called upon to "stop and throw up your hands." The order having been obeyed, the captives were marched into the bush off the road and there ranged together so as to give one man full command over them with his revolver. Only three of the bushrangers were engaged in this case—Gilbert, O'Meally and a young man wearing a mask. While one stood guard over the company the other two scientifically "went through" the pockets of the luckless travellers, the while cracking grim jokes, and assuring them that if they behaved themselves properly they need not fear any violence. The ccnstable was on his way back to Bathurst from Carcoar, where he had been doing duty, and from him they took his carbine—not for use but breakage. One of the bushrangers tried to discharge the piece in the air, but the lock proved useless, and he then broke it over a convenient log. The ex-police magistrate, Mr. O. C. Beardmore, submitted to the searching process with a very bad grace, although he had not much money about him. He had his cheque-book, however, and when this was brought to light he proposed to O'Meally to draw a cheque for £20 and fight any one of them at twelve paces. O'Meally treated the offer and challenge as a good joke and laughingly replied: "What a fool I should be! And if you shot me you would gain nothing, for my mate would at once shoot you." So what might have proved an interesting duel did not come off.

Having finished searching their prisoners, the bushrangers apologised for not letting them go, explaining that to do so would be impolitic, as they were waiting for the Bathurst mail to arrive. Shortly afterwards the mail drove up, and was quickly stopped and overhauled. Gilbert and O'Meally assisted to take the horses out of the coach, and then proceeded to open the mail bags, and sort the letters, all of which they opened. Six happened to be registered ones, containing in the aggregate £500 in cheques and drafts, which the bushrangers merely looked at and then threw down on the road. There was only one passenger in the coach, and from him they took £5, but returned him ten shillings for expenses on the road. Silver they returned, and they would not have anything to do with watches. One of those stuck up was riding a race-horse back to its owner at the Lachlan; they took the horse, and returned the saddle and bridle, observing that as the man in charge was a native they would not suffer him to go afoot; and they presented him therefore with one of their own horses in exchange.

As soon as news of this outrage reached Bathurst and Carcoar, men were despatched to look for and if possible arrest the bushrangers. But when the police got there Gilbert and his mates were many miles away. Two days after the mail robbery they crossed the Lachlan at Cowra on their way back to their old haunts, within half a mile of Cudgelong, the residence of Mr. T. H. West, J.P., from whom they had a week previously stolen a racehorse.

The gang's next appearance was between Lambing Flat and Cootamundra—then a hamlet of one or two houses, a store, a blacksmith's shop, an inn, and a small police station. The store, which was owned by Mr. Barnes, of Murrumburrah, had been "stuck up" some time previously by bushrangers, and O'Meally and the others who were with him proposed to stick it up again. Evidently they did not make a secret of their intention, for intelligence was conveyed to Mr. Barnes by his son, and that gentleman immediately started from Murrumburrah for Cootamundra, but was met on the way by O'Meally, who demanded his saddle and bridle. These Mr. Barnes refused to give up. He put spurs to his horse, and immediately galloped away. But O'Meally, determined not to be baulked so easily, followed, fired at Mr. Barnes as he rode, and shot him in the back. The unfortunate gentleman at once fell from his horse and died upon the road. The shocking affair was witnessed by some persons on Mackay's station, near which it took place, but no effort was made to avenge his death or capture the murderer, although O'Meally subsequently rode up to the station store and took all that he required.

Within a fortnight after this murder, Gilbert and O'Meally were back again in the Carcoar district, and resumed operations on a somewhat different scale. Hall, Gilbert, O'Meally, Vane, and Burke rode down one evening to the homestead of a well-to-do settler named Louden (Grubbenbong), a short distance from the little town of Canowindra. Admittance was at first refused. "We are police!" cried the visitors, but the cautious Scotchman replied through the door that they were more likely to be bushrangers. "Then," called out O'Meally, "open the door or we'll fire!" and in a moment there was the sound of a volley and the crashing of bullets through the wood of one door, with the sound of another door being broken open. There were four men in the house at the time—Mr. Louden, Mr. D. Wilson, Mr. J. Kirkpatrick and the overseer—and seeing that further resistance without firearms would be useless, they yielded to the demand, opened the door, and marched out into the verandah. Here they were at once seized by the bushrangers and handcuffed together, and then it was discovered that there were three other men on the premises, in a store-room adjoining the house; these Hall and Gilbert told to keep quiet, at the same time locking the store-room door on the outside to prevent them from coming out. The ladies of the house were naturally much alarmed, but Gilbert assured them that no harm should come to anyone, and ordered chairs to be brought for their accommodation. When Mrs. Louden was asked to "take a chair" she indignantly replied "I'll have none of your chairs!" "I beg your pardon, madam," said Gilbert with a laugh, "but it's your own chair."

When all the inmates were in safe custody, Gilbert, Hall and O'Meally proceeded to search the house, going through all the rooms and turning out everything upon the floor. They then ordered food for their horses and supper for themselves. Accepting the situation with the best grace possible, the ladies had supper spread, and the whole party were soon enjoying a hearty meal, each of the bushrangers taking care to have his revolver handy in case of a surprise. They helped themselves to two bottles of wine and handed a glass all round, meanwhile chatting pleasantly with their prisoners. The leaders treated the ladies with the utmost courtesy, and when Burke proceeded to light his pipe after the meal, Gilbert called out "For shame! in the presence of ladies!" and ordered him out of the room. After her fear and indignation had evaporated Mrs. Louden talked a good deal with Gilbert, who had rather gained upon her good graces by his somewhat pleasant manner and boyish look. She advised him to try some other way of earning a living. He said he would be most happy to drop it if he were allowed, but they would not let him work for an honest living; he had tried it lately, and even gone to New Zealand to be out of the way, but there he was hunted like a native dog, and had to fly from that country and come back to where he was known. They left about two o'clock in the morning, assuring their unwilling hosts that they would not be troubled again.

From Grubbenbong they went direct to Cliefden, the residence of Mr. Rothery, "stuck-up" the inmates, and took their pick of the station horses, which they rounded up into the yard and spent about three hours in testing. This was an exercise which appeared to give them great enjoyment, for they were adepts in the art of horse-catching and horse-breaking. They chose three of the best, and also selected two of the best saddles belonging to the place; and having eaten a

cc

hearty dinner, served up by the servants under command, they toasted each other in Rothery's champagne and sherry, and then rode off.

From Cliefden they proceeded to the residence of Mr. T. Grant, near the Belabula, and having spent some time in that locality, they made a sudden swoop upon the little township of Canowindra. Here they remained masters for at least two days, although the police were out in numbers in the bush all around them; no less than ten, indeed, were in the neighbourhood of Cowra in blissful ignorance of the extraordinary events that were transpiring within a few hours' ride.

They entered the town on Monday, the five coming down with a rush upon it from as many different directions. In their rush they swept up every horse within half a mile of the place, and rounded them up on a flat in the centre, near the hotel. No person in the town at the time of their arrival was allowed to leave it, nor any who entered the town during their stay. The horses had been rounded up to a spot within sight with the object of preventing any resident from stealing away with information; and the movement was effective.

Having imprisoned the solitary constable, they entered Mr. Robinson's public house, and made kind enquiries for the landlord, who happened to be absent. They then examined the till, and finding only a small sum, said that as "Billy" was not at home they would not take anything. Next proceeding to Pearce and Hillyar's store, they found three or four pounds in the till. This they appropriated, as well as some goods to the extent of £27 or £28. From the store they went to the other hotels, and bailing up every one who came in their way, caused those who were likely to resist or go for the police to keep within sight, making Robinson's house the centre. When all had been secured, the bushrangers prepared to spend the night in innocent revelry, and make themselves as agreeable as possible to their prisoners. It then became evident that their chief object in capturing the town was to create a big sensation, and show how effectively they could set the authorities at defiance. The townsfolk were not long in discovering that the bushrangers did not intend to do them much harm. Only a very few of the prisoners were called upon to hand over their money, and most of the money taken was spent in the township. As an eye-witness subsequently described the proceedings: "All hands were treated to what they would drink; it was then walk up, ladies and gentlemen, singing, dancing, negus, punch, instrumental music and all sorts of fun."

The "Bathurst Free Press" of the day thus describes some of the proceedings :—

On Tuesday morning, about 10 o'clock, Messrs. Hibberson and Twaddle, in a buggy, accompanied by Mr. Kirkpatrick, who was riding in a dog-cart, drove up to Mr. Robinson's inn, of which, in the meantime, the desperadoes had taken possession. The three gentlemen were at once ordered to alight, and were bailed up. Mr. Kirkpatrick was commanded to deliver up a revolver which he had in his possession; but he thought the whole affair was a lark, designed for the especial benefit of the visitors. However, that impression was very speedily removed, as the man who made the demand placed a revolver at Mr. Kirkpatrick's head, threatening to shoot him unless he complied without delay. The gentlemen then went into the inn, and found several other persons there who had already been bailed up. The bushrangers treated all hands to grog, but we have not heard of their treating any one of them with violence or taking anything from them. Gilbert went out and purchased a box of cigars, which were placed upon the table for the use of all present; and when one person enquired as to the propriety of using stolen goods, Gilbert said they need not be under any apprehension on that score, as the cigars were bought and paid for. They then induced a young lady present to play the piano for them, two of them dancing to the music inside, while the others were scouting or watching outside. The robbers would not drink anything themselves except bottled ale, and that only when they opened the bottles themselves. Messrs. Hibberson, Twaddle, and Kirkpatrick were anxious to get on their journey towards Cowra, but were not allowed to start forward until about 4 o'clock in the afternoon, when the scouts who had been in the outskirts of the township reconnoitring returned. There were three gentlemen present who were desirous of having dinner, and written passes were given to them authorising them to be absent for an hour. The hour passed over, and the gentlemen not having returned, Hall at once rode after them, and meeting them on the road they returned together. It is said that the bushrangers were in Canowindra at least three full days, during which time they acted the parts of rollicking, good-tempered fellows, treating everybody they met, and paying for all they took; and so far as we can learn, their spoils amounted only to £3 taken from Mr. Robinson, and the revolver (which they promised to return) from Mr. Kirkpatrick. It is also currently reported that ten policemen, with an officer at their head, were at Cowra when information reached that place of the state of affairs at Canowindra; but instead of proceeding, as persons anxious to meet with the bushrangers would have done, by the nearest and most direct route, they crossed the Lachlan at Cowra, and whether they got lost in the bush, or, as the river was rising at the time, could not recross it, we are unable to say; but it is pretty certain that up to the period of our informant's leaving they had not arrived at Canowindra. A large party of the police left Bathurst on Thursday morning, and another party yesterday, who, we understand, have orders, if possible to circumvent the bushrangers, or get upon their track and follow them; but not to return to Bathurst without fighting with, or taking them.

A resident of the district, writing a few days after the raid, thus described the individual members of the gang :—

The whole five are sober youngsters—none of them drink. They all have breech-loading rifles, and each has four revolvers. Gilbert is a very jolly fellow, of slight build and thin—always laughing. O'Meally is said by everyone to be a murderous-looking scoundrel. Ben Hall is a quiet, good-looking fellow, lame, one leg having been broken; he is the eldest of the party and the leader—I fancy about 28 years of age. Vane is a big, sleepy-looking man, upwards of 12 stone. Mick Burke is small. They seem at all times to be most thoroughly self-possessed and to perfectly understand each other, and being sober men are not likely to quarrel. They appear to be always talking of their exploits and of the different temperaments of the people they "bail up."

The winter of 1863 was rainy, and riding through some parts of the bush, over ground that would scarce bear the weight of a man without "squirting," much less that of a horse going at full speed, was no easy matter. This boggy state of the bush was one of the difficulties that militated against the success of the police; but it did not appear to hamper the movements of Hall and his mates, whose knowledge of the country allowed them to choose the soundest track. Not that they always came through easily. After leaving Canowindra they essayed to cross the Belabula river—generally flowing in an inconsiderable stream, but at this time "running strong" with flood water—and Vane was nearly drowned in the attempt; his horse, saddle, and bridle were swept away in the current, with all his revolvers and about seventeen pounds in money. But the loss was speedily made good; proceeding direct to Bangaroo, at the junction of the Belabula and Lachlan, the gang appropriated two fresh horses, and then lost no time in getting away from the neighbourhood.

A couple of days after leaving Canowindra they were heard of near Mulgunnia, where they fell in with two young residents of Bathurst, Messrs. R. Machattie and B. Battye, who had been out on survey duty and were returning leisurely homewards. Machattie and Battye endeavoured to "strike a bargain." They offered to run a footace or engage in fisticuffs on level terms with their adversaries, to decide whether they should give up or retain their horses and money. Hall was much amused at this proposition, but did not "catch on." The gang rode off, taking with them the surveyors' horses, saddles, and bridles, saying they would leave the horses where they would be found as soon as they were better suited. Mr. Machattie had to walk several miles before he could procure another horse, after which he rode into Bathurst, and gave information to the police. When in conversation with the bushrangers, Machattie dared them to come to Bathurst at any time—and that challenge produced strange fruits.

Meanwhile the gang had arranged another raid upon Caloola. Their first visit was to the store kept by Mr Hosie, which, it will be remembered, had only a short time previously been robbed by Gilbert and O'Meally. Hosie thought at first they were policemen, as they were accoutred exactly like mounted troopers; but on a nearer approach he recognised one of them. After a short resistance he was overpowered, and surrendered. The robbers then placed handcuffs on their prisoner, took him into the store, and proceeded to ransack the place.

In the meanwhile others of the gang went across the road to a shoemaker's shop, and marched the two inmates across to Hosie's with handcuffs on their wrists. They also visited the local blacksmith, who was at work in his shop adjoining, and fetched him, too, into the store. All the most valuable drapery and other goods taken from the shelves were now placed in three-bushel bags, while the articles not considered suitable were thrown on the floor. The horse previously taken from Mr. Hosie, which had returned, was again seized, while several other horses in a paddock adjoining were driven up; as some of them refused to stand still, one of the bushrangers fired among them and wounded two. A man passing along the road on foot at the time saw what was going on and mended his pace, but O'Meally followed hard after him and brought him up standing before he had got very far. O'Meally asked him if he were not one of the men they had stuck up at the time they stopped the Carcoar mail, "Yes, your honour," said the poor fellow, humbly touching his hat. "You deserve shooting," said O'Meally, "for giving my mare such a sweating;" and the humble captive replied "Don't shoot me, your honour!" O'Meally then marched his prisoner to the store, where he was kept with the rest until the packing was completed. Then they proceeded leisurely on their way, cautioning their victims against making too hurried an attempt to convey information to the police. Many of the articles taken from the store were useless to the bushrangers personally, but they had many friends who looked for reward, and these shop goods were accepted by them as payment for services rendered as telegraphs or harbourers just as readily as money would have been. After the robbery there were gay ribbons and fine feathers available for use in more than one house in that district, which had not been paid for by the occupants of those houses, although they at one time adorned the shelves of the unfortunate Caloola storekeeper.

After leaving the store with their booty the bushrangers called at the public house, which was at no great distance, and coolly put up for the night, after having laid the landlord under a £3 contribution; but they returned ten shillings of the stolen money, and paid the score for accommodation supplied and refreshments served to the amount of £2 8s.

After the bushrangers came the police—as usual, a long way after. As soon as the coast was clear, a messenger was dispatched to Bathurst with information of the robbery. Mr. Morrissett, police superintendent, happened to be at home, and he straightway rode up the hills to Caloola with his men— and rode back again. They might just as well have stayed at home and whistled for the bushrangers to come and be caught. They interviewed the victims at Caloola, inspected the premises through which the bushrangers has so recently passed, and then set off upon the track which they were supposed to have taken, but found themselves again outwitted and outpaced; although, had they but known it, the full gang of which they were in search was almost within hailing distance, engaged in arranging for an attack upon the very headquarters of the Western police—the centre from which issued all local orders, and to which all reports were sent. Like Mohammed, if the mountain would not come to them they would go to the mountain.

CHAPTER XI.

THE RAID UPON BATHURST.

Surveyor Machattie, when conversing with the members of the gang on the road from Mulgunnia, had dared them to pay a visit to Bathurst. By men whose whole career had been one uninterrupted series of successes such a challenge was not likely to pass unheeded. They would go to Bathurst—not so much to make a haul as to create a scare and make a big sensation. They left the police looking for them among the mountains between Caloola and Carcoar, or watching the houses of those suspected of being harbourers, and came quietly towards the headquarters which the police had left. It was a bold, yet not an unexpected movement, for many a half-earnest jest had been passing among the townspeople for some time concerning such a visit. It would not give the bushrangers much trouble, and was not likely to be attended with more danger than many of the exploits in which they had engaged right under the eyes of the force specially charged with their capture.

A beautifully calm Saturday night in October, and an hour when the citizens had temporarily ceased from business to partake of the evening meal, was chosen for the sensational raid. Oil lamps and candles were beginning to shed their light in shops and through the windows across the footpaths in the main thorough-fares—there was no gas in those days—when five horsemen were seen by the few persons abroad jogging quietly down William-street in the gloaming. The sight was not by any means an unusual one; it was the practice then for the country youth to ride into town in companies of four and five to "see the sights o' market nights," and the general market night of the week in Bathurst, as in other places, was that of the last day of the week.

Having posted Vane in a lane just off the main street (the lane which runs along the side of the Technical College buildings), the other four (Hall, Gilbert, O'Meally, and Burke) crossed the street to a gunsmith's shop kept by Mr. Pedrotta, in front of which two of them dismounted and handed the reins of their horses to their companions, who sat on their horses facing the shop. Entering the shop as ordinary customers they said no word and made no sign calcu-lated to awaken the curiosity or suspicion of the pro-prietor, who at once proceeded to ask "What can I do for you, gentlemen?" They wanted some revolvers, and politely asked Mr. Pedrotta to show them one or two of his best. The best goods were exhibited, but these customers appeared hard to please. They wanted "rifle revolvers." Mr. Pedrotta shook his head and informed them that he did not keep such articles in stock. "Then show us some double trigger re-volvers." But this article also was absent; and after critically examining the "six-shooters" that were ex-hibited to them, they declared that none were good enough, left the shop, and quietly remounted their horses.

A few doors lower down the street was a shop kept by Mr. McMinn, watchmaker and jeweller. Another halt was quietly called; the same two again dismounted, while their companions remained in charge. Mr. McMinn and his family were at tea at the time in a room at the rear, having left the shop in charge of a young male assistant. Stepping forward to serve, this young man was startled into terrified silence by the discovery that he was looking straight into the barrel of a revolver. He was ordered into a sideroom, and from it saw the other "customer" preparing to help himself to the valuables contained in a glass case on the counter. But the case was locked and could not be opened without breaking; and as breaking glass makes noise and noise attracts attention—two things which the men in the shop desired to avoid—they abandoned the case, and were appropriating articles from another part of the shop, when an interruption occurred. Miss McMinn opened the door leading into the shop, took in the situation at a glance, and screamed. The bushrangers hurried from the shop and remounted their horses, warning the lady and the other members of the family who had rushed forward upon hearing the cries of alarm, that they would meet danger if they followed them to the door.

Meanwhile the two mounted members of the gang had summoned the proprietor of a fruit shop adjoining and ordered some of his best oranges; and the shop man was in the act of handing up the oranges when the others emerged from McMinn's. To vault into the saddles was the work of a moment, and snatching some of the oranges the five men rode in a bunch down the street at a "jog." They had not gone many paces, however, when Mrs. McMinn came to the door of the shop and raised a public alarm, crying out that the horsemen were bushrangers and that the shop had been robbed by them. This brought all her neighbours into the street, and as one and another began to run out the bushrangers put spurs to their horses and set off at a hand gallop, heading down the street in the direction of the police barracks. At the corner where the School of Arts now stands, however, a further cause for commotion arose. Three of the men turned their horses into Howick-street, but as the other two were heading straight for the barracks, one of the former fired a revolver in the air to attract their attention, and they at once took the hint, checked their horses and wheeled round after their companions. The shot from the revolver rang out upon the night air as a note of war, and the townsfolk who were running after the horsemen dodged into places of safety, imagining that they were being fired at. From Howick-street the bushrangers crossed the Square, then mostly open land, into George-street, and headed for the top of the town; and when they reached a quarter which had not been disturbed by the noise, they slackened their pace and eventually pulled up in a quiet corner, arranging a visit to another citizen well known to at least one of the gang.

While they were thus engaged the whole of the business portion of the town was in a great state of perturbation. Information of the raid had been con-

veyed to the police barracks, and within a very short
time every available man at the station belonging to
the mounted police was in the saddle.   All told, the
number of mounted pursuers only amounted to five,
and these started off at a brisk pace along the course
taken by the bushrangers.   They had a brisk night
ride for nothing, for while they were plunging along
one of the roads leading from the town, believing that
the men they wanted to catch had again taken to the
bush, and were making back towards either Caloola or
Carcoar, those men were coolly continuing their depre-
datory work within the town boundaries.   In their
haste the police had overlooked the bushrangers, riding past the very spot where their horses were standing and within a stone's throw of the very house which
they were overhauling.

Meanwhile the civilians had abandoned business.
Several of the shopkeepers hurriedly put up their shut-
ters, fearing they knew not what.   Those who had no
shops to attend to formed in knots at street corners and
elsewhere to exchange opinions concerning the probabilities of the chase, leaving their womenkind to lock
the doors from within.   Suddenly a fresh turn was
given to the conversation.   Word was passed round
that the bushrangers were still in the town, and that
while they had been pictured as riding at a break-neck
speed over the gullies and ranges leading back to their
retreat, they had been making merriment for themselves and trouble for others in the house of a popular
alderman of the borough.

That report was true.   Having placed their horses
where they could not be seen from the street they had

entered the hotel kept by Alderman DeClouet, in Piper-
street, and had bailed up the inmates, who had not yet
heard of the disturbance in the centre of the town.
Gilbert, who had formerly been a jockey in the service
of Mr. DeClouet, took possession of the bar, revolver
in hand, and examined the till, but finding only silver
he put it back.   He, however, continued in occupation,
whilst another of the men walked into Mrs. DeClouet's
bedroom, where she was just preparing the children
for bed   From her he obtained the contents of the
cashbox and a silver watch.   Meanwhile two of the
other men were engaged with Mr. DeClouet himself,
from whom they took a valuable silver watch and a one
pound note; they also took two pounds from a young
man, a lodger in the house.   During their stay they
enquired from the landlord where "Pasha" was.   This
was a favourite racehorse which Gilbert knew was kept
by the alderman.   Information had been received during the day, however, that the party were near the
town and might require a good horse, and to provide
against the possibility of losing his favourite, Mr. De-
Clouet had him removed during the day to a horse
box; and as on search the animal could not be seen,
the bushrangers were obliged to leave without having
accomplished this part of their purpose.

They disappeared quietly, taking the direction of
Caloola, while their pursuers were heading for Carcoar.

It subsequently transpired that they had not forgotten the promise made to Mr. Machattie, when parting from him near Mulgunnia, after having robbed
him of his horse.   They said they would return the

animal and send him word where it was to be found. This undertaking they carried out to the letter; before leaving the Sportsman's Arms they left a message for him to the effect that his horse and also that taken from Mr. Battye would be found in Mutton's paddock on the Vale Road, about a mile from town. On the following morning Mr. Machattie's horse was found in the spot indicated, but the other horse either was not left there or was subsequently taken away again by the gang, as they passed the paddock on their way out of town. They also told Mr. DeClouet that if Mr. Machattie had not dared them to come to Bathurst they would never have thought of coming, but they were not disposed to neglect a good chance of "having a lark" when the opportunity offered.

The excitement in Bathurst did not die out with their disappearance. On the Sunday it formed the topic of conversation in church and out of church. During the day the Police Magistrate, Dr. Palmer, issued circulars to all the principal inhabitants, requesting them to attend at the Court-house on the following morning to "consider what course should be taken to protect the town in the present emergency." Many others besides those invited attended on Monday morning, and business was partially suspended while the best means of protecting the town in case of another raid—which many considered not a remote contingency—was fully discussed.

Dr. Palmer, the Police Magistrate, was called to the chair. After explaining the motives which had prompted him to convene the meeting, he said he thought it was not probable that the bushrangers would visit the town during the night; but he hoped that all the residents who could do so would arm themselves and be prepared to meet them if they should visit Bathurst again. The police appointed to town duty were fourteen in number, being one senior-constable and six others for day duty, and one senior-constable and five others for night duty, besides the watch-house keeper; these men were all well and fully armed, and were ready and willing at any moment to give every assistance, if required. He was of opinion that it would be better at that meeting to deal with the question in a general way rather than to go into minute particulars, for he believed there were some who would convey the intelligence to the bushrangers, and he had no doubt there were some in that room who were prepared to adopt that course. This was rather a reflection upon the loyalty of the meeting, but no one resented the remark, and he proceeded to express the opinion that it would be wise to appoint a committee to deal with the minutiæ of the matter, and by that means arrangements might be made that would not reach the ears of the bushrangers.

Then followed a discussion. It was argued that five policemen were not sufficient for night duty in the town, and that for the proper protection of the inhabitants a number of special constables should be sworn in, who with the town police should be placed under the orders of the Police Magistrate (who resided in town), and not have to wait for instructions from an officer of the force, whose duty might call him fifty or sixty miles from Bathurst.

Eventually the following resolutions were put and carried *nem con.*:—

1. It is the opinion of this meeting that, for the better protection of life and property in this town, a number of special constables should be immediately sworn in and equipped by the Government, and parties willing to volunteer to form a mounted body (and find their own horses) for protection at night, be immediately enrolled, and that they may be placed under the control of the Police Magistrate and Magistrates; and that the Inspector-General be requested to place the police (at present allotted for the protection of the town) under the same authorities.

2. That a committee be appointed to take into consideration the necessary steps for protecting life and property in Bathurst, and also to communicate with the Government as to the schemes to be devised for the capture of bushrangers, and the suppression of bushranging—the committee to consist of the Mayor, the Police Magistrate, Mr. Webb, Dr. Machattie, Mr. Robinson, Mr. Hawkins, Dr. Connell, Mr. W. Lee, sen., Mr. John Dargin, Mr. Stanger, Mr. J. C. White, Dr. McDonagh, Mr. Kinna, Mr. J. DeClouet, and Mr. W. Farrand; five to form a quorum.

Before the meeting closed the chairman said he had already communicated with the Colonial Secretary in Sydney, informing him of the steps that were being taken, and he had just received a wire from that gentleman to the following effect:—

The Government will most cordially co-operate with the inhabitants of the town of Bathurst in any steps such as you suggest. Keep me apprised of anything you hear. In the absence of the police officer you may do what you think best.

A number of those present then presented themselves to be sworn in as special constables by the Police Magistrate, and arrangements were perfected for these to patrol the town, singly or in batches, during the hours of darkness, fully equipped with such weapons as were deemed necessary to enable them to defend the lives and properties of their fellow townsmen from any

DD

attack the bushrangers might make upon their persons and possessions.

Sunday and Monday passed quietly, but on Tuesday evening Bathurst was again thrown into a state of great excitement by the announcement that the gang had committed a series of robberies on the Vale Road, within a mile of the town. They had found a safe shelter during the intervening time with some friends, who kept them posted in every movement of the police; and when the latter had returned to headquarters on Tuesday evening, they were ready to commence work afresh.

Their first visit was to a store kept by Mr. E. Mutton, on the Vale Road. about a mile from the police barracks; this happened to be closed, and all the doors fastened, so that they could not obtain an entrance without resorting to force. Foiled here, the bushrangers paid a visit to the owner's mother, who resided near the store. She admitted them, but refused to let them have the key of the store. They then searched her house, and whilst turning over the bedclothes one of them, who was holding a candle, accidentally set fire to the bedcurtains. They at once exerted themselves to the utmost to extinguish the flames, and one of them burnt one of his hands severely; Mrs. Mutton gave him some Holloway's ointment with which to dress it, meanwhile talking seriously to them about the evil courses they were pursuing. They listened in patience for a time, but soon mounted their horses and rode away along the main road leading to Caloola. As soon as they had left, Mrs. Mutton sent her son, Mr. John Mutton, who resided near, into Bathurst for the police, who went out at once, arriving about half-an-hour after the bushrangers had left.

Meanwhile the gang had reached a hotel on the Vale Road kept by Mr. Walker, about a mile and a half from Mrs. Mutton's, and adjoining Orton Park homestead, the residence of Mr. C. McPhillamy. Here the police would have come up with them had they kept on the road; but the "superior" officer in charge decided to take a branch road, and so kept his men beyond the range of the bushrangers' revolvers.

At Walker's they stayed twenty minutes, but found little worth taking; at a roadside store half-a-mile beyond, however, they made quite a large haul in the shape of tobacco, tea, sugar, sardines, flannel and draperies, and spent fully three-quarters of an hour upon the premises. The goods—amounting to about £50 in value—they packed in pillow slips taken from the bedrooms, and regaled themselves while at work upon tinned fish and sauce. They emptied the till of its contents, some twenty-five shillings, and took one shilling and sixpence from one of the children's boxes, in spite of the mother's protest. They then rode off, laden with stolen property.

While Hall and his mates were at the store, Captain McLerie and his men arrived at Walker's on foot, having left their horses—for some reason best known to themselves—at some distance. They were returning from an unsuccessful hunt at the back of the Bald Hills, and had crossed over to the Vale Road. Entering the inn the gallant captain found Walker calmly smoking, with the view no doubt of soothing his nerves after the shock to which they had been subjected. He at once ordered Boniface to take the pipe out of his mouth, and then proceeded to search the rooms for bushrangers, although Mr. Walker informed him that they had only a few minutes previously left the house. Having satisfied himself that the men of whom he was in search were not hidden about the premises, the captain of police braced up his nerves, and proceeded . . . . back to Bathurst! hearing along the road that the bushrangers had been before him, and that another party of police had been taken out by Superintendent Morrissett to look for them.

This latter party was lucky enough to reach house after house just as the bushrangers had left. At Mutton's they had been half an hour behind: at the second store they were only ten minutes in arrear, but had left their horses some way off, so gave the robbers a very good opportunity to get clear away. But the latter were in no greater hurry than their pursuers, and instead of disappearing into the bush or pushing at full speed along the road, they quietly cantered along with their booty until they came to Mr. Butler's hotel, about a mile farther on the road leading to Caloola. It was about ten o'clock at night when they reached the place and at once began operations. There were eight men in the bar, and Mrs. Butler was attending to them. Four of the bushrangers entered, armed like the police. They rummaged a side room and the drawers, but took nothing excepting a chain; a watch which they were told belonged to a widow woman, which had been left there to be raffled for, they allowed to remain where it was. One of the gang asked his mate to drink, but he refused, saying he was on duty. They demanded

Mrs. Butler's money; she emptied her pocket, but as there was nothing but silver they returned it. They enquired from the men in the house what money they had. It was produced; there was only silver, and they suffered them to retain it. One man asleep on the sofa they awoke and asked him for his money; he said he had only silver; they searched him and finding some notes they took them and the silver too, as a punishment for telling them a lie. This man had a draught horse in the stable; they took that, but left those of Mr. Butler. In their search through the house they came to the door of the bedroom occupied by Mrs. Butler's mother. A girl who was there said "If you are gentlemen you will not go into the old lady's room, she is nervous and you would frighten her," and they then turned away. They called for six nobblers for people in the house and paid for them, themselves drinking nothing stronger than lemonade; and having re-arranged their plunder on the spare horse they took their departure, just as the sound of the police horses' hoofs were heard along the highway, the sound indicating that they were proceeding very leisurely. This was explained five minutes afterwards, when the police made their appearance, two of them walking ahead of the others to reconnoitre! It was, doubtless, with a sigh of disappointment that Superintendent Morrissett learned the bushrangers had gone. But there was glory still ahead. The sound of the horses that had just been ridden from the hotel door could be heard in the distance, and Mrs. Butler informed the newcomers that the men had only just left the house, that they had heavy swags with them, and had taken a draught horse out of the stable to carry some of the goods; that they were still in the fenced-in road, and must be taken if pursued quickly. The superintendent was not to be hurried. He held a short conversation with a person living opposite the hotel, and then started along the road. Shortly afterwards, however, he returned to ask the person he had been conversing with to go with them! Seeing that precious time was being lost, Mrs. Butler asked one of the police what they were waiting for; and the reply came growlingly (for the "men" had no sympathy with their superior in this delay) "For orders!" The order to proceed again was shortly afterwards given, but it is almost needless to say no good result followed the proceeding. The police returned as they had started, and the men shared—unjustly enough—the reproach and ridicule which their timorous and hesitating leader had earned.

When this news reached Bathurst, public feeling was divided between shame, disgust, and indignation. The action of the Superintendent formed the subject of adverse comment in almost every circle. Through his want of generalship—to say nothing more—the gang had been allowed to come and go almost as it pleased them, and the people began to openly debate whether they would not be better off without any police at all, than with police led after the fashion above described. In this case the inefficiency of the force had been so marked that reports other than those sent from the Superintendent's office found their way into the hands of the Colonial Secretary, and the head of the department in Sydney wrote some remarkably strong minutes to the responsible officers. The whole colony was aroused to indignation by the oft-repeated tale of ineffectual pursuits, and the subject was brought before Parliament and debated on more than one occasion. The raid upon Bathurst, and the subsequent robbery of the people living along one of the principal approaches to the town, showed that the bushrangers held the law and its administrators in supreme contempt; and it was urged that unless more effective measures were adopted they would go to lengths never before heard of. But Hall and his mates, as it happened, lay quiet for some time, and those who watched for their re-appearance watched in vain—though reports were circulated to the effect that they had made back across country to their old haunts on the Southern side. And while the police in the west were thus undisturbed by fresh surprises, the whole question of the management of the force was vigorously dealt with by the authorities in Sydney, who were themselves charged with the responsibility of the failures daily recorded.

In order that the reader may better understand how it was that police efforts were so persistently futile, it is necessary to give some account of the system—for it was the system that was at fault, more than the individual employed under it. Frank Gardiner had only just set the ball rolling when the late Sir Charles Cowper, who was then Premier of the colony and leader of the Government—for it must be remarked that in Australian Governments the Premier is not always the leader—succeeded in passing through the Legislature a new Police Act. Formerly the police in country districts were under the supervision and control of local police magistrates; this Act brought the whole of the police in the colony under one central head, resident in Sydney; and that head was, at this time, Captain McLerie. Mr. Cowper was very proud of his legislative offspring, but he had chosen a most unfortunate time for bringing it to the birth. Bush-ranging had already assumed a vigorous growth, while the system was by no means in working order to con-front it. It may have answered very well in the streets of the Metropolis, where the daily round of police duty was circumscribed, and dealt with city rogues and vagabonds; but in the country the nepotism which flourished under it, and the restrictions placed upon the men by officers who knew absolutely nothing of bush duty (and who, if they had known, would not have been qualified to engage in it from lack of the ex-perience born of active exercise) opened the way for wrong-doers to run a free and easy course. The men were harassed by contradictory orders, or rendered fretful by enforced inactivity pending the arrival of in-structions which their inexperienced officers sought from the head centre, hundreds of miles away. The system looked well on paper, but was hopelessly futile when contrasted with the requirements of the infested districts. The men were right enough, if they had been permitted to *know* anything; but this was denied them, and every single movement was nothing but the clockwork of graduated office. All was done by reference upward, and the officer in command was the oracle. It was a secret society, and all the actual knowledge of an inferior became ignorance the mo-ment he had communicated the information he had re-

ceived to his superior. There was too much rank and
file and commission in the system; and although the
Government went out of its way to make it more
effective, actually giving more liberty than could be
taken without putting the machinery out of gear, in-
ternal friction continued, and external disgust and dis-
satisfaction kept pace with it.

Even before the ridiculous exhibition on the Vale
Road, the outcry against the system had become
general. The House of Assembly badgered the Premier and Colonial Secretary, in whom the control of
the police force was vested. The Colonial Secretary
importuned the Inspector-General, and even went so
far as to reprimand and threaten him. The Inspector-
General passed the trouble on to those immediately
under him in command, who in turn worried the rank
and file to the verge of resignation. Disorganisation
reigned supreme, and while officers fought with each
other, and Parliament and people raved and stormed
and bemoaned the powerlessness of the system to cope
with the first evil that confronted it, the bushrangers
and their friends laughed consumedly and sought every
opportunity of openly defying the police and intensify-
ing the confusion.

The Inspector-General at last determined to leave
his comfortable quarters in Sydney and visit the disturbed districts, with the view of rallying his officers
and showing them how to do bush duty. He went to
the central stations in the south and west, and himself
led small companies in pursuit; but it was all so much
wasted energy. Outrages multiplied, and while Hall's
gang ran riot over the wide area in the south and west,

other bushrangers sprang up in other districts, to the dismay of the residents and the further annoyance of the authorities.

Now the full force of the condemnatory blast was felt in Parliament, and the Government were at their wits' end to stand against it. They could not defend a force as inefficient as that under McLerie's command had proved itself to be, but Mr. Cowper would not admit that it was the system that was in fault. He was loyal to his offspring, but terribly indignant at the manner in which those in whose charge he had placed it were acting. A bitter correspondence ensued between Mr. Cowper and the Inspector-General, during which the Premier threatened at one time to "set the regular police aside and organise another band under an entirely different arrangement," and in a later letter added—"The Colonial Secretary is, however, unwilling suddenly to withdraw the Inspector-General, but intimates his intention of doing so, if within one month, Gilbert and party are not apprehended. It will then become a question for immediate determination what modification of the police system shall be made to remedy the defects so loudly complained of."

The raids made upon Bathurst and along the Vale Road forced the Government to introduce a new course of procedure. One portion of the plan was to offer a reward of £500 each for the capture of Gilbert, Hall, O'Meally, Vane and Burke. These rewards were to be paid, not into the police reward fund, but directly to those persons who either captured these bushrangers themselves or gave such information as should lead to their capture by others. The strictest secrecy was to be observed relative to the parties giving information; and to prevent publicity the money was to be paid from the Treasury direct to the parties entitled to it without passing through any second hand. In the next place, private persons were to be employed in a way and under circumstances which the Government deemed prudent not to make public. It was stated that various offers had been made by parties desirous of undertaking the ridding of the country of the dangerous and troublesome pest; but they wanted to be well paid for their trouble, and one of them stipulated for no less than £6000 as the price of his efforts if successful. Others, however, were much more moderate in their proposals. A further measure resolved upon by the Government was to send six special parties of six or eight men each into the disturbed districts. These constables were not to be clothed in uniform, or accoutred in the heavy dragoon style, but in the usual bush costume, armed with rifles and revolvers. Each party was to have a black tracker. The horses were to be of a first-class character, and the officers in command were to choose their own men. They were to take pack-horses, with tents and provisions, so that they might be able to keep the bush for a considerable period; and they were to have no other duty than to follow up the bushrangers until captured. Each of these parties was to be placed under the command of officers who had distinguished themselves by their courage and activity.

As it turned out, the gang in the west was broken bit by bit, not by any newly infused energy on the part of the police under better leaders, but by the courage of private individuals; who instead of yielding fought, at the risk of losing life as well as money: and whose steady hand and correct aim rendered their fighting—in each instance against "long odds"—successful

CHAPTER XII.

THE DUNN'S PLAINS TRAGEDY.

For about a fortnight after the raid on Bathurst very little was heard of the gang, and it was thought that they had quietly stolen away back across the Lachlan, near Cowra, knowing that as soon as their exploits in the vicinity of the City of the Plains were officially reported the main body of police would hasten thither, and give them opportunities of prosecuting their calling near their old haunts without much molestation. But they had not left the district. Watching their opportunity, they suddenly attacked the residence of Mr. Keightley, Gold Commissioner, at Dunn's Plains, near Rockley, and about thirty miles from Bathurst. They made no secret of the reason of their visit to this homestead. Mr. Keightley, who was a man of splendid physique and undoubted courage, had openly assisted the police in their search for the bushrangers, and had declared that he would show them no mercy if he should happen to come across them. Like every other word or movement of those who sought to break up the gang, Mr. Keightley's sayings and doings reached their ears; and they determined to put his courage to the test by sticking up his household.

From the beginning of Peisley's career bushranging in New South Wales had proceeded by
gradations—from idleness and petty stealing to cattle
stealing; from cattle stealing to robbery from
the person; then to robbery (under arms) of
mails and escorts; followed by the ruin and
extermination of honest storekeepers, attacks on
the officers of justice, raids on banks, country
towns, and private establishments. The time had now
arrived for a further advance—to the Neapolitan
system of ransom. This made, the question was
seriously discussed in certain quarters whether the next
successive movements would not be to the formation
of camps, stations, regiments, batteries, and open attack upon the united Government forces.

At about sunset on Saturday evening, 24th October, 1863, Mr. Commissioner Keightley stood in the
doorway of his house, when he observed five men riding along the fence at some distance from the dwelling.
At first he thought they were a party of police who he
knew were in the neighbourhood, they having been in
his paddock on the previous evening; but as he desired to give his guest, Dr. Pechey, a shock, he called
out to him, "Here are the bushrangers!" Mr.
Keightley and the doctor watched the men to within
twenty-five yards of the house, when they saw them
simultaneously leap from their horses and make a sudden rush into the yard, at the same time presenting
fire-arms and calling out, "Stand! if you run into the
house we'll shoot you!" Before the last word had
sounded, however, Mr. Keightley and his companion
had turned and made for the open door, which was

fortunately near at hand. The men fired at them as they ran, but the bullets did not find their mark, and the door having been made secure prompt measures were taken to repel the coming attack. A plan of procedure had been previously arranged, and was now followed. Dr. Pechey hastened in the direction of a room occupied by the man servant (who was at the time absent, having gone to Rockley for the letters), his intention being to secure some firearms and ammunition there stored; but finding that he could not reach the room without exposing himself to the fire of the bushrangers he returned, to find Mr. Keightley armed with a double-barrel gun and a revolver, which he had obtained from his bedroom, after having told Mrs. Keightley that the dreaded gang had made its appearance—a fact of which she had already been made aware by the firing that had taken place. Taking up their station at the door nearest to the yard where the bushrangers had congregated, Keightley and his companion prepared to make a stubborn resistance. But the failure to reach the other arms and ammunition somewhat disconcerted them, although the assailants were not aware that the occupants of the house were so poorly provided with the means of defence. Knowing something of Keightley's determination and skill, the bushrangers kept themselves under cover, posting themselves in the form of a semi circle, so that they could command the doorway from all points. As the two men came to the open door the bushrangers fired; but none of he bullets did any harm. Keightley and his companion took care not to expose themselves, although closely watching the movements of their assailants.　What followed is best told in Mr. Keightley's own words.　And this is his story:—

> As I appeared at the door several shots were fired; the men were in a semi-circle around me, at varied distances; at the time I took up my gun I fancied it was loaded in both barrels—one with snipe shot, and the other with buck shot; when I went to the door I noticed a man near me on my left, who was firing very rapidly; he fired several shots; he appeared to draw out from a cask, behind which he was concealed, with the view of firing at the door; the last time he came out I slung up my gun and fired the right barrel, which, I thought had the small shot in it; I could not see the effect of the shot otherwise than the man put his hand on his stomach and fell back; I then said to Dr. Pechey, "Now for the roof!" which I had had barricaded for some time; when on the roof I saw Vane for the first time; he was going across the yard, and when the party saw me on the roof they commenced firing at me again, but I cannot say how many shots; when I had fired I looked for my powder horn but could not find it; I concluded that Dr. Pechey had got the arms and ammunition I had sent him for previously; I left the house open when I went on to the roof and Mrs. Keightley and child were below; when on the roof I asked the doctor for the other gun and loading materials, and he said he had been intercepted and could not get at the arms; I then looked at my own gun and found that the other barrel was discharged; the shooting at this time was very close, one ball went close to my face, I think it was Hall's, and another through my hat; they called upon me to surrender or they would burn the house down; and as I had no arms I thought it best to do so as we had no ammunition; two of the voices called out "If you lay down your arms and come down we'll not touch you;" I said "honour bright?" and they replied "honour bright;" I said "Very well, we will come down," and I came down the ladder into the garden in front of the house; I concluded that the party knew at the time that one of their party was hit; when we came down they made a rush at us; Vane struck Dr. Pechey with a revolver and knocked him down; I said "What did you do that for? he has done nothing;" one of them said "Is not that Keightley?" and I said "No, I'm Keightley;" Vane then said "You b——y wretch, you have shot my mate;" I denied it, saying, "I never killed your mate"; I did not know then the result of my shot; he said I had and that they would shoot me for it; they then brought me to the spot where Burke was lying, and they held a consultation, the result of which was that I was to

be shot; I was told to go into the paddock; from their statement I learnt that Burke had, after he was shot, fired at himself and shot himself through the head; I was then told that I should be shot, and to say good-bye to my wife and come up the hill; as I had been ensnared in my position and had no means of defence, I begged them for God's sake not to shoot me and commit murder; it was then arranged that Dr. Pechey should proceed to Rockley for his instruments with the view of affording assistance to Burke, and while he was away Gilbert came to the foot of the hill and called out "Mickey is dead," or words to that effect; one of the party remarked "He (meaning me) had better be shot at once and waste no more time."

Mr. Keightley's position was a very critical one. That the bushrangers fully intended to kill him when they found that Burke was dead was proved by their efforts to shoot him when he appeared on the barricaded roof, and their threat that if he did not come down and surrender they would burn the house down.

Mrs. Keightley and the servant woman, who was also on the premises, saw Dr. Pechey knocked down and witnessed the preparations which the bushrangers were making to shoot Mr. Keightley in cold blood; and it goes without saying that they begged hard for his life. It is said that the servant actually threw herself between her employer and one of the bushrangers who had raised his piece to fire at him. In the end his life was spared. Vane was not the leader, and had to swallow his resentment at the command of Hall and Gilbert, neither of whom was more bloodthirsty than the average run of bushrangers. Keightley was removed into the bush, and the leaders remained at the house, while further parleying took place; eventually the bushrangers agreed with Mrs. Keightley to spare her husband's life on condition that the sum of £500 was paid to them. When Dr. Pechey returned from

Rockley he was made aware of the bargain, and informed that it had been arranged that he should ride into Bathurst and get the money from Mrs. Keightley's father, the late Mr. Henry Rotton, of Blackdown. If the money was not handed to them, said Gilbert, between ten and twelve o'clock on the following (Sunday) morning, Mr. Keightley would assuredly be shot; as he would be if during his visit to Bathurst the messenger gave any information to the police. In reply to a question from Dr. Pechey, Hall said they would have the money in £5 notes, and that they had fixed upon £500 as the ransom because that was the sum which Keightley would get for shooting Burke—there being at that time a reward of £500 upon each of their heads. It was then arranged that Mrs. Keightley should go to Bathurst with Dr. Pechey; the horse was caught and harnessed, and the pair started on their urgent mission. Before leaving, however, Mrs. Keightley was allowed to have a brief interview with her husband, who was brought down to the house for the purpose.

The journey to Bathurst was accomplished in smart time, the reader may be sure, the horse being kept at top speed; but it was two o'clock on the Sunday morning before Blackdown was reached. There was excitement bordering upon consternation in the household when the anxious daughter made known her errand to her father, and then the question arose—How was the money to be obtained? The large sum required was not in the house, and innumerable difficulties might arise to prevent it being obtained in time. The Blackdown squire was known to be a wealthy

MR. AND MRS. KEIGHTLEY

man, but even wealthy men cannot always lay their hands upon a large sum of money at a moment's notice. An appeal must be made to the bank in Bathurst, and the time spent in waking the bank manager, making explanations, and counting the money would considerably shorten the few hours of grace allowed for the ransom to be paid. And another difficulty presented itself. The object for which the money was required must be kept secret; yet the bank manager must be told, and he might consider it his duty to inform the police before the messenger had got well away with the price of the ransom. There were difficulties and risks on every side, but they were boldly faced and overcome. Fresh horses soon covered the distance between Blackdown and Bathurst, and very shortly after the visitors had poured their tale into his astonished ears notes to the amount required were counted out by the bank manager, and Mr. Rotton and Dr. Pechey were "making the pace" towards Dunn's Plains.

Meanwhile Mr. Keightley was kept a close prisoner by the bushrangers on a rocky hill (known as the Dog Rocks) about a quarter of a mile from his homestead, the spot being chosen because it commanded a view of the Bathurst Road. Here some members of the gang made themselves comfortable for the night, and the others took turn about as sentries, keeping a close watch upon Keightley, who had voluntarily pledged his honour not to make any attempt to escape. When morning dawned the party had breakfast, and then settled down to await events. Seven, eight, nine o'clock passed, and still there were no signs of the messengers returning. Ten o'clock found the waiting party painfully impatient; but a little later Mr. Rotten and the Doctor drove up to the house, and learned from the inmates that Keightley was with the bushrangers at the Dog Rocks. Alighting from the vehicle they entered the house and Mr. Rotton proposed to take the money to the bushrangers, but this was deemed inadvisable, as the appearance of a stranger on the scene might lead to trouble. As quickly as possible, therefore, the notes were recounted in the house. Mr. Rotton hastily took their numbers with a view of tracing them should they pass into circulation in the district, and then handed them to Dr. Pechey, who mounted his horse and rode to the bushrangers' camp. As he came forward Gilbert met him and asked "Have you brought the money?" "Yes," replied Dr. Pechey, "will you set Mr. Keightley at liberty?" "Come along," Gilbert responded, "he's all safe;" and he conducted Pechey to where his friend was standing under close guard. As soon as Keightley saw him he anxiously repeated the question, "Have you the notes?" For answer Pechey threw the notes to Gilbert, who counted them, found they were all right, and told Keightley he was at liberty. The ransomed man returned hastily to the house, his captors meanwhile leaving the locality with all speed.

After Burke's death, the remaining members of the gang did not concern themselves very much about his body. They saw, however, before they left Dunn's Plains that arrangements had been made to convey the remains to Carcoar, that task being entrusted to one of Mr. Keightley's servant men and another. Concern-

ing the exact manner of Burke's death, it may be here
remarked that some people have doubted whether Mr.
Keightley shot him at all, and thought the first wound
must have been accidentally inflicted by one of his
mates. It is certain that the shot which killed him
was fired by himself after finding that he had been
wounded. On the way to Carcoar the party conveying
the body was met by the police, who had received word
at Cowra of the attack upon Keightley's house and
were making for that locality. There were twelve
policemen in the party, and two of these were told off
to accompany the men with the body to Carcoar, the
other ten proceeding to Rockley, the nearest station to
the scene of the outrage. At Carcoar an inquest was
held upon the body, which everyone pressed to see.
After the inquest the body was handed over for interment to Burke's friends, some of whom made no secret
of the fact that they considered the remains they were
committing to the grave were those of a hero and a
martyr.

After the return of Mr. Keightley and the disappearance of the bushrangers, Mr. Rotton tried to induce the employees at the homestead to go for the
police, but in vain. Then he decided to go himself; a
horse was brought up from the paddock, and he rode
into Rockley and made known at the police station
what had occurred. Returning, he started for Bathurst
to give information to the authorities there. But the
news had already reached Bathurst, and within three
or four miles of the town he met a party of mounted
troopers pushing forward at full speed for the scene of
the outrage. The news had by some means reached

Carcoar shortly after breakfast on the Sunday morning. A magistrate of that town at once procured a horse and enlisted the services of a lad to ride post haste to Bathurst, giving him a sealed letter to the police and a written communication to all whom it might concern, requesting that if the bearer should require a fresh horse on the road he might be immediately supplied. Young Bonnor—that was the lad's name—covered the distance between Carcoar and Blayney in very short time, and finding that his horse was fagged he after some difficulty obtained another, and made a fresh start on the road. Within two hours from leaving Carcoar the lad was in Bathurst and the letter delivered to the police, the distance covered being about thirty-five miles. A party of troopers was at once formed and sent off, some of them half inclined to disbelieve the report which had come to them in such a round-about way; but the meeting with Mr. Rotton dispelled all doubts, and they pushed along the road at a faster pace, while Mr. Rotton continued his journey to Black-down to assure Mrs. Keightley of the safety of her husband and the faithfulness of the bushrangers to their pledges.

During the same afternoon Mr. Keightley and Dr. Pechey drove into Bathurst, where they received many congratulations on their escape from death at the hands of the bushrangers, and much praise for their courage and heroism. Mrs. Keightley also received a full share of praise, for none but a stout-hearted woman could have maintained her presence of mind sufficiently to assist even her husband under such trying circumstances. The servant woman subsequently received due approbation for the part which she had sustained in the affair; indeed, there was at one time quite a heated public discussion as to which of the ladies was most to be honoured.

There was already a reward of £500 for each of the gang, and Burke's head money was paid by the Government to Mr. Keightley. Two days later the offered reward was increased by the following proclamation, which appeared in most of the newspapers :—

£4000 REWARD,

For the apprehension of JOHN GILBERT, JOHN VANE, JOHN O'MEALLY, and BENJAMIN HALL.

and

£100 REWARD

FOR ACCOMPLICES.

Whereas the abovenamed persons are charged with the commission of numerous and serious offences, and have hitherto eluded the efforts to apprehend them: It is hereby notified that the Government will pay a reward of One Thousand Pounds for such information as will lead to the apprehension of each of the offenders named.

The Government will also pay a reward of One Hundred Pounds for such information as will lead to the conviction of any person or persons for harbouring, assisting, or maintaining either of the abovenamed offenders.

All such information communicated by any person charged with the commission of an offence will entitle his case to favourable consideration by the Crown, and will in all cases be regarded by the police authorities as strictly confidential; and in the event of payment of any of the rewards above offered, the name of the recipient will not be disclosed.

The above rewards are offered in lieu of all others previously payable by Government for the apprehension or conviction of the offenders abovenamed.

WILLIAM FORSTER.

Colonial Secretary's Office, October 26, 1863.

In addition to the pecuniary reward, however, Mr. Keightley's services were recognised by the Government by an appointment in the public service as Police

Magistrate. He was well fitted for the post, and faithful and efficient service in that capacity proved that the confidence of the authorities had not been misplaced.

While Mr. and Mrs. Keightley were yet in the Bathurst district, the latter was made the recipient of a handsome present from the ladies of a distant part of the colony, in recognition of her bravery when Hall and his gang visited Dunn's Plains. The present took the form of a handsome silver tea service, upon the chief piece of which were engraved the following words:—"Presented to Mrs. Keightley, by the ladies of Maitland, through Mrs. Mullen, as an appreciation of her heroic conduct in defence of her husband against bushrangers, at Rockley, on Saturday, October 24th, 1863."

But here it is necessary that I should diverge somewhat from the straight course of the narrative, and show how some of the ransom money was traced after it had left the hands of the bushrangers.

THE NUMBERED NOTES, AND HOW THEY WERE FOUND.

It will be remembered that before Mr. Rotton handed over the notes that were given to Gilbert he hurriedly copied their numbers. It was a wise precaution, and fruitful of results. From this list copies were subsequently made and handed to various tradesmen in Bathurst and the neighbourhood, and it was arranged that immediate information should be given to the police if any of the notes were presented at their establishments.

Within a week after, a young man from a district known to be friendly to the gang entered Bathurst, and purchased at different shops a revolver, several boxes of percussion caps, a quantity of black crape, seven gold rings, and some articles of clothing. While he was still in the town it was discovered that some of the notes paid away by him corresponded with those on Mr. Rotton's list, and before he had completed his purchase he was apprehended and safely lodged in the lock-up. There were found upon his person the sum of £11, a piece of paper, the seven gold rings, and five invoices of the goods he had purchased at the stores. In his valise were found the revolver, caps, crape, etc., and it was ascertained that out of £35 which the articles had cost, the prisoner had paid away five of the £5 notes given to the bushrangers. Upon the piece of paper was written a memorandum of what the prisoner was to purchase for six different persons, whose names were left blank. The singular and incriminating document ran thus: "For mother, bottle of medicine; for ———, pair of pistols, box of caps, gold ring; for ———, revolver, box of caps, gold ring," and so on. One other article was found in his possession—a piece of used blotting paper, bearing on it the words "Patrick Burke"—the name of the father of the bushranger who had met his death at Keightley's hands. The arresting constable charged him with receiving the notes, "knowing them to have been stolen," and the prisoner made no reply to the charge. It was afterwards elicited that the young fellow was a cousin of Vane's, and it was publicly stated that the father of the dead bushranger, Burke, was connected in some way with his family.

As may be supposed, the news of the arrest caused

great excitement in Bathurst and its immediate neighbourhood, and for a time even the bushrangers and their doings were forgotten. In due course the prisoner was brought up at the police court charged with receiving stolen property, and was committed to stand his trial at the following Bathurst Circuit Court, at which he was found guilty.

The Chief Justice, after making some impressive remarks upon the enormity of the offence, and expressing an earnest hope that the crime of bushranging would now effectually cease, sentenced the prisoner to five years' hard labour on the roads, or other public works of the colony.

There was an appeal to the Full Court in Sydney on some legal technicalities: but their Honours were of opinion that the conviction should be sustained.

The news of the ruling was received with joy in Bathurst, as it tended to intimidate the already too bold friends of the gang, who had their doors ever open to receive the bushrangers and their hands ever open to receive the bushrangers' ill-gotten gains.

THE SURRENDER OF JOHNNY VANE.

After leaving Dunn's Plains, Hall, Gilbert, O'Meally and Vane rode across the bush in the direction of Carcoar, calling in to see some of their friends on the way. They stayed long enough in this locality to quarrel amongst themselves; but the cause of the quarrel has never been made known, although its results were most startling to the public. In a letter from a gentleman at Carcoar which now lies before me, and which is dated 27th October, 1863, I find the following sentences: "I have heard that Vane was seen alone at the back of Mount Macquarie (a prominent district landmark near the town), and again at the foot of Mount Fitzgerald, on both occasions well armed. . . . . Gilbert, Hall and O'Meally supposed to have cleared out. Vane still at the back of the Mount —was at Number One school yesterday and had a black eye given him by Gilbert—says he got not a sixpence of Keightley's ransom money."

How the quarrel between Vane and his mates originated was never clearly explained, but whatever the reason, within three weeks from the time of Burke's death, Vane yielded himself up to the authorities.

When riding through the bush in the direction of the Abercrombie Ranges, the Rev. Father McCarthy— one of the pioneer priests of the Bathurst and Carcoar districts, whose genial good nature and zealous labours made him most popular with the residents, particularly those scattered through the isolated parts which seldom or ever saw the face of priest or parson, other than his—happened to fall in with Vane. There was mutual recognition, for the good priest was well acquainted with the bushranger's family—although not of his flock, for they were Presbyterians—and a long conversation ensued. The substance of that conversation never transpired, but the reader can imagine how earnestly Father McCarthy pleaded with Vane to forsake the course which was keeping the community in a state of terror, breaking the heart of his mother, and leading him to certain death. They parted, and before the day closed Father McCarthy told Mrs. Vane that he had met her son. The poor woman wept bitterly, pouring out her troubles in the presence of her sympathetic listener, and bemoaning the dreadful circumstances in which her boy had placed himself and her. Before leaving, Father McCarthy advised the disconsolate mother to seek an interview with her son in the bush and beseech him to surrender, pointing out that by so doing he would be likely to win favour which could not otherwise be extended. Mrs. Vane promised to do this, and without delay she sought her son in his retreat and pleaded with him only as a mother could. Her prayers and tears were effectual, and in sorrowful joy she returned to send a message to Father McCarthy, to the effect that her erring son desired another interview in order to make arrangements for his surrender. Within a few hours the priest and the bushranger were again together, and in the latter's hiding place these arrangements were completed, Vane agreeing to meet his newly-found friend at a certain spot before midnight, and accompany him to the headquarters of the police at Bathurst.

At eleven o'clock that night the bushranger faithfully presented himself at the place appointed, where Father McCarthy was already in waiting. A start was made for Bathurst, forty miles away, through the bush; they reached it before five o'clock next morning, their chief anxiety being to enter the town unobserved. A brief rest at the Fitzroy Arms in George-street; a short consultation between Father McCarthy and his venerable superior, Dean Grant; a message to Dr. Palmer, the Police Magistrate, and another message to Superintendent Morrissett; the formal surrender of Vane to the latter; a quiet walk to the gaol gates—and the Bathurst residents woke up to learn that Vane had voluntarily surrendered and was safely domiciled in the gaol on the central Square.

In due course he was brought before the local bench of magistrates, when three charges of robbery under arms were preferred against him, and two charges of shooting with intent to kill. Evidence in each case was given, and the prisoner, who made no

JOHN VANE

defence, was fully committed on each separate charge to take his trial at the next Bathurst Circuit Court, to be held in April of the following year.

Vane had been five months in gaol—bail had not been sought, and would not have been granted—when the Assize Court to which he had been committed opened. Sir Alfred Stephen, Chief Justice, presided, and as several very important cases besides those

against Vane were set down for trial, nearly all the
leading members of the bar attended, the circuit work
of prominent barristers in those days being quite as
heavy and quite as remunerative as that of the Judges.
Mr. Edward Butler acted as Crown Prosecutor.
Bathurst was full of people and the people were full of
excitement, to the no small benefit of the hotel keepers.

When Vane was placed in the dock his personal
appearance was made the subject of general remark.
He was a good-looking young fellow, and in the slim-
ness of his build was a typical Western "native." Those
who expected to see a repulsive-looking desperado of
the Bill Sykes type were disappointed—no doubt
pleasingly—for there was nothing repulsive-looking
about him, and the court visitors could scarcely believe that the youth before them was the daring bushranger who had assisted in keeping the country-side in
terror and for so long set the law and its officers at
defiance.

Mr. Dalley had been retained for the defence, and
it was no doubt under his advice that the prisoner
pleaded guilty to being concerned in the raids on
Caloola, Grubbenbong, and Canowindra, and the attack on Mr. Keightley. To a fifth charge, concerning
the sticking up of the mail coach near Carcoar and the
shooting of Constable Sutton, he pleaded not guilty.

Mr. Dalley's defence was able and successful, and
the jury acquitted Vane on this charge—the more
readily, perhaps, because they knew that for other
offences he would receive punishment commensurate
with his crimes.

As the hour was late, his Honour ordered the

prisoner to be removed and brought up for sentence on the following day; but knowing that many of his relatives were in the court, in order to ease their minds, he announced that the sentence he should pass would not be death.

On the following day the Court was again crowded, and shortly after the Chief Justice had taken his seat Vane was called up to receive sentence. Before judgment was pronounced Mr. Dalley pleaded with the judge for leniency, urging prisoner's youth in extenuation, and referring to the fact that he had borne a good character before abandoning himself to lawless pursuits and that he had given himself up and shown true contrition for his crimes. He also called several prominent public men to bear testimony to the fact that Vane, prior to becoming a bushranger, had been a most exemplary young man.

His Honour, after a long address, passed sentence as follows:—For the outrage at Dunn's Plains, 15 years' hard labour on the roads or other public works of the colony, and for each of the other three offences 10 years' hard labour—the sentences to be concurrent.

It is right that a word or two should be said concerning the subsequent action of the good priest through whose instrumentality the district was freed from the presence of this member of the notorious gang. Father McCarthy was entitled to the reward of £1000 which the Government had offered for the capture of Vane. He did not accept that reward. In his ministerial capacity he had effectively preached repentance to the sinner, and the consciousness of having done his duty was reward sufficient. In another case, yet to be recorded, in which a bushranger not connected with Hall's gang was concerned, he was instrumental in recovering for one of the banks some £2000 in notes which had been stolen from one of the Western mails. The bank had offered £100 reward for the recovery of the notes, but Father McCarthy refused to accept that reward also. The act was characteristic of the man, who in his priestly office laboured for something more precious and more enduring than earthly treasure.

CHAPTER XIII.

THE ATTACK ON GOIMBLA STATION.

DEATH OF O'MEALLY.

After Vane's severance from the gang, Hall, Gilbert and O'Meally did not remain long in the Carcoar district, but hurriedly pushed on for their old quarters in the Weddin Mountains. They knew that the Bathurst police, the men who had recently arrived from Maitland under Superintendent Lydiard, and the Carcoar and Cowra police, were concentrating on Dunn's Plains; and while the police were still hunting up their tracks in the country about Caloola, Rockley and Trunkey, the three were again creating a sensation in the neighbourhood of Canowindra.

They entered the town just as daylight was creeping over the eastern hills, a morning or two after the quarrel between Vane and Gilbert. Riding quietly up to the door of the local inn, which was still kept by Mr. W. Robinson, they awoke the landlord and asked if there were any police about: hearing of none, they went into the house and had some grog. They stayed about a quarter of an hour, and on going away asked for two bottles of wine and two of Old Tom, in payment for which they offered a £5 note—doubtless one of the number paid for Keightley's ransom. Mr.

Robinson said he could not change the note, and they replied that he must do without the payment in that case, as they had no other money; they then rode away.

Mr. Robinson informed Mr. K. Cummings, a magistrate, who was stopping in the house, of what had occurred, and a messenger was sent for the solitary policeman, who lived about half a mile away. While they were conversing about the affair Mr. Superintendent Chatfield and a party of policemen rode up to the house, heard the news, found out which way the robbers had gone, and started in pursuit, taking a black tracker with them. They very soon got upon the bushrangers' tracks, and after riding six or seven miles the tracker sighted them and the chase commenced. When the bushrangers were first seen a young man named Hurkett was with them; and as soon as they saw the police they galloped off, and, according to Hurkett's account, his horse ran away with him so that he could not stop for some time. However, as soon as he possibly could he pulled up and the others went on by themselves; the police galloped up, dismounted, and fired at Hurkett, whose horse was shot. He had a bad time of it altogether, in fact : he was handcuffed at once—when he got back to Canowindra Sir F. Pottinger threatened him with arrest again, and when Chatfield returned from a fruitless chase the threat was carried out. Chatfield's party followed the bushrangers for about forty miles, in the direction of Bangaroo, but as the darkness came on they could no longer follow the tracks; however, they went on to Bangaroo and on riding up to the hut a little half-caste girl called out "There some men coming." O'Meally and Hall were then in the hut at tea, and had to get out in a hurry and on to their horses and off again. Hall, not having time to put on his boots, carried them under his arm. In the meantime Gilbert had been in an adjoining paddock looking for some horses, and when he rode back for his mates he found the police in the hut. A policeman called out "Who's there?" and Gilbert, turning his horse, rode away; the policeman fired at him, but the result was *nil*. The bushrangers were not seen again by the police, but on Thursday morning breakfasted at a station of Mr. Icely's, three miles below Canowindra, and on Friday morning were at a station of Mr. Grant's, not far from Carcoar. So sudden was the departure of Hall and O'Meally that they had not time to take all their things with them, but left a coat belonging to Gilbert, in the pocket of which was found with other things a bag containing a quantity of revolver bullets and a bullet mould.

On the following day they stuck up several teamsters between Canowindra and Toogong, but took nothing but some horse feed for their own animals, which they proceeded at once to feed. While the horses were feeding the police were observed coming up, and the bushrangers at once mounted and rode off, pursued by the police. Several shots were exchanged. In crossing a swampy flat Hall's horse got bogged, and the police, had they pushed on, might have made Hall prisoner. O'Meally and Gilbert pulled up and came to his assistance, and the police observing this pulled up and commenced re-loading. This proved so tedious an operation that before it was concluded the horse was got out of his difficulty, and the three bush-rangers cleared off, pursued at a respectful distance by the police.

On the night of Thursday, 19th November, at about a quarter to nine o'clock, the three bushrangers rode up to Goimbla, about thirty-two miles from Forbes. Mr. Campbell, the station-owner, had made no secret of his abhorrence of the freebooters, and on one occasion had started out in pursuit of them, ac-companied by a few of his immediate friends. Mr. Keightley had been paid out for his audacity: now it was Mr. Campbell's turn.

The first notification he had of their presence was the sound of footsteps under the front verandah of the house; suspecting the true cause of the sound, he sprang towards the chimney corner, seized one of two double-barrelled fowling pieces which were ready loaded there, and ran into the next room, where he confronted one of the bushrangers, who stood at an outer door of the same room that opened upon the verandah. After an ineffectual exchange of shots the fellow rejoined his mates, who proceeded deliberately to set fire to the barn and stabling, which formed two sides of a quadrangle. As the barn contained a large quantity of hay, the whole structure was quickly in flames, which raged so fiercely that the premises in the immediate vicinity were brilliantly illuminated; and a favourite horse of Mr. Campbell's was roasted to death.

In the meantime Mrs. Campbell had with great bravery and at the risk of her life secured the second fowling piece and some ammunition, luckily unhit by a volley which the gang fired at her through the window. She and her husband then posted themselves in the passage leading from the house to the kitchen, where they could command all approaches, the lady reconnoitring every now and then. Presently she reported that a man with a cabbage-tree hat stood watching the flames. Mr. Campbell rushed round the house to the front corner, took deliberate aim at the fellow's throat, fired, and returned to load his gun.

MR. AND MRS. CAMPBELL

Just before this several shots had been fired, but now there was a dead silence. At half past eleven he cautiously approached the spot where the man had stood, and on the opposite side of the fence, found a carbine and cabbage-tree hat; at daylight he and a constable who had arrived followed a track into the oaks, and discovered the body of the man, who was wounded in the neck.

Early on the following morning word was sent to the Police Magistrate at Forbes, who at once started for the spot to hold a magisterial inquiry over the body. Mr. Campbell was not yet certain whether it was O'Meally who had fallen before his fire.

As Saturday dawned upon the smoking ruins, the place presented a melancholy spectacle. Everything combustible inside and around the tottering walls and barns and stables had disappeared, and the charred remains of the dead horse, swollen to nearly double its natural size, lay inside the inclosure. No vestige of nearly £1100 worth of property remained save the crumbling shells of the two buildings. Under the verandah of an out-building hard by lay the disfigured corpse of the dead bushranger, the body covered by part of a woolpack and the face by a towel. It was clad in a pair of strapped breeches, high boots with spurs, and three Crimean shirts, and underneath the neck lay a white comforter. The frame was athletic, the arms muscular, the hands as small and delicate as a lady's. The lower limbs were light and apparently well knit, and the figure as a whole gave the impression of activity and strength combined in more than an ordinary degree.

It was at first intended to remove the remains to Forbes for interment, but the heat of the weather rendered this impossible. They were interred at Goimbla, on the near bank of the Eugowra Creek. Subsequently, however, they were removed by relatives and friends to Forbes and there interred amidst much ceremony, as though they were those of a hero who had lost his life in the performance of a noble duty.

The following letter from Mrs. Campbell to her mother after the occurrence will further illustrate the fact that the danger which threatened her and her husband on that awful night was exceptionally great; and it will also show how empty was the boast made by the bushrangers and their friends that in all their raids Hall's gang were careful to treat females with the utmost consideration and respect. Writing on the 21st November Mrs. Campbell said :—

You will be anxious till you hear direct of our safety. It is indeed owing to the great mercy of God that the lives of David and William are spared. So many people have been here taking notes, that I doubt not you will read a most truthful account of all in the papers. I need not therefore weary you with another. We had no time for fear. The most dreadful part was the burning of the barn and stable. They are not much farther from the house than your stable; and at one part an outhouse, which is connected with the main building, is only divided by a road. You cannot imagine my agony while the flames were towering above us. Had the wind only blown towards the house all must have gone. The ground between the stable and outhouse was strewn with straw from the haymaking; there was also a large heap of woolpacks and a cart, all of which were set on fire. I was in such deadly fear of its catching at this point, that I rushed out and succeeded in getting the road cleared with the assistance of the cook. By this time the roofs had fallen in, so that the danger was passed. I imagine the ruffians had also retreated. Mr. Campbell had ventured out to the spot where he had aimed at the man. He found his gun and hat, but not the body, for his mates had dragged it some distance away, and his idea at the time was that the man had merely been wounded, and would return for his things. A short while after we heard a rustling as of some one creeping stealthily through the oats, and were afraid to go out again lest the bushrangers should be lying in ambush. The men in the huts had now recovered from their panic, and came up to see what was going on. David stationed them at various posts, and they watched till morning. It was by this time 3 o'clock. I was very tired, went to bed and managed to sleep a little; but was awakened before dawn by the arrival of the police. They found the body, and I cannot describe to you the state of my feelings when I heard of it—heard that the unhappy man had been shot by the light of the fire which he had helped to raise —for at the moment he fell the country round was as light as day. It appears the ruffians retreated to one of the huts, where they were cursing and swearing in a most fearful manner that they would yet have revenge; and I am grieved to add that a female servant heard one of them regretting not having shot the woman—meaning, I suppose myself; but his comrade called out to him to hold his tongue, and mind what he was about. When the alarm took place, William rushed to the back door, not knowing that Mr. Campbell was in the house, and that the shots had been fired at him. William there received a charge of slugs in his breast, four wounds in all, but fortunately not deep. Startled, he staggered on, got outside of the place, and could not find his way back. He is now all right.

As soon as the excitement had somewhat subsided, the public began to discuss how best Mr. and Mrs. Campbell's bravery could be rewarded, and their losses made good. Public meetings were held, laudatory speeches were made and subscriptions were raised. The reward of £1000 offered by the Government was, of course, handed over to Mr. Campbell, but the value of the property destroyed by the fire raised by the bushrangers was estimated at nearly double that amount, and although a goodly sum was raised, and every reputable person in the colony applauded them to the echo, the response was really not at all what it ought to have been. Mr. Campbell did not count the cost to himself, however, when single-handed he defied the common enemy, and he earned the gratitude, poorly expressed though it may have been, of every decent man and woman in New South Wales.

The two remaining members of the gang made no attempt to avenge the death of their comrade, but stripped the body of its valuables and disappeared in the darkness, making haste to reach a place where the police would not be likely to look for them for a day or two. Thus it happened that while the bush round Goimbla was being scoured by the authorities, Hall and Gilbert were many miles away laying their plans for future operations. After a few days' quiet they resumed operations on the road near Burrowa, in the Southern district, and some twenty cases of sticking-up were reported in one day.

About this time the gang was joined by a young fellow named Dunleavy, and a man named Gordon, generally known as the "Old Man." Of the latter's history previous to his association with Hall very little was known, and as he was captured soon after joining the gang he did not have many opportunities of distinguishing himself as a freebooter. Dunleavy was a smart young fellow, about twenty years of age, who up to the time of joining the gang had lived with his mother on a station in the Forbes district. He was well known about Bathurst, where in his youth he had attended one of the public schools, and those who knew him were greatly surprised when they heard that he had cast in his lot with the gang.

They were engaged with Hall in six highway robberies of the usual type, the road between Bathurst and Blayney being the scene of several. They then pushed on towards Cowra, stopped five drays which were on their way to Forbes, and ransacked the residence of Mr. T. P. Grant, J.P., soon afterwards leaving the Carcoar district for the Lachlan.

Shortly after this the gang came into collision

with a party of police under Sir Frederick Pottinger, near Forbes, and shots were exchanged, when both Hall and Dunleavy were wounded, the latter severely, having his wrist shattered by a bullet, but the former not very seriously. The bushrangers lost their horses, but managed to escape. Two months afterwards the "Old Man" was pressed very closely and escaped from Wheogo to the Murrumbidgee, and was cleverly tracked by two policemen and Billy, the black tracker, and arrested in a public house. He was brought back to Forbes, and it is said that Hall watched him being taken into town by the police. He was subsequently sent down to Bathurst, where he was tried and convicted and sentenced on three separate charges—for the first offence, ten years' hard labour on the roads, the first three in irons; for the second offence ten years; and for the third offence five years, the sentences to be cumulative.

The brush with the police appears to have intimidated Dunleavy, and a report was circulated that he had asked Hall's permission to give himself up, as Vane had done, but that Hall had refused to consent. Whether this was a fact or no, certain it is that Dunleavy did follow Vane's example, and voluntarily surrendered himself to the Rev. Father McGuinn, who was at that time labouring in the Carcoar district. He sent a message to the priest saying that he desired to see him, and the priest answered the call, when Dunleavy said he was sick of bushranging life and wanted him to go with him to Bathurst and deliver him over to the authorities. The two then rode into Bathurst and the bushranger was incarcerated in the gaol.

The two men were called up together at the Circuit Court in April, 1865, at which Judge Wise presided, and each of them pleaded guilty—the "Old Man" to six and Dunleavy to five charges of robbery under arms.

These rather rapid developments from the choice of a bushranging life to surrender, trial, sentence, and the entrance upon an almost life-long term of imprisonment, formed a powerful deterrent to other young men who may have been enamoured of the lawless life in the bush. Henceforth there were no more fresh recruits in the Western District Banditti, and one by one the remaining members of the gang established by Frank Gardiner came to the inevitable goal—the grave or the gaol for long-sentenced prisoners.

CHAPTER XIV.

BEN HALL IN EXTREMITY.

Shortly after the shooting of O'Meally, Gilbert disappeared from public view, and there were rumours that he and Hall had quarrelled and separated. That they had separated soon became evident, as Hall committed several robberies single-handed, and was known to be acting alone. This was before Gordon and Dunleavy joined him; and Gilbert was not present at any of the robberies in which Hall and the two men named engaged.

Hall had one very narrow escape from arrest while acting alone. He had returned to his old quarters at Wheogo, and had apparently been hard pressed, for he was almost famished with hunger, had only one boot on, and could scarcely walk when he alighted from his horse, his lameness being caused, so he said, by a bite from some insect in the bush. In this condition he called at Sandy Creek Station, and stayed there for a day and a half, making the owner cook his meals, and refusing to let any of the station hands leave the place. On the second morning two troopers and a black tracker rode up. Hall at once ran out of the kitchen, where his breakfast was being cooked, leaped on his mare and set off at a gallop towards the slip-rails; but to reach them he was com-

pelled to ride within ten yards of the black tracker and
one policeman. Before they had realised the situation,
Hall had nearly passed them, but then they saw who
he was, and the trooper fired, calling upon the black
boy to do likewise. The shots did not tell, however,
and Hall's return fire was equally futile. There was a
short and fruitless chase; Hall was on a horse that was
a splendid goer, and soon out-distanced his pursuers,
who returned to the station and demanded his rifle,
which they said he must have left behind. Wilson
denied that Hall had any rifle when he came there.
The troopers then searched the place, but no rifle was
to be found, and disappointed at losing Hall they arrested Wilson for harbouring him, at the same time
telling him to get his horse and go with them. This
he did, and very shortly thereafter was being escorted
to Forbes in custody.

Meanwhile Hall was not far off. He had doubled
back, and was watching the movements of the troopers
from a convenient "rise" in the ground, no greater distance than 150 yards away. The police did not see
him, but Wilson did, and in reply to a statement from
one of the troopers, when some distance along the
road, to the effect that they had at any rate sent Hall
some distance for his breakfast, Wilson informed them
that if they sent the tracker back he would find the
hoof marks of a horse with only one shoe on at the
spot indicated. But the police would not believe him,
and pushed along the road with their prisoner.

In less than an hour after the troopers had left the
place Hall re-appeared, much to the surprise of the
man who remained in charge. He led his horse up to

the kitchen and said to the man "Good morning, old
fellow. I have been watching them take my cook,
and must now finish cooking my breakfast myself."
He then breakfasted on five eggs with bread and
butter, and two pints of coffee, and finally departed,
leaving a message for the police that he had been back
to secure the meal of which they thought they had de-
prived him.

A month had not elapsed before another sensational attack disclosed the fact that Hall and Gilbert
had again come together, and that a young fellow
about eighteen years of age, named Johnny Dunn, had
fully cast in his lot with them. As previously stated,
the bushrangers were as anxious to obtain good horses
as they were to secure good firearms, and several well-
known racehorses had been stolen from their owners,
including Mr. Chisholm's Troubadour. They were
invariably well mounted, and the speed and endurance
of their steeds were frequently put to the test by the
hurried journeys from one place to another, the gang
not infrequently covering eighty or ninety, and on one
or two occasions fully a hundred miles in the twenty-
four hours. None but good horses would suit them
and none but good horses would they have; and these
they were repeatedly changing, having fresh mounts
always available.

Races had been fixed to take place at Young, and
no less than five noted race horses had been despatched
from Cowra to take part therein—Dick Turpin, Jemmy
Martin, Duke of Athol, Hollyhock, and Bergamot.
The knowledge that the bushrangers were somewhere
in the Lambing Flat neighbourhood had made the

owners of these horses more than ordinarily careful; hence they travelled together, and as Troopers McNamara and Scott, of the Bathurst mounted police, had, on the day of their starting, arrived from Bathurst,

JOHNNY DUNN

they accompanied the racing contingent, donning plain clothes for the journey.

At the Koorawatha Inn, Bang Bang, a temporary halt was called, and the horses properly stabled, while the party proceeded to take their ease in the verandah.

While sitting here they were suddenly startled by the appearance of three splendidly-mounted men, who without ceremony rode up to the verandah, covered them with their revolvers, and called upon them to throw up their hands. This they did as a matter of course, and while Hall, who was well-known to one or two of the party, stood guard over them, his two companions, Gilbert and Dunn—although the latter's identity was doubtful, and he was thought to be a ticket-of-leaver named Long White—rode to the gateway leading into the yard. Here the two troopers were busily engaged grooming their horses, which were standing in the yard unbridled and feeding. They were startled by hearing a voice commanding them to "leave them horses," and to find themselves covered by a carbine and revolver.

The troopers not immediately complying with the request, one of the bushrangers, flourishing his revolver, again exclaimed "I say once more, leave them horses!" On this Scott and McNamara drew their revolvers, and a brisk exchange of shots commenced. Soon the troopers advanced, Scott chasing Hall up the road, while Gilbert and Dunn posted themselves behind trees on the further side of the road, commanding the inn. When Scott returned, Gilbert fired at him: the ball struck the ground close to where the constable was standing and ricocheted into the hotel bar, but without doing any injury. The bushrangers now retreated to a distance, and after firing a final shot, left altogether. They had fired between twenty-five and thirty shots during the action, and the troopers, who had reserved their ammunition for closer quarters, only nine. On leaving, Hall called out that they would come again directly, and this the police fully expected they would do after reloading their pieces. They therefore made every preparation for giving them a warm reception, barricading the doors and loading with slugs the only available weapon in the house—an old double-barrelled gun—and as early as possible despatching a message to Cowra for assistance. The encounter occupied about fifteen minutes.

A vigilant watch was kept until midnight, when Sir Frederick Pottinger arrived with four troopers from Cowra; but as nothing further occurred during the night two of these were sent back in the morning. Shortly after daybreak the two troopers, Scott and Macnamara, proceeded to Young with the race horses, where they arrived in safety at 5 o'clock in the evening, while Sir Frederick scoured the bush in the neighbourhood.

As there was a danger that the gang might seize some of the crack horses while taking their "breathings," a detachment of police was told off to do duty on the course up to the termination of the race meeting, and a police escort accompanied the horses on their departure from the district.

Shortly after the unsuccessful raid at Bang Bang, Hall and his mates re-appeared at Canowindra, and stuck up Messrs. Pierce and Hilliar's store. On the following night they revisited the homestead of Mr. Rothery, but found the house so well prepared for them that they were afraid to attack it. They, however, secured three or four of Mr. Rothery's horses, and then set fire to a stack of hay, containing about fourteen tons, which, with a large shed, was entirely consumed.

Then for a space that locality had rest. They had operated sufficiently long in the Young and Carcoar districts to draw the main body of Western and Southern police thither; this dcne they suddenly shifted ground, making their appearance near Yass, about three days' ordinary journey distant. One of their first exploits in the locality was sticking up the coach than ran between Young and Yass. This exploit, however, realised only about twenty-five pounds. For two hours the coach was detained, as Hall said he expected other travellers to pass. A horseman and a carrier coming along the road were stopped and overhauled, each of the bushrangers taking from the loading on the latter's dray an assortment of clothing and other things. Shortly after the coach had been permitted to resume its journey a man named Barnes, who had been a special constable at Goimbla after O'Meally had been shot, was stopped and well flogged, Gilbert even proposing to lynch him.

The gang next lay in wait for the mail from Binalong to Yass; but a party of police happened to be on the road in advance of the mail, and seeing a camp fire near the road, they turned off to inspect. As they rode forward they were challenged, and a volley discharged at them; and before they could recover from their surprise, Hall and his mates were galloping off. Each was mounted on a stolen racehorse, three of the animals being recognised by the police as Harkaway, Teddington, and Troubadour, the latter being used as a pack horse.

The police reported that one of the number was very close to Hall when he fired his revolver, and that the flash covered the bandit's face, and it was believed that he had been seriously wounded. Even a report of his death was circulated—an untrue one, needless to say.

The traveller who carried much money about him during this reign of terror invited loss, and all manner of dodges were resorted to by those whom business called to travel to secrete money and valuables about their persons, their horses or their vehicles, in order that the bushrangers might not find it, should they happen to be stopped on the road. I was acquainted with one carrier who proved a man of ready resource in this direction. He had delivered a load of goods to a storekeeper in one of the larger towns and had received a large sum in payment, carriage at that time being high. He was afraid to trust his treasure to the mail, and equally afraid to carry it about his own person; and having obtained some back loading, the night before starting on the return journey he unhooked the grease-horn which swung under his dray, and having emptied it deposited the money in the bottom and then replaced the fat. It proved a safe bank, and when he reached home his "plant" of sovereigns was sound, though greasy. Had the bushrangers molested him on the road—which they didn't—they would not have thought of looking in the dirty grease-pot for booty.

THE SHOOTING OF SERGEANT PARRY.

So rapidly did mail robberies follow each other on the Southern road (I have mentioned only one or

two out of many) that the authorities determined upon
sending police guards with the coaches.

Early on the morning of 17th November, 1864,
Hall, Gilbert and Dunn appear to have resolved upon
"making a day of it" on the main road near Jugiong.
Before many hours had passed they were standing
guard over a motley group of scared mortals, many of
them residents of the immediate locality, in a spot just
off the road.   They bailed up people in buggies, drays
and carts, horsemen and pedestrians, "without respect
of persons," and for the time being well-dressed men
of means were compelled to rub shoulders with dust-
begrimed carriers and unkempt swagmen, while ladies
—to be very correct, there was only one—had to stand
cheek by jowl with loose-robed Chinamen, the whole
number bordering upon three score.   And over this
little army sometimes three and sometimes only one of
the bushrangers stood guard.   The reason of their
being kept thus together was obvious.   If any of them
had been permitted to enter the town the presence of
the gang on the road would have been made known
before they had accomplished their primary object,
which was to intercept the mail from Albury to Sydney.   Hence all must wait until the mail arrived.
Before it came, however, a police constable was added
to the throng: the three attacked him one after the
other, and when he had emptied his revolver at them
without effect he was compelled to surrender.

Shortly after this the Gundagai mail was seen approaching.   There were on the coach at the time
Constable Roach, of the Yass police, who had gone as
guard of the mail on the previous day to Gundagai

and was now returning to his station, and Mr. Rose, Police Magistrate of Gundagai; while two mounted troopers, Sub-inspector O'Neil and Sergeant Parry, of the Gundagai police, acted as the escort. When the bushrangers were first sighted the two troopers were riding together behind the coach, a short distance from it, but at a pre-concerted signal they galloped to the front, O'Neil confronting Hall and Dunn, and Parry exchanging shots with Gilbert, who called on him to surrender, and then, taking more deliberate aim with his gun, shot his opponent clean through the breast. Parry fell dead from his saddle. By this time O'Neil had pretty well expended his stock of ammunition, and seeing his companion fall before Gilbert's fire he surrendered and was conducted to the "camp," where the other prisoners still stood watching the proceedings and afraid to move.

On the termination of the fight Gilbert looked at the dead body of Parry and said to one of the bystanders "I am sorry for him, for he was a brave fellow; I don't like to shoot a man, and he's the first man I ever shot, but I can't help the poor fellow now."

Meanwhile the coachman had retained his seat, as also had the Police Magistrate; but Constable Roche had slipped out behind and disappeared in the bush. The Police Magistrate had commanded him not to fire from the coach and had advised him to get behind a tree within firing range; but finding that one of his comrades had been shot and that the other had surrendered he took to his heels. After all his conduct was only on a par with that of the Police Magistrate, whose orders he was bound to obey, and both were afterwards called to account for having shown the white feather.

The mail was a heavy one, and the gang made a good haul from the bags, in addition to about £100 gathered from the parties whom they had previously bailed up. Shortly afterwards the bushrangers left. Parry's body was placed upon one of the drays and taken to Jugiong, where a magisterial investigation was held by Mr. Rose, and a verdict of wilful murder was returned against Hall, Gilbert, and Dunn, for whose apprehension warrants were there and then issued. The police were, of course, active for some time after, with the usual want of result.

The shedding of Sergeant Parry's blood appears to have made the gang more determined than ever in their attacks, knowing that they could not expect any mercy if they fell into the hands of the authorities. Hall began to make enquiries as to the whereabouts of the Bishop of Goulburn and the Attorney-General, who were travelling in the district, saying that he intended to bail them up and hold them in custody until the Government granted him and Gilbert a pardon.

The gang found it prudent, however, to get right away from the district and to keep away, for a time at least; and they were next heard of as having crossed the Lachlan, making for their old quarters near Canowindra, and subscribing towards some races that were to be held at Bandon. But they kept very quiet, and did not engage in any sensational exploits; and while the police were making efforts to discover their hiding place in this locality, they suddenly re-appeared on the Goulburn and Braidwood side.

This time they found one man, at any rate, who was not inclined to cower before them. A Mr. William Macleay had been to Wagga Wagga, and had reached Goulburn on his return journey to Sydney, when he heard that Hall, Gilbert and Dunn were on the road in advance of him, and that they had held the road for several hours that morning near Towrang, successfully sticking up a large number of people. But he was not to be deterred from prosecuting his journey, and proceeded along the road in his buggy, with a boy as driver. On reaching Towrang, and at different places on the road between that place and Shelley's Flats, he was told that the bushrangers were riding leisurely along the road ahead of him, but he saw nothing of them until he sighted the hill which looked down upon Plum's inn, at the Flats just mentioned. Some half mile or so from the top of the hill he met the up-coach and was informed by the passengers that they had just been stuck up and then allowed to proceed on towards Goulburn. They pointed out to Mr. Macleay the bushrangers on the hill, where there were some teams and a number of people stuck up, and endeavoured to persuade him either to return, or at all events to send his arms (a Tranter revolver and a Tranter revolving rifle) back in the coach to Goulburn, as he could scarcely contend by himself against three. Mr. Macleay, however, preferred to go on and keep his arms. When he approached within three or four hundred yards of the gang, who were dismounted and apparently engaged in ransacking some cases taken from the drays, he got out of his buggy and told the boy to drive the horses slowly along the middle of the road, while he, rifle in hand, walked on the right hand side. The robbers immediately discontinued their work, mounted their horses, and cantered into the bush on the left hand side of the road. Mr. Macleay walked on to where the people were standing, and inquired whether they had not been stuck-up, but could get no answer, as they appeared afraid to give him any information. He then proceeded down the hill towards Plum's (half a mile off), still walking, while the boy drove the buggy, and reached the bottom of the hill without seeing anything more of the bushrangers. At that point the land was cleared on both sides and fenced in. Mr. Macleay then got into his buggy, about three hundred yards from Plum's, and told his boy to drive on rapidly to the inn. He had scarcely entered the buggy when two of the bushrangers rode after him from the left hand side of the road, and one of them fired at him without effect. On reaching Plum's, he found a number of persons collected there for a wedding; while he was speaking to them, the bushrangers dismounted at the corner of a paddock on the road side, near the spot where he was when they fired at him, and remained there for a few moments, apparently in consultation. He was anxious to get Plum's verandah cleared of the people, most of whom were females, before fighting began; as soon as this could be done, he went to the corner of the verandah to fire at the bushrangers, who at once mounted their horses and rode off. He fired one shot at them, apparently without effect, and saw them no more; but ten minutes after they had ridden off two troopers from Marulan came up, and shortly after four more from Goulburn. These immediately set out in the direction taken by Hall and his mates, but they did not happen to come up with them.

The news of Mr. Macleay's daring movement reached Sydney before him, and he arrived at home to find his praises being loudly sung in public.

Macleay's, however, was an isolated case. Mail robberies again became frequent, and every day brought some fresh case of highway robbery. Towards the end of February the Goulburn police came into actual collision with the gang and very nearly succeeded in capturing them in the barn of a house on Breadalbane Plains: in this encounter Hall was wounded and a trooper was shot in the leg. It is refreshing to find that the combatants were at last beginning to shoot fairly straight,

A day or two afterwards a man out looking for a horse came across a number of letters in the bush. He gave information, and Captain Zouch proceeded to the spot, where he recovered as many letters as were sufficient to half fill a three bushel bag, and drafts and cheques to the value of about £7600.

Not long after this the gang took complete possession of the road near Collector, and stopped no less than twelve carriers with their drays, keeping them together in a crowd while they overhauled the loading. One or the other of the bushrangers meanwhile kept a look-out for other travellers, and brought them up to the "camp," until there were about thirty under their charge. From these they took various amounts ranging from 2s 6d up to £11 12s, together with such watches and other valuables as pleased their taste.

They broke open several of the cases and helped themselves to bottled porter, biscuits, &c., and added to their arms a good double-barrel gun that was among the goods. While the bushrangers were thus engaged Judge Meymot passed the spot on his regular circuit work, attended by the regulation escort—two troopers on horseback. He saw one of the bushrangers, and so did the troopers, for Gilbert rode out from the bush and one of the troopers immediately started in pursuit. But the judge called him back, and as the bushrangers did not appear to think it worth while to attack the judge, he reached Collector without molestation. The local police at once started out in search, attended by the two troopers who had acted as escort to the judge, and by a magistrate and a civilian. But the bushrangers had shifted ground, and shortly afterwards entered the township, and proceeded to stick up Kimberley's inn. Ben Hall and Gilbert entered the house, Dunn being left outside. Presently he gave the alarm, "Constables coming." "You can manage them, Jack," said Hall, and Dunn went out to meet the danger, which he had somewhat exaggerated. A solitary constable—Samuel Nelson, the one man of the force who had been left in the town—had heard the firing, and rightly concluded that the bushrangers were near at hand. Seizing his carbine and fixing his bayonet he at once proceeded in the direction of Kimberley's hotel, walking smartly along the road by the fence. Behind the fence Dunn crouched, and, with revolver at the "ready," awaited the nearer approach of the hurrying constable. Almost out of breath with the haste which he had been making, Nelson was within ten yards of the place when the bushranger suddenly jumping up cried out "Stand! Go back!" at the same time firing his revolver. The shot took effect; but Nelson staggered on towards his assailant. Before he could recover himself, Dunn raised his rifle and fired, and Nelson fell shot through the heart. Dunn went back to his mates and told them what he had done; they stripped the corpse of belt and carbine and rode off with all the booty they had accumulated.

Subsequently the police who had gone out sighted them on the brow of a hill and immediately gave chase; but the bushrangers leaped their horses over logs and plunged into the bush. The night being very dark, their pursuers lost sight of them, and returned to Collector.

On the following day an inquest was held upon the body of the unfortunate Constable Nelson, and a verdict of wilful murder was returned against Dunn, and against Hall and Gilbert for aiding and abetting. The murdered man had been in the police force for some years, and was greatly respected. He left a widow and eight children, and it is satisfactory to know that these received consideration at the hands of the Government and the public at a later date, although no monetary allowance could conmpensate them for the bread winner who had laid down his life on the altar of duty.

The gang now beset the Goulburn to Braidwood road, sticking up the mail coach and many travellers, and coming occasionally into conflict with the police; they also made an attempt on the gold escort coming from Araluen to Braidwood. But before the end of

March they had forsaken this field of prolific adventure and returned to their old haunts on the Lachlan. Here they visited several stations for choice horses which they knew to be there, and appropriated such as they deemed best suited for their purpose, generally leaving in exchange those they had ridden almost to breaking-down point in the service. Thus it was that sooner or later the owners of the "bloods" that were taken in different parts of the country regained their valuable steeds, but all considerably "the worse for wear." Among other places visited about this time were Strickland's Bundaburra Station, Bowler's Gumbidgiwa Station, and Atkins', at the Billabong. But the one exploit which again directed all eyes to that quarter was a raid upon one of the principal stores in Forbes, made at a late hour one Saturday night in March. This resulted in a booty of about £80 in cash, and nearly as much in clothing and other stores. There was, of course, great excitement in the town, and the police were informed of the visit shortly after the gang had left the store; but, as it happened, there were no men available for immediate pursuit, and the robbers were far enough away, or safely enough hidden, before their tracks through the town had been picked up.

THE ACT OF OUTLAWRY.

The continued outrages of the bushrangers, and the powerlessness of the police to capture or shoot them, as may be readily imagined, gave the Government great concern, and at last they determined to resort to extreme measures.   At every sitting of Parliament the subject was referred to, and every individual representative of the people was prepared to propound a scheme for the capture of the gang which should prove more effective than any that had yet been tried. Volunteers had more than once been engaged in the infested districts, to work independently of the police; the police force had been strengthened to the fullest limit possible, the cream of the force being sent into the bush with almost unlimited powers at their command; but the bushrangers had laughed at both alike, defied both alike, outwitted both alike.   It was then decided to pass an Act—the Felons Apprehension Act —which should make the bushrangers outlaws, and place it within the power of anyone who might come across them to shoot them down like dogs.   How stringent the provisions of this Act were may be seen from the following summary of its provisions.

The first section was to the effect that against any person charged on oath made before a justice of the peace with the commission of a felony punishable by law with death, and who might be at large, a warrant might be issued.   Any judge of the Supreme Court, being satisfied by affidavit of these facts, was empowered to issue a bench warrant for the apprehension of the person so charged, and to order the insertion of a summons in the "Government Gazette" requiring the accused person to surrender himself on or before a given day and at a place specified to abide his trial for the crime of which he stood accused.   The judge might also direct the publication of such summons in such manner and form as should appear to him to be best calculated to bring such summons to the knowledge of the accused.

Section two ran as follows :—

If the person so charged shall not surrender himself for trial pursuant to such summons or shall not be apprehended or being apprehended or having surrendered shall escape so that he shall not be in custody on the day specified in such summons he shall upon proof thereof by affidavit to the Judge of the Supreme Court and of the due publication of the summons be deemed outlawed, and shall and may thereupon be adjudged and declared to be an outlaw accordingly by such Judge by a declaration to that effect under his hand filed in the said Court of Record. And if after Proclamation by the Governor with the advice of the Executive Council of the fact of such adjudication shall have been published in the "Gazette" and in one or more Sydney and one or more country newspapers such outlaw shall afterwards be found at large armed or there being reasonable grounds to believe that he is armed it shall be lawful for any of Her Majesty's subjects whether a constable or not and without being accountable for using of any deadly weapon in aid of such apprehension whether its use be preceded by a demand of surrender or not to apprehend or take such outlaw alive or dead.

Section three enacted that proclamation should be evidence of outlawry; and Section four read as follows :—

If after such proclamation any person shall voluntarily and knowingly harbour conceal or receive or give any aid shelter or sustenance to such outlaw or provide him with firearms or any other weapon or with ammunition or any horse equipment or other assistance or directly or indirectly give or cause to be given to him or any of his accomplices information tending or with intent to facilitate the commission by him of further crime or to enable him to escape from justice or shall withhold information or give false information concerning such outlaw from or to any Officer of Police or Constable in quest of such outlaw—the person so offending shall be guilty of felony and being thereof convicted shall forfeit all his lands as well as goods and shall be liable to imprisonment with or without hard labour for such period not exceeding fifteen years as the Court shall determine and no allegation or proof by the party so offending that he was at the time under compulsion shall be deemed a defence unless he shall as soon as possible afterwards have gone before a Justice of the Peace or some officer of the Police Force and then to the best of his ability given full information respecting such outlaw and make a declaration on oath voluntarily and fully of the facts connected with such compulsion.

The fifth Section had reference to the form of indictment under the previous section, and the sixth enacted that—

Any justice or officer of the police force having reasonable cause to suspect that an outlaw or accused person summoned under the provisions of this Act is concealed or harboured in or on any dwelling house or premises may alone or accompanied by any persons acting in his aid and either by day or by night demand admission into and if refused admission may break and enter such dwelling house or premises and therein apprehend every person whom he shall have reasonable ground for believing to be such outlaw or accused person and may thereupon seize all arms found in or on such house or premises and also apprehend all persons found in or about the same whom such justice or officer shall have reasonable ground for believing to have concealed harboured or otherwise succoured or assisted such outlaw or accused person. And all persons and arms so apprehended and seized shall be forthwith taken before some convenient justice of the peace to be further dealt with and disposed of according to law.

The seventh section made it lawful for any police officer or constable in the pursuit of any outlaw to demand and take and use any horses not being in actual employment on the road; and also arms, saddles, forage, sustenance, equipments, or ammunition required for the purposes of the pursuit. The eighth section fixed the duration of the Act—which was to continue in force for the period of one year from the date of its passing; and the last remaining section enacted that transfer or conveyance of the property of harbourers should be voided on their committal.

A more drastic measure could not well be conceived, and there can be found in it a very fair reflection of the feeling of unrest which stirred the breasts of the people's representatives and moved them to its passing. When it is remembered, however, that it was directed, not against a large and powerful force, but against less than half a dozen young men, it will be seen that it was also a lamentable confession of the inoperativeness of British law, and of the weakness of the peace-preserving machinery of the country. Nevertheless, it, or something like it, appeared to be necessary; and it had the merit of inspiring the police, who had hitherto proved inefficient all along the line, with the hope of reward; although at the same time it might terrify settlers in the infested districts with the fear of undeserved punishment.

In due course of time after the passing of the Act, Hall, Gilbert, and Dunn were formally commanded through the "Gazette" and newspapers, by summons under the hand of the Chief Justice, to surrender, the affidavit and information necessary thereto having been judicially made and laid. As they did not surrender, the next step was to issue the following:—

PROCLAMATION.

By His Excellency the Right Honourable Sir John Young, Baronet, Knight Commander of the Most Honourable Order of the Bath, Knight Grand Cross of St. Michael and St. George, Captain General and Governor-in-Chief of the Colony of New South Wales, and Vice-Admiral of the same.

Whereas on the 12th day of April last, an information was duly filed in the Supreme Court of New South Wales, by the Honourable John Bayley Darvell, Esquire, Her Majesty's Attorney General for the said Colony, charging John Gilbert, Benjamin Hall, and John Dunn with the crime of Murder: And whereas by writ of Summons, bearing date the seventeenth day of April last. under the hand and seal of Sir Alfred Stephen, Knight Commander of the Bath, Chief Justice of the said Colony, the said John Gilbert. Benjamin Hall, and John Dunn were, under and in pursuance of "The Felons' Apprehension Act," duly summoned to surrender themselves into the custody of the Gaoler of Her Majesty's Gaol at Goulburn, on or before Saturday, the twenty-ninth day of April last, to abide their trial severally for that crime: And whereas the said John Gilbert, Benjamin Hall, and John Dunn did not, nor did any one or more of them surrender themselves or himself as required by the said summons: And whereas the said Sir Alfred Stephen, Knight, as such Chief Justice as aforesaid, hath, by a declaration to that effect under his hand bearing date the eighth day of May instant, duly adjudged and declared each of them the said John Gilbert,* and John Dunn to be an Outlaw: Now I, the Governor aforesaid, by and with the advice of the Executive Council of the said Colony, in pursuance of the authority in me vested under and by virtue of the said Act, do hereby notify and declare that each of them, the said John Gilbert and John Dunn, was on the eighth day of May instant, duly adjudged and declared to be an Outlaw by the said Sir Alfred Stephen, as such Chief Justice as aforesaid, by a declaration to that effect under his hand, and that the said declaration was, on the said eighth day of May filed in the said Court of Record.

Given under my Hand and Seal, at Government House, Sydney, this tenth day of May, in the year of our Lord one thousand eight hundred and sixty-five, and in the twenty-eighth year of Her Majesty's Reign.

(L.S.) JOHN YOUNG.

By His Excellency's Command,

CHARLES COWPER.

GOD SAVE THE QUEEN!

Thus the clouds of doom gathered thick around the heads of the denounced murderers; and those who aided them in any way were also threatened with penalties of the heaviest kind. Although until the actual proclamation of the outlawry the severest penalties of the new law were not incurred, yet, as was set out in the Chief Justice's summons, the ordinary criminal law provided for the punishment of all who gave assistance in any manner to the accused criminals, for the

---

* Ben Hall had been shot (see *infra*) before May 8, and his name is therefore omitted here.

purpose of enabling them or either of them to elude
justice, and such persons were warned that they might
"become thereby accessories to the murders with which
those parties stand accused." After the proclamation
of outlawry on 10th May the penalties against
harbourers, "telegraphs," and others were made still
more stringent, and any persons giving the slightest
aid to the outlaws rendered themselves liable to the
punishment of fifteen years' hard labour on the roads,
with forfeiture of all real and personal property, without any reference whatever to the crimes with which
the outlaws stood charged. As to the outlaws themselves, as has been stated, anyone could kill them; one,
indeed, had already been shot like a mad dog.

After the robbery of Jones' store at Forbes the
three bushrangers had no rest night or day. The
police by this time had become well acquainted with
their haunts, and were always watching the dwellings
of those who were known to be sympathisers, so that
they were compelled to move with the utmost caution
when near those places; in addition to which the bush
was, to use the words of one who moved with them,
"literally alive with police." With every avenue of
escape closely watched and every place of shelter as
carefully guarded, the wretched men were driven to
seek temporary rest among the fastnesses of the mountains; but even here they were not safe; and they appear to have realised that their race was nearly run.
Only one or two stations were visited after they left
Forbes on the night of Jones' robbery, and before a
month had elapsed, the meshes closed around the
leader of the gang.

Hall had separated from Gilbert and Dunn for the time being, and had visited a house with the occupants of which he was reported to have held a somewhat close connection. It was believed, indeed, that certain moneys banked in Forbes by the head of the household had really been placed there for Ben Hall, from whose hands he had received it; and that Hall was camped in the bush close by, waiting to obtain some of the money, when the police surprised and shot him. The manner of the shooting is still in dispute. The police evidence, which I give, certainly tells part of the story, but probably not the whole truth.

Giving evidence before the Coroner at Forbes, James Henry Davidson, Sub-Inspector of Police, declared as follows :—

On last Saturday morning, 29th April, I left the police camp Forbes, and started with five men and two trackers in pursuit of the bushrangers, Hall, Gilbert and Dunn. On the evening of the fifth day from leaving Forbes we came upon two horses hobbled in the scrub, about 12 miles from Forbes, near the Billybong Creek. We watched the horses for about half an hour when we saw a man approach, who caught the horses; he passed close by where we were standing; he caught the horses and led them away about 100 yards. This was about 10 o'clock in the evening. We did not recognise the man; he took the horses about 100 yards and hobbled them again. Shortly afterwards the tracker, Billy Dargin, informed me that he heard the man he saw lead away and hobble the horses making a noise among the dead leaves, as though he was preparing a bed for himself. I then placed five of the men in my charge where we were standing and went with Sergeant Condell and Billy Dargin on the other side of the man, with the intention of attacking him in his camp, should we discover that he was Ben Hall. We could not get within 100 yards of the man, in consequence of his horses snorting at our approach. I then determined to wait until daybreak. About half-past six in the morning I saw a man with a bridle in his hand about 150 yards from where I was, approaching the horses. By this time the horses were feeding on a plain, bordering the scrub, and when the man was about half way from the border of the scrub to the horses, myself, Sergeant Condell and Billy Dargin ran after him. After running about 50 yards, the man became aware of our presence, and ran in the direction where the five men were posted. By this time I had identified the man as Ben Hall. I several times called on him to stand. After running about 100 yards, I got within 40 yards of Hall and fired at him with a double barrelled gun. Hall after my firing jumped a little and looked back, and from his movements I have reason to believe that I hit him. Sergeant Condell and Dargin the tracker fired immediately afterwards; they were running a little to the left of me and not far away. From the manner of Hall I have every reason to believe that Condell's and Dargin's shots took effect. From that time he ran more slowly towards a few saplings. The five police, who were stationed beyond him, immediately ran towards him and fired. I noticed trooper Hipkiss firing at Hall with a rifle and immediately afterwards the belt holding his revolvers fell off him. At this time he held himself up by a sapling, and upon receiving Hipkiss' fire he gradually fell backwards. Several other shots were fired afterwards. There were about 30 shots in all. Hall then cried out, "I am wounded, shoot me dead!" I then went up to the body, and noticed that life was extinct. I also observed that the bullet fired by Hipkiss passed through his body. I searched the body; there was £74 in notes in two chamois leather bags—one in his trousers pocket, the other in his coat breast pocket—three gold chains and a gold watch, a portrait of a female, three revolvers, and a number of bullets in his pockets, and a gold ring keeper on his fingers. Along with his saddle was a quantity of wearing apparel; there were also two single blankets. I know the body to be that of Ben Hall. His clothing I observed to be perforated with bullets. We caught the horses, and fixed the body of deceased on the saddle, and in this manner brought him to Forbes.

Sergeant Condell's story was corroborative of that told by Davidson. He said that when he fired at Hall he aimed at his back between the shoulders, and believed he hit him. He also stated that when Hall had hold of the sapling he cried out twice, "I am dying! I am dying!" and then it was that the full volley from the other men was poured into him, after which he threw out his feet convulsively, and rolled over dead.

DEATH OF BEN HALL

Of the thirty shots fifteen took effect, and when examined subsequently the body was found literally perforated with bullets; there were three holes in the head, four in the left shoulder, two in the right side, and others in other parts of the body.

During the day the body was tied up and packed on the saddle found in the bushranger's camp, and brought into Forbes on one of the horses which he had ridden to the spot—a favourite animal of Mr. Bowler's, named Tomboy, which had been stolen from Gumbidgewa station about a fortnight before. There was great excitement in Forbes when the news arrived, and after the body had been brought in people flocked to the barracks to view the remains of the man whose name for so long a time had been a terror. At the inquest which followed the police told their story, as I have given it here. Billy Dargin, the black tracker—a most intelligent aboriginal—subsequently told a different story when wandering about the country, which indicated that the bushranger received most of his wounds when lying on the ground.

The body was buried in Forbes on the Sunday following, relatives and friends attending the funeral as genuine mourners. It is said that the miniature found upon his person after death by the police was that of a favourite sister—then living near Maitland—and that he had constantly carried it about with him during his three years of bushranging. The reward of £1000 was duly paid over—£500 going to his betrayer and £500 to the police.

It is probable that Gilbert and Dunn were somewhere in the locality when Hall was shot. A few days afterwards they were seen near Marengo, making their way in the direction of Yass. At this time they presented a very jaded appearance, while their horses were much blown and nearly knocked-up, having evidently been ridden very hard. A few days after this they appeared at the Rocky Ponds, near Binalong, where they stole fresh horses, leaving those they had been riding in exchange; but they do not appear to have committed any other robberies, their object in visiting that part being to obtain temporary shelter and rest at the house of a farmer named Kelly, who was Dunn's grandfather, and had on previous occasions harboured the bushrangers.

Whether the penal clauses of the Felons' Apprehension Act bearing upon harbourers had intimidated the old man, or the large reward offered for the apprehension of the bushrangers tempted him, I cannot say; but that he received them only to betray them does not admit of any question. Gilbert and Dunn reached his house on Friday, 12th May. On the evening of the same day the Binalong police were watching the house, a watch which they preserved during the whole night, themselves being hidden. But as nothing occurred to warrant any further forward movement, at daybreak they returned to the police station. An hour after their return, however, fresh information was conveyed to them, and they at once retraced their steps to Kelly's, where they arrived at about 9 o'clock. After they had been waiting for about an hour, watching the family move about, they made for the door, and Kelly, seeing them, exclaimed in a loud voice, "Look out! the house is surrounded by troopers."

The police then rushed the hut, firing through a closed door into an inner room, and the two bushrangers bolted out through a paddock to a creek. Here Gilbert took up a position behind a tree and aimed at the constables with his revolving rifle, but it missed fire; he then went down the bank, and two policemen almost simultaneously fired at him as he was running along the dry creek bed. He fell immediately. Dunn ran off, hotly pursued, and escaped in the scrub.

On the day following an inquest was held at Binalong upon Gilbert's remains, and the jury returned the following verdict:—"That the said John Gilbert came to his death by a gunshot wound inflicted on Saturday, May 13th, 1865, near Binalong, in the said colony, by one of the constables in the police force of New South Wales, in the execution of their duty, and that they were justified in inflicting the said wounds which caused his death." The jury further expressed their approval of the conduct of the constables in so gallantly attacking the bushrangers and fighting one of them to the death. After the inquest the body was kept for a time at the Binalong police barracks, and there was some talk of having a plaster-of-Paris cast of the face taken; but whether this intention was ever carried out I cannot say. The remains of the dead outlaw were, without much ceremony, subsequently interred in the police paddock at Binalong.

From the time that his name came prominently before the public in connection with the Eugowra Escort Robbery to the time of his death, Gilbert had participated in the following crimes:—

1862.

June 15.—Attacked the Gold Escort at Eugowra Creek, carried off a large amount of gold, and wounded one of the police.

1863.

February 2.—Robbed a store at Spring Creek, and stole a saddle and bridle.

March 14.—Robbed store at Fisher's Creek; stole saddle, bridle and watch.

May 16.—Robbed Mr. Barnes' store at Cootamundra, and attempted to fire the place.

May 29.—Stole a racehorse at Burrowa.

June 1.—Robbed a store at Spring Creek.

June 7.—Robbed a store at Possum Flat.

June 16.—Stole two racehorses at Currawang.

June 29.—Robbed several travellers on the Forbes Road.

July 3.—Robbed a man of money, watch and chain on the Lambing Flat road.

July 13.—Robbed a man of £7 near Burrowa.

July 30.—Robbed a store at Caloola of money and goods to the value of £300.

August 19.—Stole two horses from the Burthong Station, near Young.

August 24.—Robbed four storekeepers on the Hurricane Gully road.

August 27.—Robbed two stores at Tirnee.

August 29.—Robbed Mr. Edmunds' house at Demondrill.

September 19.—Robbed the mail from Cowra to Bathurst.

September 24.—Robbed Mr. Hosie's store at Caloola.

October 10.—Assisted in the raid on Bathurst.

October 24.—Attacked Mr. Keightley's house at Dunn's Plains, on which occasion Burke was shot.

November 19.—Attacked Mr. Campbell's house at Goimbla, when O'Meally was shot.

December.—Robbed the mail from Burrowa to Binalong.

December 9.—Robbed the mail from Binalong to Yass; also, stole two horses from Mr. Garry of Mylora.

December 16.—Stole a horse belonging to Mr. R. Salmon.

1864.

October 29.—Robbed the mail from Albury to Yass; robbed a store at Jugiong of a quantity of goods; also, stole two horses.

October 27.—Robbed Mr. McCaush's store at Bagan Bagan, of jewellery, &c.; robbed a Chinaman of money and a gold watch.

November 8.—Stole from Rossiville, near Goulburn, jewellery, three horses, and some saddlery.

November 9.—Robbed the Sydney mail, six miles from Goulburn.

November 11.—Robbed the mail from Yass to Goulburn.

November 15.—Robbed the mail from Gundagai to Yass, firing on the police and killing Sergeant Parry.

November 19.—Stole three horses from the Bolero station.

December 10.—Stole some property from Mr. McLachlan, of Young.

December 25.—Robbed and burned Mr. Morris's store, at Binda.

December 30.—Robbed Mr. Davidson's store at Murrumbah Plains.

1865.

January 19.—Robbed a store at Wheogo.

January 24.—Robbed John Ross and others on the Yass road.

January 27.—Robbed a public house near Collector, when Constable Nelson was mortally wounded by Dunn.

February 6.—Robbed the Braidwood mail, twelve miles from Goulburn.

February 18.—Stole three horses, at Molonglo.

February 23.—Had an encounter with the Goulburn police at Mutbilly, when Constable Wiles was wounded.

March 5.—Robbed the Goulburn and Gundaroo mail, at Geary's Gap.

March 13.—Robbed the Araluen Escort, when two constables were wounded; stole two horses from Jinglemoney.

March 21.—Took two horses from Suttor's station.

March 23.—Stole two racehorses of Mr. Morton's.

March 25.—Robbed Jones' store at Forbes of £80 in cash and goods valued at £30.

April 10.—Robbed Watts' public house at Newrea, the White Horse Inn, at White Rock, and Gultimore's store, taking £48 in cash and £30 worth of goods.

Shortly after the last-mentioned robbery he was killed.

The reward offered by the Government was apportioned as follows:—To the informer, £500; to Senior-constable Hales, £150; to Constable Bright, £130; to Constable King, £120; and to Constable Hall, £100.

By the death of this notorious scoundrel the gang was fairly broken up. Two of the gang—Vane and Dunleavy—had saved their lives by giving themselves up; two others—Burke and O'Meally—had been shot down by settlers whose homesteads they had attacked; and two others—Hall and Gilbert, the two acknowledged leaders—had been betrayed by trusted associates and fallen dead before the fire of the police. Only one—John Dunn—now remained to be accounted for, and as he had been wounded in the leg by a bullet during the encounter in which his last remaining mate had fallen, and had, furthermore, made his escape on foot, it was thought impossible for him to evade capture for any length of time.

Dunn evidently realised his danger. Wounded as he was—he carried a bullet in his leg—had he not been afraid to trust those who had befriended him in the past, he would no doubt have sought refuge in one or other of their houses for a time. But the only alternative before him now was flight. Had the Binalong police followed up the pursuit speedily it is probable that they would have succeeded in running the fugitive down before he succeeded in obtaining a horse, as he soon did. Reaching Mr. Julien's station, near Bogolong, about ten miles from Binalong, he demanded and obtained from Mrs. Julien—the men folk were away—a horse, saddle and bridle; and, well-mounted, but evidently weak from loss of blood, which had flowed freely from his wound and covered his clothes, he set out across country, taking back tracks and unfrequented roads, with the object of passing away from his old haunts unobserved. He rode hard and long without rest. Water was scarce, and time was too precious to spend in searching for it. He overtaxed his horse's strength at last, and as the poor beast staggered and fell beneath him, he opened his knife, cut its throat, drank the hot blood, and then lay down in the dead horse's narrow shade until the sun sank below the western horizon, when he "humped his swag" and resumed his flight, making his way by the help of the stars. Near daylight he reached a small, lonely out-station; he was nearly exhausted and was obliged to ask for rations, after he had drunk his fill at the waterhole. The stockman was away at the head station, mustering; the wife was alone and was full of pity for the slim lad with the heavy swag. After she had left him, and when he was sleeping the sleep of utter exhaustion, she gave way to an impulse of curiosity, opened the heavy swag which he had left on the table, and shivered when she saw the weight was accounted for by two big loaded and capped revolvers. She did it up again carefully, plied the lad with all manner of good things to take with him when he went on refreshed, and, enlightened by subsequent events, she told her children, and tells her grand-children now, by the way, how she entertained Johnny Dunn at breakfast.

For eight months after this nothing was heard of Dunn, and the authorities concluded that he had either perished in the bush or had escaped from the colony. But he was neither dead nor distant, and at the expiration of the time stated the police at Bourke and Walgett received certain information which led them to patrol the courses of the Culgoa, Bemo and Bokara.

They expected to find the missing outlaw working with another bushranger named Ward, more generally known by the significant title of "Thunderbolt." This was not true, but Dunn was in the neighbourhood, having been engaged for some time as a horse-breaker on one of the stations there. The police actually called at this station, but the outlaw had by some means become aware of their proximity, and had made off with one of the best colts on the run. Subsequently Sergeant Flynn and Constable Drake, of the Walgett police, set out upon a journey of sixty miles, which distance they covered in a day, and encamped within sight of McPhail's station, on the Wammerawa Creek. Made wise by the experience of the past the police adopted precautions, fearing that even at this remote spot Dunn might have a "telegraph" on the watch, ready to warn him of the approach of the police.

That these suspicions were correct and the precautions necessary was proved by subsequent events. Dunn was not at the station, but a confederate was, and at the very time the police arrived he was in communication with the outlaw. After consulting the station owners the constables arrested and questioned the confederate, who after a good deal of hesitation agreed to lead them to their quarry. They approached to within one hundred yards of Dunn's camp unobserved, and then it was apparent that the "telegraph" had done its work. There stood Dunn, holding a fine bay horse, which he was in the act of mounting—holding the reins in one hand and a revolver in the other. The moment he saw the police he vaulted into the saddle and challenged them to "Come on!" The challenge was accepted, but the police soon realised that the horses they rode were very inferior as racers to that upon which the outlaw was mounted. For six long miles the chase was tenaciously maintained, Dunn keeping just out of pistol shot, displaying a seat which proved him a perfect horseman, and nursing his horse in a manner that indicated he meant a long run for his life. Throughout the chase it did not appear that Dunn desired to outstrip his pursuers, but rather to exhaust them, and for this purpose he frequently waited until they approached within three hundred yards of him. and then he would gradually increase the distance again, leading them through tall wire brush ten feet high, across broken swamps and plains, and lastly into a dense pine scrub, known as "The Monkey." It was in the latter place the pursuers were reluctantly compelled to relinquish the pursuit; and once more Dunn had got clear away.

A fortnight elapsed, and then he was heard of as heading for his old haunts in the Lachlan district, having a companion with him; but no definite information concerning his movements could be obtained, until, by the merest accident, a party of police who were on the look-out for other game in a lonely part of the bush encountered him. Troopers McHale, Hawthorne and Elliott, of the Canonbar police, had started out in search of a sly-grog cart which was reported to be somewhere in the neighbourhood of Perry's station on the Marthaguy; and at the same time were keeping their eyes open in the hope of catching sight of a somewhat notorious character named "Yellow George," a half-caste, who was gazetted as "wanted." Having

called at the station they found that in order to secure
their quarry they must proceed very carefully, and they
therefore turned out their horses and continued their
journey on foot, carrying their blankets and provisions, as ordinary "swagsmen." They were making
for a certain hut occupied by a man named Walton,
where "Yellow George" was supposed to be, and as
night came on before they had covered the whole distance they camped until daylight, when they started
again in single file through a dense scrub, Elliott leading. When within a quarter of a mile of the hut they
reached an open space of ground, from which they
could see the building and sheep-yard, and they then
made a more rapid movement. As they drew nearer
the hut, however, the sheep dogs began to bark
furiously, and as soon as this alarm was raised a man
was seen looking cautiously round the end of the hut.
Catching sight of Elliott, the man immediately bolted
for the bush, Elliott giving chase and McHale taking
an opposite direction with the view of intercepting the
fugitive in running. But when putting on speed
McHale noticed another man (who turned out to be
Dunn) running across the sheep yard, and abandoning
his first intention, gave chase to him. As Dunn
jumped the fence McHale noticed that he carried two
revolvers, and calling upon him to stand he drew his
own revolver and fired at him, but missed. Still keeping up the chase McHale saw that he was gaining on
the fugitive, and when within about seventy yards of
him he again challenged him and fired, the shot evidently passing close to Dunn's head, for he suddenly
jerked aside as he ran. McHale then cried, "Stand, if

you're Dunn, and fire!" and Dunn at once turned round to measure the distance (as he afterwards declared), but before he could use his weapon, McHale fired a third time, and with more effect, the shot wounding the outlaw in the fleshy part of the back and causing him to fall forward heavily on his face, while blood was seen to spurt through his shirt.

Even when wounded, however, Dunn was a formidable enemy, shooting McHale in the thigh and

CAPTURE OF DUNN

keeping the others at bay until he had emptied his revolvers. As soon as his last shot had been fired, he suddenly rose to his feet and darted off, with Hawthorne and Elliott in hot pursuit. McHale had been incapacitated from running by the wound he had received, which was bleeding copiously, and he was compelled to lie down; but his companions continued the pursuit and after a short run managed to overtake and secure the wounded bushranger. Then "cooeying" for McHale they awaited his arrival, and under his instructions Dunn was taken to the station, and after a time removed to Dubbo, where he and McHale were both handed over to the care of the local surgeon, who found them suffering severely from the wound which each had inflicted upon the other.

Dunn's wound was pronounced by the medical attendant to be a very dangerous one, and at one time his recovery was considered hopeless. So bad did he become several days after his arrival that the doctor ordered his irons to be struck off, as he had eaten nothing for two days and appeared to be on the point of death. At this time he was incarcerated in a room in the police barracks at Dubbo, with McHale as a fellow lodger, and five other troopers in an adjoining room.

The last to look in upon the apparently dying outlaw were the constables who returned to barracks from patrol duty in the town at one o'clock, and as they passed through the room they noticed that both McHale and Dunn were sleeping soundly. But some time after this McHale awoke and was reaching over for a drink which had been placed at his bedside, when he saw that the blankets which had been on Dunn's bed were lying in a heap on the floor, and Dunn had disappeared. McHale at once raised the alarm, and the other troopers came rushing in, to find that the prisoner who had been so carefully guarded since his arrest, and who a few hours previously had appeared too weak to move, had vanished.

Search was at once made for the missing man. The whole of Dubbo was in an uproar. Sunday passed in fruitless efforts to find Dunn's tracks. Towards dusk on Monday, a horse-driver named John Smith drove up to the barracks and informed the constable in charge that he had come across the man for whom everyone was searching. He had left Dubbo, he said, at about two o'clock that day with his horse and dray for the purpose of getting a load of wood; while engaged in his work, at about half past four, a man bareheaded and barefooted came up to him, leaning on a stick, and apparently in a very exhausted condition. This man asked for a drink of water, and having obtained it lay down on the grass, Smith taking a seat by his side. While lying on the grass the man asked Smith if anyone was looking for him, and then Smith concluded that he was Dunn. He further asked if Smith would take him to the river, and the wood carter replied that he could not, as people were out looking for him in every direction. "Ah!" said Dunn, "if it had only been Wednesday night instead of Saturday night, I could have got clear." A boy on horseback now came up, and Dunn asked if the lad would let him have the horse, saddle, and bridle, at the same time expressing regret that he did not feel as well as he did on the Wednesday night. He then put a few questions concerning the lay of the houses about Dubbo and the direction of Mudgee, which Smith explained to him, and Dunn said: "If I could have got away on Wednesday night I expected to meet a friend with a good horse, and then I would have put the traps at defiance." While Smith was loading his dray, Dunn demanded that he should take the horse out of the shafts and let him ride away, saying "I am choking and want water, and must get to the river." This fairly frightened Smith, and he thereupon whipped up the horse and drove into Dubbo as quickly as possible, gave information at the barracks, and conducted the constable to the spot where he had left the outlaw.

When the two reached the place they found Dunn lying beside a log, thoroughly exhausted, and incapable of resisting arrest, if he had felt so inclined. Without loss of time he was conveyed to the lock-up, where he was again placed under the doctor's care, and a more vigilant watch kept over him.

After he had recovered somewhat he told the police that if he had had his revolver he would have shot every man that had come near him, reserving the last bullet for himself. He also told them the manner of his escape and his experiences in the bush after getting away, his story being briefly this:—During the night, after the effects of the opiate administered by the doctor had worn off, he became very feverish and exceedingly thirsty, and called out two or three times for a drink; but as there was no reply, and he could hear McHale breathing heavily in sleep, he tried to get up, but found that he was too weak to rise. His thirst at last, however, became unbearable, and making an extra effort he managed to get out of bed and crawled across the room to the door communicating with the apartment in which the five troopers were sleeping. Finding this door locked, and almost mad in his craving for a drink, he made for the window which overlooked the street, and finding it slightly open he succeeded in dragging himself through it. He fell from the sill on to the verandah floor, and lay there for several minutes, being unable to stand: but the fresh air revived him, and although his only thought up to this point had been to obtain water, he now determined to make a further effort to regain his freedom. He crossed the deserted and silent street, and was endeavouring to climb over a fence when he fell heavily down an embankment on the other side, severely hurting himself. In this hollow, however, he found the water for which he was longing, but he was

DUBBO GAOL

so weak that it was with difficulty he could get his face back out of the water into which in his eagerness he had plunged it. From this point he crawled away a short distance into the bush near the racecourse, about a quarter of a mile from the town, and here he lay hidden during the whole of Sunday. During Sunday night he managed to catch a horse which had been hobbled out, and having made a sort of head-stall of the bandages which had been placed on his injured foot, he led the animal to a leaning tree and endeavoured to mount it; but when he had nearly effected his purpose he fell backwards and hurt himself still more, while the horse got away. He then crawled to a log and lay beside it until the afternoon of Monday, when he determined to try and make his way back to the barracks, as he felt that he must die if he remained longer without relief. It was then that he encountered the wood-carter. He declared that he had no thought of escape when he first got out of bed in the room, and only thought of getting away when he felt the cool night air after crawling through the window.

No further opportunity of escape was allowed to the outlaw. When he was well enough to be moved, he was transferred to Bathurst, where the bullet was removed from his loin; and less than a fortnight afterwards he set out for Sydney, still closely guarded.

On the 9th February, 1866, he was committed for trial on two charges—the murder of Constable Nelson, and "shooting with intent" at McHale; a week later he was arraigned before Chief Justice Stephen at the Central Criminal Court on the charge of murdering Nelson.

The jury returned a verdict of Guilty, and his Honour straightway proceeded to pass sentence of death.

During the trial Dunn maintained a calm, almost indifferent, demeanour, and when sentence had been passed he quietly turned round and gazed at the crowd in court; after which he was removed to the condemned cell by two policemen, and a month later was brought out for execution. From the time of his conviction, he was most attentive to the admonitions of his religious instructors, giving no trouble to his keepers, not questioning the justice of his sentence, and seemingly perfectly resigned to his fate.

In conversation with the gaol authorities, Dunn attributed his fate chiefly to Gilbert, who, he said, had persuaded him to leave his parents' roof for the lawless and murderous career which had ended on the gallows. He made no regular confession of his guilt, neither did he deny it.

Next to Constable Nelson and his family, Constable McHale, perhaps, suffered the greatest injury at Dunn's hands. The wound inflicted upon him by the revolver shot incapacitated him from active duty during the remainder of his life. He received his share of the reward which had been offered for the capture of the outlaw and retired from active service some time afterwards on a pension.

The speedy and effectual break-up of Hall's gang after the passing of the Felons' Apprehension Act furnished ground for hope that bushranging in the Western and South-western districts of the colony would speedily cease; but even while the last of that gang was being nursed into health in order that he might be tried and hanged, reports of numerous other outrages were daily being made, the ruffians committing them being scattered over different parts of the country, and acting principally each "on his own account." The following brief list of bush "occurrences" recorded during two weeks preceding Dunn's conviction will indicate that the crime of bushranging was still popular:—

1866.

February 5.—The down mail from Bathurst to Sydney stuck-up near the Pulpit Hill, and the mail bags and passengers plundered of a large amount of money and valuables, by two armed men.

February 6.—The post office, and Mr. Affleck's and Mr. Fraser's store at Gundaroo, robbed by four armed ruffians.

February 6.—Several highway robberies committed in the neighbourhood of Mudgee, by a mounted and armed bushranger named Lloyd—a youth only seventeen years of age.

February 7.—A man, name unknown, murdered at Warland's Flat, near Murrurundi.

February 8.—The body of a man named Wood, who had been murdered, discovered at Dubbo.

February 8.—Mr. Davis's public house at Currabubula stuck-up and robbed by two mounted and armed men—identified as the same persons who had robbed the place on the 9th December last.

February 9.—The White Horse Hotel at Windsor robbed, at noon, by two men.

February 9.—Clarke and another bushranger encountered the police, near Ballalaba, but got clear off.

February 10.—The post office, and Mr. Cameron's store, at Michelago, stuck-up and plundered—it is supposed by Clarke and his companion.

February 13.—Constable Nichols, one of the Orange police, stuck-up and robbed of his horse, firearms, &c.

February 14.—Mr. M'Kay's inn, near Murrurundi, stuck-up and robbed, by a single bushranger.

February 15.—Two bushrangers attacked two men engaged at a quartz-crushing machine at the Ironbarks—shot one of them, and robbed them of a large cake of gold, when although one of the plunderers was shot dead by a spectator, the other got clear off with the booty.

February 16.—The Yass mail, and also Mr. Baker's place at Millbank, attacked and robbed by three men armed and disguised.

February 19.—Mrs. Green's residence near Kissing Point, entered at night and the inmates attacked.

February 19.—Mr. McElroy's inn, at Warri. Shoalhaven River, stuck-up by two armed and mounted men.

CHAPTER XV.

THE MUDGEE MAIL ROBBERS.

On the 13th July, 1863, when the attention of the colonists was rivetted upon the exploits of Ben Hall's gang in the Lachlan and Abercrombie districts, Sydney was startled by the news that the Mudgee mail had been "stuck up" by two armed bushrangers, and that gold and bank notes to the amount of £5700 had been taken from an accountant of the Australian Joint Stock Bank, who was a passenger on the coach. It was at once seen that the robbery could not have been committed by Hall's gang, as they were then busily engaged in the neighbourhood of Lambing Flat, some two or three hundred miles distant from the spot; and the authorities awoke to the fact that there was another gang "on the roads."

On the night of the 12th July (Sunday) the mail left Mudgee at ten o'clock, having only one passenger, Mr. Kater, the accountant of the Mudgee branch of the Joint Stock Bank, who had in his charge notes amounting to £5700. These were carefully tied in a bundle, first in paper, then in canvas: outside the oilcloth they were attached by string to his carpet bag, the whole being stowed away in the front boot of the coach. Mrs. Smith, wife of an inn-keeper on the road, got into the conveyance on Monday morning. About half-past eleven o'clock the two passengers were walking up the steep hill, generally known as the Big Hill, sixteen miles from Bowenfels. Two men on horseback were observed to be coming down the hill, and stopped when opposite the mail. One of them stopped the horses, the other approached Mr. Kater, without dismounting, and presented a revolver at his head. Mr. Kater, having a revolver in his coat pocket, immediately commenced unbuttoning; the robber, seeing this, told him to hold up his arms or he would shoot him dead. The bushranger then ordered the coachman to lead the horses into the bush, where any person passing on the road would not observe what was going on. The smaller man of the two rifled Mr. Kater's pockets, and gave him ample opportunity of noticing the robbers. They were not common looking men, but well dressed, in black coats, having the appearance of settlers or squatters: they wore gold chains, and were not disguised, but their horses were not first-rate. After finishing with Mr. Kater, they took the mail bags and the bank parcels from the coach. When taking the revolver one of the rascals lifted up his coat and exhibited seven revolvers—putting the other in his belt he said "Now I have eight." Mrs. Smith, the female passenger, had between one and two hundred pounds upon her, but they said they never molested women.* Having secured their booty

---

* More than 30 years after the event here recorded the writer was assured by one who knew the bushrangers well, and who was in fact an associate of theirs for a while, that this version was not quite correct. The money was actually taken from the woman, he declared, but subsequently, and without her knowledge, replaced in her pocket, where she afterwards, much to her surprise, found it. When, some months later, she was confronted by one of the bushrangers then under arrest for the mail robbery, she declared she could not identify him. *Verb. sap.*

the scoundrels made the coachman and Mr. Kater take out the horses and destroy the harness, and they then drove them into the bush, riding off themselves in an opposite direction. Mr. Kater made his way to Hartley, and gave information to Inspector Norton, who immediately, with four mounted police, rode off in pursuit.

For several weeks the Hartley and Bathurst police scoured the bush, but without any good result. They arrested several suspected persons, but no case could be proved against them and they were discharged. At last they got upon the proper scent, and began to look for two men whose names had previously been "known to the police," and it then became pretty generally known that Frederick Lowry and John Foley, erst-while residents in the Fish River neighbourhood, about thirty miles from Bathurst. were "wanted." Each of these men had a history, the first named being looked upon as a hero in criminal circles by reason of the fact that he had cut a hole through the massive brick walls of the Bathurst Gaol when a confinee, and got clean away from his pursuers.

This escape created a great sensation in Bathurst at the time, no less than five prisoners having 'broken out of the gaol. It happened five months before the Mudgee mail robbery. The prisoners had, while in the exercise yard, obtained possession of a pick-axe, which (it was afterwards supposed) had been conveyed to them by friends through a drain communicating with the outer yard. The men in the inner yard congregated in one corner, and while one or two were engaged in removing bricks from the outer wall with the pick-axe, they were sheltered by the others from the gaze of the warder, who was stationed on a platform at the opposite end of the yard. A hole was made in the wall from eighteen inches to two feet square, through which five prisoners made their escape. The alarm was given by a citizen who was crossing the public square, in the centre of which the gaol stood, and observed the hole in the gaol wall. He saw two men get through the hole, but, thinking that the bricklayers were at work upon the wall, did not take much notice of the matter until one of the men hurriedly passed him, saying, "Don't say anything about it, old fellow."

His suspicions being thus aroused, he ran to the gate of the gaol and gave the alarm. In the meantime three other prisoners made their escape. At once a hue and cry was raised, and the whole place was in a ferment. One of the local Justices of the Peace happened to be near when the alarm was given, and seeing a man in prison clothes running down one of the streets he jumped on the first horse he saw and headed the escapee, who was afterwards secured in a yard into which he had darted, hoping to baffle his pursuers. A second escapee was also captured on Piper-street, and by this time the mounted police were in their saddles scouring the country in every direction. A third capture was effected by the police between White Rock and Macquarie Plains, about seven miles from Bathurst, the same afternoon; but the remaining two—Lowry and Woodheart—could not be traced, and three months elapsed before the latter was re-arrested at Braidwood, a reward of £50 having

been offered by Government for his apprehension. Of
Lowry no trace could be found, although good reasons
existed for the belief that he was in hiding somewhere
in the Abercrombie or Fish River districts, about
thirty miles from Bathurst.

Shortly after the robbery of the Mudgee mail, in
July, the police received information that a third man
who was "wanted" for being concerned in bushranging
exploits, named Larry Cummins, had joined Lowry,
who was evidently forming a gang, and that they were
somewhere in the Goulburn district. Arrangements
were at once made for a thorough and eventually successful search of the locality.

The first of the trio to fall into the hands of the
police was Foley, who was captured in a very simple
manner. Early in the month of August the police at
Hartley (the police station nearest to the infested district) received information that one or more of the
bushrangers might be found in the neighbourhood of
Campbell's River; and without delay three mounted
police and a black tracker started in that direction.
After suffering considerably from exposure during
very inclement weather, having to cross rivers swollen
by the winter rains, sometimes up to their waists in
water, they reached Campbell's River and at once proceeded to a public house kept by one Jack Mackie. As
they approached they saw a woman push a man into
one of the rooms and hurriedly close the door. While
one of the police watched the house the others went to
the stables, where they found a horse ready saddled
which a lad on the spot said was his; but his story was
disbelieved, as it was found that the stirrups were ad-

justed for a rider with legs very much longer than his.
A visit was then paid in force to the suspected room,
but the man within refused to open the door, and it
had to be forced, a couple of shots being fired into it
to intimidate the occupant. Finding that further resistance was useless, he quietly surrendered, and to
their delight the troopers discovered that he was the
redoubtable Foley.   Upon being searched he was
found to have in his possession two fine revolvers,
loaded and capped, a massive gold watch and chain,
and about £60 in notes—which were subsequently
identified as a portion of those stolen from the Mudgee
mail.   Having properly secured the prisoner, the
police escorted him to Bathurst; he was afterwards
placed upon his trial, convicted of the mail robbery,
and indicted on two other charges of highway robbery
under arms. He was sentenced to fifteen years hard
labour on the roads or other public works of the
colony, and shortly thereafter was forwarded to Darlinghurst Gaol, the prison in which all long-sentenced
criminals were incarcerated.

Foley proved that he was not altogether bad by
subsequently revealing (through a priest who was acquainted with him) the hiding place of his share of the
stolen money, or what remained of it; and thus the
bank got back something over £2000.

The capture of Lowry and Cummins was effected
some time afterwards by a party of Goulburn police,
led by Senior-sergeant Stephenson, after an encounter
in which Lowry was so badly wounded that he died
twenty-four hours after. The account may be given
in Stephenson's own words:—

On the 28th August, 1863, I left Goulburn to go in the direction of Tuena. I had three men with me, one of them a German, and about thirty miles from Goulburn we put up at a roadside inn for the night. The next morning, long before break of day, I was astir and had my men out. The landlord remarked that we were making an early start and asked in what direction we were going. I told him I did not know, nor did I, for we were merely on the look out for something. The landlord then told me, confidentially, that he had heard Lowry was at a house some fifteen miles distant. I said nothing to my men but pushed on, and just at day-break got to the house indicated. I had never been there before, and when in sight of the house I told the men whom I was after, and arranged their positions so that no one could leave the place without being challenged. We were in uniform, but had monkey jackets on, as it was a cold morning. I went to the front door, which was opened by a young woman who had apparently just got up, and her first exclamation on seeing us was, "Oh! we'll all be shot." I asked where the landlord was, and very shortly after he came out of his bedroom with his trousers over his arm. I asked him if he had any strangers staying in his house, and in a frightened sort of way he pointed to a room opening out on the verandah, and said—"In there, in there." I went to the door indicated and called out to whoever was inside to open it, saying at the same time that we were the police. There was no reply, and I then said that if the door was not opened at once I would force it. Still it remained closed, all inside being perfectly quiet. I then put my shoulder to it and it gave way. I had retired a few paces when a man from the inside stood in the door way with a revolver in each hand. Without speaking he fired at me, the ball passing close to my head, and I fired in reply, hitting the handle of the door. I stood sideways to him on the verandah, and his next shot hit me on the knuckles, striking my revolver barrel and traversing inside my coat sleeve came out at the elbow. I found that out afterwards, but my next shot took effect in his throat when he threw up his hands and fell backwards. Although wounded he was not killed, and I ran in and dragged him outside, where, with the assistance of the other men, I had him secured. When the German, who was at the rear of the place, heard the firing, he seemed to lose his wits, and kept firing off his revolver in the air. Having secured one man I began to search for the other, and ultimately found Cummins hidden in the bedroom. He surrendered without any show of resistance. In Lowry's purse I found £160 in A.J.S. Bank notes, corresponding to those stolen from the Mudgee

mail, and a similar note upon Cummins.   As Lowry was
bleeding internally I secured a dray and started with my
prisoners in the direction of Goulburn. We reached Wood-
houseleigh that night, and I sent a man on for Dr. Waugh.
He arrived about 3 o'clock a.m. and gave Lowry every attention, but he expired about 7 a.m., or twenty-four hours
after being shot. Cummins was subsequently tried at Goulburn, charged with robbery under arms. He was convicted
and sentenced to fifteen years.

Stephenson received promotion in the ranks for
his service on this occasion, and was also presented

LOWRY AFTER DEATH

with a silver salver and purse of sovereigns by the
people of Goulburn.

What became of Lowry's share of the money was
never made known to the authorities; but there are
some persons now living who know all about it. Many
of the notes were put into circulation about Bathurst
and Goulburn during the succeeding twelve months,
but although several persons were prosecuted for having the stolen money in their possession, no convictions were obtained.

For the purpose of proper identification a photograph of Lowry was taken as he lay dead, and copies of the gruesome photograph were held for years and much prized by his friends and admirers in the district in which he found shelter and where his ill-gotten gains were spent.

CHAPTER XVL

DANIEL MORGAN, INCENDIARY AND MURDERER.

In each of the characters hitherto revealed by the acts of robbery or violence in bush townships or on bush roads recorded there has been brought into prominence more or less of the ruffian—generally more. The Australian bushranger of any "standing" was necessarily a ruffian, even if robbery was his only crime; but there were many degrees in this particular species of viciousness, each of which had its proper representative. Taking only the latter-day bushrangers, from Gardiner, the father of them all, down to Johnny Dunn, the last of Hall's gang to fall a victim to the laws which he had outraged, we find each differing from the other in certain particulars, the strong individuality of the man showing out in the acts of the bushranger. Thus Gardiner, although the leader in the attack upon the gold escort at Eugowra and in other smaller affairs of the road, did not display the coarser and more brutal instincts which marked the career of Gilbert, O'Meally and Dunn. The same remark applies to Ben Hall, who never during his career attempted to wound or kill either the persons whom he robbed or the police who hunted him; although, being associated with others who added violence and murder to robbery—for a length of time being their leader—the guilt of the more serious crimes in which they engaged attached to him. Gilbert, O'Meally and Dunn were, however, regardless of human life in cases where resistance was offered, while the last-named committed at least one act of exceptional atrocity. Whether they had it or not, each assumed a particular virtue—or what they chose to consider a virtue. One prided himself on courteous behaviour to women; another boasted of his kind-heartedness, declaring that he had never "pulled trigger upon any unarmed cove"; a third claimed credit for robbing only those who could afford to part with that which he took from them; and a fourth avowed that he had "never shot anyone, not even a 'bobby.'" They were all thus concerned for their reputation, having regard for the good opinion of one section or another of the people to whom they made their boasts.

But we have now to do with one who was a monster rather than a man—who tortured his victims because the sight of their writhings gave him pleasure—who committed murder from sheer wantonness, and a tigerish lust for blood. This was Daniel Morgan, and the scene of his exploits was the southern district from Gundagai to Albury, over which he ruled by mere terror longer than any other bushranger or gang known to Australia.

Of his early history very little reliable information can be gleaned, but the following account, given by an old man who adopted him when only about two years of age, may be taken as fairly correct. Morgan's proper name was Owen, and he was the illegitimate son of a woman of that name and a man named Fuller, being born at Campbelltown about the year 1830. Both father and mother were well known characters in the neighbourhood, the latter being known as "The Gipsy," and the former a sort of costermonger, who many years afterwards was stationed as a barrow-man in the Haymarket, Sydney. Until he was about seventeen years of age young Owen remained under the roof of the man who had adopted him—and who was also a "character" in the neighbourhood of Campbelltown, rejoicing in the nick-name of "Jack the Welshman"—after which he went to the Murrumbidgee, where he was employed as a stockman until 1854. Then he returned to Campbelltown, and for some ten months luxuriated in idleness at the old Welshman's hut; after which he proceeded in the direction of Bathurst, giving out that he was going to see his mother, who was then living in that locality. That he might perform the journey with greater ease and more speedily, he appropriated two horses without asking the owner's permission, and was chased for several miles on the road by the Campbelltown police, whom he managed to evade. Whether he carried out his intention and visited his mother, who was now married and the mother of a legitimate family, does not appear; and he was next heard of in the Murrumbidgee district in the latter part of 1863, as a bushranger whose every exploit was marked by ruffianism of the very worst kind.

It is not my intention to follow closely the career of this arch-fiend; even a brief account of three or four of the deeds of blood in which he engaged will enable the reader to fully understand his character, and the terrorism which he exercised.

At one time he worked in company with a "mate," but the two did not run together long, and the latter came to an untimely end, being discovered in the bush dead after an encounter with the police. In that encounter the then Police Magistrate of Wagga, Mr. H. Bayliss, was engaged; he volunteered for service in hunting the bushrangers, who were at the time infesting the district, received a wound during the affray, and was subsequently presented with a gold medal for his bravery. It was supposed by some that he had shot Morgan's companion; but others declared that the man must have been shot by Morgan himself in order that his own escape might be rendered more easy.

On one occasion the two bushrangers paid a visit to Mr. Gilbank's station at Wallandool. They were mounted on two fine horses and intercepted two overseers who were making their rounds. After conversing with them for a few minutes the bushrangers suddenly presented their revolvers, and before the overseers had fully realised the situation they were stripped and tied up to two convenient trees, in which position they were left, minus their portables, Morgan informing them as he bade them adieu that he and his companion were about to pay a visit to "old Gilbank" himself. Cantering up to the station they found Mr. Gilbank, and, assuming the characters of station-hands in search of work, they asked him to give them a "job." The station holder told them that he had no job on hand on which he could engage them and they then said they "must have a feed," at the same time giving Mr. Gilbank a shock by presenting their revolvers at his face and ordering him to "bail up." Having secured him as they had secured his two men, they proceeded to make a deliberate survey of the premises. Shortly afterwards they rode away, leaving Mr. Gilbank the poorer by about £60 worth of property, including two horses and their trappings.

After the death of his mate Morgan invariably operated single-handed, and committed outrages which made his name feared in every settler's house in the district, and by every traveller along the road. On one occasion he visited Mr. Gibson's house, near Piney Ridge, and compelled the owner to draw a cheque for £90, keeping him prisoner while a man was sent to get the cheque cashed. He also visited Messrs. Stitt Brothers' station at Wolla Wolla, and compelled the proprietor to bring rum to the wool shed and treat all the shearers. He made particular enquiries as to the treatment the servants received, and instructed the servants to acquaint him if they were ill-used, as he was always to be found thereabouts. In this particular he followed the practice of the early-day convict bushrangers, whose fellow-feeling for assigned servants made them "wondrous kind." But this considerateness was not by any means natural to him, and it soon became known that he would sooner shoot those with whom he came in contact, no matter what position in life they might occupy, than minister to their necessities or order for them luxuries.

Shortly after the visit to Wolla Wolla Station, the

desperado committed an outrage which for cold-blooded atrocity had never been equalled by any of the "gentlemen of the road" since the days of Mike Howe and Jeffries. Shearing was in full swing at Vincent's Mittagong Station, when one morning the police rode up and asked Mr. Vincent if he could give them any information concerning Morgan. They had previously sought information from the same quarter, but had either not acted upon it when supplied, or had failed to follow the instructions given; so on this occasion Mr. Vincent replied: "What is the use of giving you information? it appears to me you do not want to meet him; if you do, your horses are in much better condition, and you could run him down; I am quite convinced I could do it with any of the horses I could point out to you in the yard." "Oh," they remarked, "you give us the information, where we are likely to fall in with him, and if you don't hear a good report of us, and Morgan's capture, we will not blame you." "Well," Mr. Vincent said, "I will try you again. You know ——, some miles from here, where there is a wattle-sided stable; if you see a chestnut horse in it Morgan is not far away. He is riding a horse he stole from this station; if the horse is not there, there is some thick scrub within a very short distance of the stable, where you can remain unseen, and in all probability Morgan will turn up some time during the night." After refreshment, the party rode away, and had not gone far before they met a horseman, from whom they made similar enquiries, and who professed that he knew nothing of any one named Morgan. The result was that Morgan was not captured that night, nor for a long time afterwards. But he was in the neighbourhood, as Mr. Vincent soon to his cost discovered.

A few days after the visit of the police, the bushranger himself called at Mittagong, sticking-up the whole body of shearers, and making particular inquiries for Mr. Vincent, who shortly afterwards appeared on the scene and was at once made prisoner. Having secured him Morgan ordered him to a paling fence some sixty yards from the shearing shed, and called on one of the shearers to strap him tightly to the fence. This was not done to Morgan's satisfaction; he examined the work and peremptorily ordered the man to strap his employer "much tighter," standing over him during the operation and seeing that the straps were drawn so tightly round his wrists as to stop the circulation almost completely. Then, "You are the man," said he, "who gave information to the police the other day. You can see they have not taken me, and your life is forfeited. I will give you five minutes to live, and if you have anything particular to say to your wife and family, I will have them called up to see the last of you."

One of the men was at once despatched to the house with a message for Mrs. Vincent and other members of the family, and while he was away on this Message, Morgan amused himself by placing the muzzle of his gun close to the face of his victim. Morgan also tauntingly said: "You also told the police you had several horses with which you could run men down, and that if you once had your hand upon me you would hold me. You are quite in error if you think anyone harbours me; they do not, but I force my company upon them, as I am doing upon you."

In due course the ladies arrived on the scene, and prayed for the life of the husband and father, with such effect that Morgan hesitated, after pointing his rifle, and offered Vincent his choice either to have the wool-shed and wool burnt, or be shot.

To this alternative offer Vincent replied that if Morgan had a grudge against him it would be poor satisfaction to burn the wool and shed, as they belonged to his mother and brother and sisters equally with himself, but that he had no desire to be shot. After some delay men were told off from the gang of shearers to cut open the bales; another man was sent for a firestick, and in a very short time the fire was completely master. The heat from the burning shed was so intense that the unfortunate prisoner at the fence became utterly exhausted, and being apparently forgotten in the new excitement, narrowly escaped death by slow roasting.

But the devilish work was not to end with the destruction of the woolshed. When that building and its contents were nearly consumed Morgan marshalled the shearers—there were some eighteen of them on the ground, but not one of them offered resistance on their own or their master's account—to the station store, some distance away, intimating that he desired to "treat" them. The store contained a large quantity of clothing, provisions, saddlery, and all the etcetera of a well-furnished establishment at shearing time, including no less than ten tons of flour, a new dog-cart and harness, and other articles of the more valuable kind. Having reached the store Morgan told the men that they could help themselves to whatever they might require. He then commanded the storekeeper to produce the station books, containing an account of the goods supplied from the store to the shearers, and this having been done he threw it into the building and ordered that a firestick should be applied.   His orders were carried out, and in a few minutes this property was also being consumed by the flames.

The property destroyed was valued at about £1600. I have not been able to ascertain whether the unfortunate station-holder ever received compensation from the Government, although his claim for compensation was undoubtedly a good one, seeing that his loss was clearly brought about by his efforts to assist the police in the capture of the notorious ruffian who was holding the whole country-side in terror. Morgan's object in committing this act of incendiarism was undoubtedly to intimidate other settlers from conveying to the police information concerning his whereabouts, and it had the desired effect.

Mail robberies were of frequent occurrence shortly after, diversified by the "sticking-up" of settlers, small and large, and the robbery of travellers on the roads; the wonder was that one man could so frequently and with such perfect ease "bail up" and rob as many as a score of persons at one time. But all these events were ordinary when viewed in the light of other exploits in which this monster engaged.   To rob for the sake of enriching himself was the natural work of the bushranger, but to make targets of the men who had obeyed his command to "bail up" from sheer love of blood-shedding was work natural only to a devil in human shape, and Morgan gave himself up to that work.

An outrage committed by him at Round Hill Station, in the Albury district, was marked by more cold-blooded brutality than any committed by bush-rangers during any of the bushranging periods, early or late. The station in question was owned by Mr. Henty, and was about forty miles from Albury. On a Sunday morning towards the close of 1863, four persons belonging to the station—Mr. Watson, the superintendent; Mr. McNeil, the overseer; Mr. McLean, cattle overseer; and Mr. Heriot, a visitor, son of a neighbouring squatter—were sitting in a room of the house quietly conversing, when Morgan suddenly made his appearance. He entered the house unobserved and looked in through the door of the bedroom in which Mrs. Watson was engaged, enquiring where her husband was. Mrs. Watson was naturally alarmed at this unlooked-for intrusion, and her alarm was increased when she recognised the intruder as Morgan, having seen him on a previous occasion. But she pointed out the room in which her husband was engaged with the other men named, and thither Morgan at once proceeded, introducing himself to the occupants, after opening the door, by presenting two revolvers at their heads, and commanding them not to move from their seats on peril of their lives. He asked where the grog was kept, and on being informed desired to know how many bottles there were available. Mr. Watson replied that there were six bottles of gin in stock and that one of them was broached; whereupon the bushranger ordered the four men to march to the apartment indicated, himself following with a revolver in each hand and fingers on the triggers. Mr. Watson poured out a glass of the liquor and offered it to Morgan, who smiled and said "Now drink that yourself; you may have it readied up for me." Having thus assured himself that the grog had not been "doctored" for his special delectation, the bushranger drank a glass himself, and then called the female servant and ordered her to get dinner for him, at the same time instructing her to tell one of the men to put his horse in the stable and give him a feed. While the meal was being prepared Morgan conversed freely and pleasantly with his four prisoners, among other things questioning Mr. Watson concerning the rations given to the station hands. He continued to act in a friendly manner while eating his dinner, although he was careful to let his prisoners know that he had not forgotten his mission, for during the meal he kept a loaded revolver in one hand and displayed other similar weapons in his belt, keeping an eye always upon the corner before him where the four men were standing by his orders. He reminded Mr. Watson that he was "not a man to be played with," and declared that he came to the house fresh from a brush with the police, who had, however, been unable to capture him, although they had chased him for about four miles through the bush. This statement was subsequently found to be correct. The police had come across him when resting in a shepherd's hut on an adjoining station, but he had managed to get away scathless, running the gauntlet of their fire and outpacing them on the magnificent horse that he was riding.

Having appeased his hunger, Morgan marched his prisoners out and mustered all the men, making a total of eleven, at the stable door while he went to examine his horse. He then ordered them to precede him to a small cattle shed, and take their seats on a bench there, while Mr. Watson returned to the house for the bottles of gin. These having been brought, one of the men, at the bushranger's desire, handed round the spirits until the four bottles had been emptied, Morgan making his prisoners drink the spirits raw, and himself taking at each round a small "nip" of brandy from a bottle which he had with him. He told the men that he had been drinking hard for a whole week, and his subsequent conduct left no room to doubt the correctness of his assertions.

After the spirits had been consumed the bushranger ordered his horse to be brought, and while this was being done he fired several shots from one of his revolvers over the heads of his prisoners. He then proceeded to mount the horse, having a revolver in each hand; but as he was in the act of crossing the saddle the horse shied and one of the revolvers was accidentally discharged. In a moment Morgan had secured his seat, and, thinking that the shot had been fired at him, began firing right and left, using both revolvers. One of the shots struck young Heriott, passing clean through his leg between the knee and ankle, shattering the bone, and striking one of the station hands standing behind him without doing much damage, as its force was spent. Another shot was aimed direct at Watson's head, but that gentleman instinctively put up his hand, and the ball passed through it, afterwards grazing his scalp. The other shots fortunately missed, for the men scattered as soon as the first two had been fired. Young Herriott fell to the ground, but rose again immediately and managed to drag himself after some of the others for a considerable distance, when he fell from pain and exhaustion. Watson had hid himself behind the shed, and Morgan galloped round looking for him, declaring that he would have his life for having fired at him. Some of the others then interfered and convinced Morgan that it was his own revolver that had gone off, and that Watson had not fired at him; but although he abandoned his intention of shooting Watson the murderous instinct was still operating, and observing young Heriott in the distance he galloped towards him, leaped from his horse, and, putting the revolver to his head was about to fire, when the wounded man appealed to him for mercy, declaring that his leg was broken. At the same moment Watson rushed from his hiding place and besought the drunken madman not to murder the boy.

Then in a moment Morgan changed his tactics. A wave of compassion seemed to sweep over him, and he called upon the station hands to assist him in attending to the wounded man, declaring with an oath that if they did not come at once he would shoot every man on the station. At the same time he knelt down and cut the boot from the wounded leg, and tenderly lifting the unfortunate youth, carried him to the gate near the house, when two of the men came forward

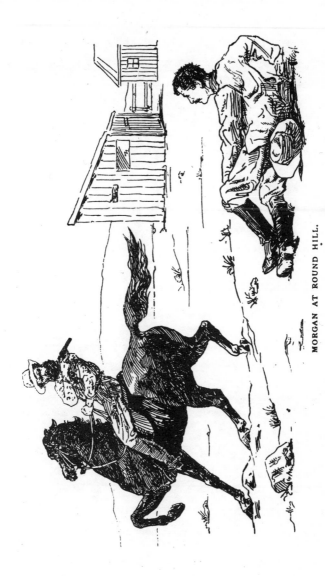

MORGAN AT ROUND HILL.

and relieved him of his burden, carrying Heriott, under Morgan's direction, into the house and laying him on a bed. Then Morgan cut off the other boot, and set a man to attend to the wounded boy, after which he returned to Mr. Watson and bound a handkerchief round his wounded hand, expressing regret for having in a moment of passion disabled him, adding that the police and drink had driven him mad, and that he scarcely knew what he was doing.

While attention was being paid to the wounded men two strangers appeared upon the scene—one of them a half-caste aboriginal—and it soon became evident that they were the bushranger's "telegraphs." These men remained on the station observing everything that transpired, and apparently keeping a watch upon the now terror-stricken company.

Seeing Morgan apparently relenting as if satisfied with the damage done, Mr. McLean suggested the advisability of sending for surgical assistance for the wounded men, and asked if he might go for a doctor. Morgan assented and said he would accompany him on the road. McLean started, but had not gone more than two or three miles towards Walla Walla when suddenly Morgan rode up and exclaimed, "You wretch! you are going to give information," and at once fired at McLean's back, shooting him clean through the body. The unfortunate man fell from his horse mortally wounded, and his murderer rode away, but returned again after a short time, and, having assisted him to remount his horse, held him in the saddle until the return journey to the station had been made.

As may be imagined, the appearance of the dying

man attended by his murderer increased the consternation of the people at the station. McLean was in
too great agony to give any explanation of the affair,
and Morgan declared that he must have been wounded
by one of his (Morgan's) mates, as he himself had not
fired.   McLean was carried into the house, and received what poor attention the inmates could give him.
He lingered in great agony until the following night,
when death put an end to his sufferings.

Having brought McLean to the house, Morgan
joined the two men who had come to the station after
him, and the three caroused until about one o'clock on
the Monday morning, when they hurriedly left, a party
of police calling at the station within an hour after
their departure—just too late to see the man for whom
they were looking, and not a little put out at the circumstance; although, for some reason not stated, they
remained at the station for about twelve hours, within
easy reach of the murderer—if they had but known it
—for it was afterwards discovered that Morgan had
camped within two miles of the place for the remainder
of the night.

The remains of the unfortunate man McLean were
subsequently conveyed to Albury, and a magisterial
inquiry into the cause of death was held by Captain
Brownrig, the local Police Magistrate, the result of
which was a finding of wilful murder against Morgan.

Poor McLean was buried by his friends, and
Heriot was by his nursed back to life, but the shattered
leg never became thoroughly sound.   Meanwhile the
murderer was committing other outrages, and the
authorities were putting forth strenuous efforts to effect

his capture or compass his death, but without avail, although the Government sought to stimulate police energy and encourage the bushranger's friends to betray him by offering £1000 for his capture.

Some of the Victorian papers were particularly severe upon the police of this colony, and boasted that no bushranger could reign for more than a week or two in their territory, where the police knew their work and were competent to perform it. However, the Victorian "blowers" were in later years compelled to eat the leek. The men of the New South Wales force were as energetic and as brave as men could be, and it was not their fault that bushrangers lived so long. The fault lay with the system, and with some of the higher officials appointed under it. One writer, who had wide experience of the Morgan-infected country, wrote thus in defence of the police :—

I have travelled about 300 miles in and about the district and have had opportunities of witnessing some of the movements of the much-abused police. I have likewise held many conversations with the inhabitants, and I consider it my duty to give to the public what came under my observation some few days back, upon three different occasions, and at a distance of about twenty-five miles apart. I met two men riding in the bush who, at first sight, I took to be bushmen in search of employment, but, upon closer observation, I found they were police officers with an ordinary swag, which was merely composed of one pair of blankets and holsters for pistols, and not loaded like elephants and with turbans, as your contemporary's informant describes, and their horses appear to have been ridden for a long period. Upon the 17th of this month I had occasion to pull up at a hut in the bush, which to me appeared to be a deserted one, at about eight o'clock in the evening, and where I was surprised to find a sergeant and three or four blacks who had just taken shelter for the night, and were as ragged as gipsies. If your contemporary's correspondent had only seen what I then saw, and had a spark of humanity, he would not have spoken about "scented handkerchiefs" and other nonsense. The men appeared—like the horses—literally and thoroughly knocked up, and the horses nearly starved, in consequence of the want of sustenance in the grass, and being upon duty since November last. Instead of stowing themselves away comfortably in bed at night, they just unrolled their pair of blankets, and went off to sleep in five minutes. Next morning I said to the sergeant, "If Morgan were to gallop across the plain now in your sight, what could you do?" He answered, "Nothing, for we have not got one horse that could stand an hour's chase." I maintain that the attack made upon the character of the police is not warranted. The right horse should wear the saddle—the fault lies with the Government in not supplying the police with more horses; good judges should be appointed to select these. The horses at present used by the police are of the very worst description. In my opinion, two good officers, well mounted, should be stationed or billetted on every station in the tainted district, so that if sticking-up occurred at one station, and the ruffian escaped, they could gallop off to the next station, and then the pursuit could be taken up by the fresh horses and men, who would be able to run him down. It is not generally known that this south-western district, under Superintendent Carne, is nearly as large as the whole of Victoria, and the number of constables under his command only thirty-five, while they have 900 men in Victoria, and stations every fifteen miles or so. They have nothing to do if an offence is committed but to gallop up to the next station, and the pursuit is taken up. It is laughable to hear the feather-bed police in Victoria brag what they would do if they were in Morgan's country; about one month's service with the police that came under my observation would be *quantum sufficit* for them. I, for one, wonder not that Mr. Carne should resign.

Two sergeants of police were shot dead by Morgan, one of them in an encounter on the road, and the other when at camp in his tent in the bush. The former—Sergeant McGinnity—was out with a constable named Churchley when he came across Morgan near Tumberumba. They exchanged shots, and the horses of both sergeant and bushranger were shot under them. The former then rushed at Morgan and grappled with him; they struggled together, and in the struggle Morgan shot his assailant through the spine.

Churchley's horse, not standing fire, bolted with his rider, and with one more life to answer for the bush-ranger escaped. The second sergeant—Thomas Smyth—was out in the bush running the outlaw's tracks very closely, and had camped for the night when Morgan surprised him and fired at him in his tent, inflicting wounds from which he died three weeks afterwards.

And these were not the only tragic events in which this bloodthirsty desperado engaged. Although he bailed up numbers of people and robbed coaches on several occasions the events were deemed scarcely important enough for record unless attended with some act of violence. One of his victims was an inoffensive shepherd on the Wollondool station, about forty miles from Albury. The man was quietly feeding his dogs on the station when he was suddenly and without warning shot by the bushranger, who had approached him unawares. The ball from the revolver struck the unfortunate shepherd in the thigh, and after he had fallen Morgan went forward and expressed regret for having wounded him, saying that he had mistaken him for someone else. Such was the demoralised state of the people in the neighbourhood that the wounded man had to apply to seventeen different persons before he could get any one to convey him to the Albury hospital. The wound was fortunately not dangerous, and the shepherd was discharged from the hospital cured shortly afterwards.

The following account of one day's doings, supplied by a correspondent from Kyamba to the Albury "Banner," will serve as an illustration of the prowess of this notorious ruffian, and the disregard of human life which characterised his lawless movements :—

Tragic events in connection with bushranging follow each other in such rapid succession that no one one will be surprised to hear that Morgan paid us a visit here last evening. At about 12 o'clock noon he made his appearance in the camp of Mr. Adams, road contractor, when he bailed up all his men, about fifteen in number, and, as a warning to the contractor for having no cash in hand for the supply of his wants, he set fire to the tents, thus ruthlessly destroying at least £15 or £20 worth of property. Five Chinamen having made their appearance, he caused them also to join the rest of the men; and, having ordered them to strip, with a view to search their garments, they, not understanding the command, and therefore apparently hesitating to put it in force, he shot one of them in the arm just below the shoulder joint. This man is now lying at the Kyamba hotel in a precarious state, and the ball has not been extracted. After all, the money found on them was trifling—one small gold piece and about 30s. in silver—which latter Morgan threw away from him in chagrin, expecting to have obtained a larger sum. He remained at the camp till 5 p.m., having caused tea to be made and a damper prepared for him by the cook of the party. The position of the camp is above a mile north of Kyamba Inn; and everything, including the account-book of the contractor, was destroyed. He did not tie the men or secure them in any way, but kept them in such a position as rendered it impossible to have rushed him without incurring a further loss of life, otherwise the men were well disposed, and would, if opportunity had been given, most undoubtedly have made resistance. The only weapon in the place was a double-barrelled gun, which was unloaded; but, remarking that "he did not like double-barrelled guns," he expressed his intention of taking it away with him. About one o'clock in the afternoon, Mr. Jones, another contractor, paid a visit to the camp (which was soon after it had been set on fire); he was likewise secured, besides a traveller, and two or three other men residing in the neighbourhood who came there on horseback. On leaving he took these men with him, as also Mr. Jones, four in all, they being each mounted on horseback. He made them carry the gun with them, and took them by a circuitous route over the mountains to a small bridge on the Little Billabong, about eight miles south of Kyamba. Here were two buggies, in one of which were Mr. and Mrs. Manson. on their way to Braidwood, and in the other two young men, travelling to the same destination. These he immediately stopped, ordering them ont of their buggies; and, because Mr. Manson seemed to hesitate, he threatened to shoot the whole of them on the spot. Having got them out, he pointed to the four other men standing where he had placed them in a rank close by, and spoke of them as belonging to his own party. This effectually set aside all idea of resistance; and, after having stripped Mr. Manson to his shirt, and searched the pockets of the others, he succeeded in taking about £6 in all. They then asked his permission to proceed, but he said they must wait twenty minutes, as the mail was expected, and the buggies would be useful in stopping the passage of the coaches. The time having expired, however, and the mail not arriving, they were allowed to proceed. It may be important to mention here that he conversed freely at the camp for hours with the men, detailing his exploits at great length, and dwelling particularly upon the murder of McGinnerty and Smyth, of which he made no attempt at concealment—indeed he stated that he had watched Smyth's party five days in order to make sure of the right man. Soon after Mr. Manson had escaped from his clutches the mail to Albury arrived at the scene of action. The mailman had been previously warned, but did not consider it to be his duty to take any steps by way of special security. Being very light he allowed it to pass after a merely formal examination; but shortly afterwards, and it was now nearly eleven o'clock, the Albury mail arrived, when he demanded of the driver to stop. This not being instantly complied with, he fired a shot at him to bring him to. He then made him get out and hold the horses' heads while he ransacked the mails. This inspection lasted a considerable time, in the course of which nearly all, if not the whole, of the letters were opened, and though many cheques were found, which he threw on one side as useless, it is supposed that he obtained but little booty in the shape of bank notes, for he complained bitterly of the mails. A box of pills and some photographs were disposed of with sovereign contempt. Having accomplished this much, he is supposed to have visited Mr. Williams' station, where it is said he pressed two men into his service, taking also a horse, saddle, and bridle. But the circumstances connected with this portion of the story have not yet been sufficiently authenticated. He took with him the gun obtained from Adams' camp. Perhaps the worst feature in this affair is the telegraph having been cut down by his order, and the wire severed, thus, he supposed, stopping the communication; but fortunately the line to Albury being open, allows communication northwards by way of Deniliquin. I omitted to state that, in the course of conversation, the bushranger spoke of three men whom he was determined to shoot before "retiring from business," namely, Mr. McKenzie, late of Mundaloo, identified with the capture of Peisley; Mr. McLaurin, of Yarra Yarra; and Sergeant Carrol. On these he expressed himself determined to be revenged; and with respect to the former, he declared that if he once had him in his power, £5000 would not save his life. Otherwise he said there was "no good in bushranging," and he felt inclined, after a time, to give it up. You may implicitly rely upon the accuracy of all that has been related above; many other particulars could have been furnished, but they would probably only tend to pamper a morbid curiosity.

At last the day of reckoning arrived. Outrages had become so frequent and were attended by such brutal violence that no settler in the district felt safe; yet the daring of the ruffian seemed to have a para-lysing effect upon those who under other circumstances would have resisted attack and made some effort to capture their assailant. The vigilance of the police was redoubled, and they managed to press him so closely that Morgan was at last compelled to forsake his favourite haunts and seek fresh fields for robbery across the Border—on Victorian soil. But he did this without letting the New South Wales police into the secret, and they were still busily engaged in searching for him when they received word that he had been shot at a station near Wangaratta, some miles on the other side of the Murray from Albury.

As soon as he had crossed the Murray—which he did on April 5th, 1865—he commenced what he was pleased to call a "raid upon Victoria." He had heard of the boast of the Victorian police that they would arrest or shoot him within a week if he entered their territory, and told one of his first victims on that side that he had come to show he was not afraid to enter Victoria and that, notwithstanding the smartness of the police, he would "go through it in a week." He certainly commenced well; on the first day he stuck up Mr. Evans' station at Whitfield and a number of carriers on the road near Winton, taking from them sums ranging from £3 to £50. He fired Evans' granaries in revenge for a wound which the owner had inflicted on him four years previously, when he was engaged at that station. In addition to these exploits he visited and stuck up McKinnon's station at Little River. He then passed on to Mr. Rutherford's Peechelba station, about twenty miles from Wangaratta. He arrived at the station on Saturday night and bailed up all the occupants—as he thought—in one room, having as prisoners eight females and four males. One of the women, a nursemaid named Alice MacDonald, pretending that she heard one of the children crying in an adjoining room, demanded that Morgan should let her go to attend to it; but he refused and she then boldly smacked his face and declared that she would go in spite of him. Unused to such treatment, and evidently as much amused as annoyed, the bushranger complied with her demand, and passing out of the room she managed to convey intelligence to one of the station hands who had been overlooked in the "mustering." Morgan happened to hear her talking, and when she re-entered the room he questioned her, but she said she had only been talking to the dog. Among the prisoners was Mr. McPherson, who was part owner of the station with Mr. Rutherford. Morgan proceeded to enjoy himself, and tea being ready he made all the company sit down together, including Mr. and Mrs. McPherson, and the other ladies who were present. During the night the bushranger was very chatty and

confidential, speaking of the hardships he had to endure, and of his father and mother, who he said were
still alive.   He made one of the ladies play the piano,
and allowed them to retire at bedtime.   He said he

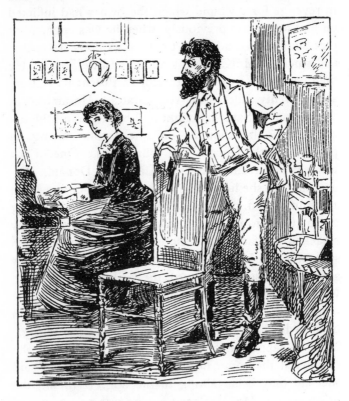

MORGAN AT PEECHELBA STATION.

was blamed in the Round Hill affair for more than he
had done, and that Heriot's messenger would not have
been shot only that he took the wrong road, which
made him think that he was going to give information

to the police, and that he (Morgan) consequently shot the messenger. Morgan was very sleepy, and nodded occasionally but always kept a revolver in hand; he said he had not slept for five days and nights, but told the people to be cautious, as he always slept with one eye open. He treated Mr. McPherson, to whom his remarks were chiefly addressed, civilly all through the night, declaring that he would be content if supplied with a good horse in the morning.

Meanwhile the man with whom Alice MacDonald had spoken had gone to a neighbouring station and carried the news, and all the men were immediately supplied with firearms and proceeded to Peechelba house, which was quietly surrounded, awaiting the arrival of the Wangaratta police, for whom a messenger had been despatched on a fleet horse. When this messenger reached the township he found that all but one policeman were absent, but the news having spread, six civilians volunteered for service, and placing themselves under the lead of the policeman—Senior-constable Evans—the party were soon on the road, making for the scene of what they had every reason to believe, from Morgan's character, would be murder. Arrived at the house they found the other party lying in ambush near the various outlets, and a whispered consultation ensued as to what was best to be done. There were fourteen persons all told outside the house, each carrying arms, among them being Mr. Rutherford, McPherson's partner. At first some of the civilians wished to rush the place, expressing a fear that at any moment Morgan's murderous propensities might be given play, and there would be a repetition of the

Round Hill affair; but better counsels prevailed, and
it was resolved to lie in wait round the house until daylight, when the bushranger was expected to show himself. During the night the watchers were reinforced
by some additional policemen.

Towards daylight Morgan went to the door and
cautiously looked out, as though feeling that there was
danger near; but not a sound or movement came from
the watchers, and he returned to the room and drank
a glass of whisky, the first spirits he had tasted during
the night. He then made preparations to leave, and
cocking his two revolvers, he ordered Mr. McPherson
and the three other men to precede him to the stable
to catch the horse that had been promised him. When
he was well out, and while he was watching his men,
those behind closed cautiously on him, and an Irish-
man named Quinlan, employed on the station, stepped
in front to a stump. McPherson glanced round as if
talking to Morgan, and seeing the men advancing,
stepped a little on one side to allow them to fire, which
action was observed by Morgan, who was in the act of
turning his head to see the cause when Quinlan took
aim at him and fired. The shot struck the bushranger
in the back near the shoulder; he fell to the ground on
his face, and in a moment was secured and disarmed.

As soon as his captors laid hands upon him he
cried out, "Why didn't you challenge me fair, and give
me a chance?" but he made no attempt at resistance,
doubtless feeling that he had received his death wound,
for the shot had entered at the back of the shoulder
and passed upwards and out near the windpipe. He
lingered in great agony from 8 o'clock a.m. when he

was shot down until 2 o'clock p.m., when he pointed to his throat as if choking and expired.

When searched he was found to have on him £86 in notes, a bank draft on Albury for £7, and two revolvers, one of which proved to have belonged to Sergeant McGinnerty, whom he had shot some months previously.

During the afternoon the body was removed to the police camp at Wangaratta, where an inquest was held and a verdict of justifiable homicide was returned. The body was subsequently buried at Wangaratta; but it was not a whole body, the head having been removed and taken to Melbourne to Professor Halford, presumably to advance the cause of science. But if all that was reported was true the body had been mutilated even before the head was removed. Here is what the Wangaratta "Despatch" of the day said on that subject :—

It may not be generally known that an act, the parallel of which might in vain be looked for among the stories of the most savage tribes, was perpetrated upon the remains of the bushranger Morgan, as he lay exposed in the police camp, after the coroner's inquisition had decided upon and recorded the verdict, and the majority of the public had departed, after their curiosity was glutted by gazing on the peculiar features, the flowing locks, and the luxuriant beard and moustache of the unfortunate man. The razor or knife was, by the order or the act of some high official, brought into requisition, the lower part of the face hacked and the skin and portion of the flesh dragged round and over the chin, till the operator performed the task of taking from the corpse his massive beard. This disgusting job finished, the official departed with his trophy, to be gazed at and admired by distant friends. Those who were eager to see the corpse, and who were late in gratifying the feeling, were horror-stricken with the spectacle which presented itself to their view. The decomposed state of the head when it arrived in Melbourne may have precluded, perhaps, the possibility of the detection of the horrible desecration; but numbers of our townspeople are aware of it. We have now drawn attention to the fact, and it becomes incumbent on the proper authorities to institute an investigation and let us all see the credentials of the perpetrator for the atrocity he has committed.

A greater act of barbarity was perhaps never committed in any civilised community; and when the rumour circulated public indignation found loud expression. A board of inquiry consisting of four Government officials was appointed to investigate the affair, and that board sat in secret at the Wangaratta Court House, certain charges in reference to the outrage having been preferred against a prominent police officer and the coroner for the district. Whether the Board found the charges proved, and if it did what penal consequences followed, I have not been able to ascertain, for the matter was hidden as much as possible from public view. That the mutilation took place, however, was proved beyond doubt, and the horror of the public when they heard of the act of barbarity was only equalled by the indignation which they felt towards the savages who had committed it.

Shortly after Morgan's death a responsible officer from police head-quarters in Sydney visited Wangaratta for the purpose of more fully inquiring into the circumstances concerning the shooting of the notorious bushranger and distributing the reward. The £1000 offered by the New South Wales Government for his capture was paid over by that official as follows:—£300 to Quinlan, who fired the fatal shot; £250 to Alice McDonald, who courageously conveyed information to the station hands, and communicated to McPherson and others, who were guarded in the house by Morgan, what was being done, and who finally gave the signal to the armed men outside when Morgan left the house; £200 to James Frazer, who volunteered to ride into Wangaratta with information and for assistance—(when another man selected would not go)—riding the forty-two miles in about three hours and a half, and afterwards taking his post under arms as directed, until Morgan was shot; £100 to Donald Clarke, who conveyed the information to Mr. Rutherford, and then volunteered (others having refused) to go up to the schoolroom for guns, cleaning and loading them with his own—watching the house all night, and arranging plans with others—then following Morgan down to try and shoot him, in which attempt he was prevented by Mr. McPherson and son being too near; £50 to Alice Keenan, a fellow servant with Alice McDonald, for her presence of mind in communicating between the parties guarded by Morgan and those outside. The balance of the money was handed over to Mr. Rutherford and one of the officers of police to be apportioned among the Victorian police and the other civilian volunteers who assisted on the occasion.

There was not one redeeming feature in Morgan's career as a bushranger. He entered upon that career of pillage and blood from choice, and not one single regret can be felt that the wretch who could so ruthlessly slaughter innocent men from sheer tigerish love of blood, should himself be shot down without warning. "Why not challenge me fair and give me a chance?" he asked with his dying breath; but fair challenges and chances had not been given to any of the unfortunate men who had fallen before his murderous fire. He

MM

had shown no mercy to others, and no mercy was shown to him; the only regrettable circumstance connected with his final disappearance being the brutal mutilation of his body after death.

CHAPTER XVII.

"THUNDERBOLT" (FREDERICK WARD).

Next to Morgan, perhaps, no individual bush-ranger earned greater notoriety than did Frederick Ward, otherwise called "Thunderbolt." He was an old "Cockatoo" bird, and one of the few prisoners who escaped from that gruesome island. The escape was effected on September 11th, 1863, and Ward had for a companion in his flight a fellow convict named Britten. Having evaded the sentries and got across the water dividing the island from the mainland, the two men headed for the Hawkesbury, and despite the efforts of the police to recapture them managed to get clean away. Ward was a native of Windsor, and at the time of his flight was about twenty-seven years of age. He was in point of size and agility a good sample of the "Hawkesbury native," a splendid horseman, and fearless and daring to a degree. To stimulate the police in their efforts to re-arrest the bolter, the Government offered a reward of £25; but very shortly after his escape he disappeared from the district, and all efforts to trace him were for a time fruitless.

When next he was heard of he was making a name for himself as a bushranger in the New England District. Like Morgan, he preferred generally to work single-handed; but one person knew all his secrets,

sympathised in all his troubles, sheltered him, watched
for him, and proved a faithful friend. That person was
a woman, and it is questionable if ever bushranger had
a "mate" more serviceable or more devoted. "Thunderbolt" had a long reign, and during five or six years
his name was kept prominently before the public, while
his person was eagerly sought after by the police of the
district chiefly infested by him.   He was a terror to
the mailmen of the North, and, sometimes alone, sometimes in company with others, "stuck-up" the drivers,
rifled the mailbags, robbed the passengers, and then
leisurely decamped.   His paramour did not accompany him in his raids, but was generally near at hand
in some secure camp, to which "Thunderbolt" would
resort when hard pressed by the police or in want of
provisions. She was an intelligent, pleasant-looking
half-caste, able to read and write fairly well, and more
refined in her speech than many of her European sisters, having been carefully trained in her younger days.
At one time she was in the habit of riding about in
man's attire, collecting horses or information, procuring supplies, or doing any other odd jobs which it
would be unsafe for her comrade to engage in.   It was
by her means and through her indefatigable exertions
that "Thunderbolt" was enabled for so long a time to
evade capture; and although the police arrested her on
a charge of vagrancy, nothing could be proved against
her, and she was released, again to serve the master
whose critical fortunes she had elected to follow.   On
more than one occasion, when hard pressed for food in
some lonely retreat in the bush, and when a visit to any
settler's house or wayside store would have furnished

a clue as to the hiding place, she was known to ham-string a young calf (using a sharp shear-blade fastened to the end of a long stick for the purpose), cut up the carcase, and carry the meat to the "camp." During a portion of the time she had several children with her, but towards the latter part of 1866 she went "down the country" and left all but one, the youngest, with some of "Thunderbolt's" friends. She proved faithful to her hunted paramour to the last, and, as will be seen farther on, "Thunderbolt" proved faithful to her, inasmuch as at great personal risk he found for her a comfortable resting place in which she could breathe her last.

On four different occasions he stopped and robbed the Warialda mail, and on each succeeded in making a good haul. In February, 1867, the mail was being driven to Tamworth by Abraham Bowden, who had with him a passenger named Derrington. They had just passed Manilla when the command to "bail up" was heard, and having obeyed the mandate the two men were ordered to pass into the bush a mile from the road, where "Thunderbolt" had a second horse tied up. Here Bowden was commanded to hand out the mail-bags and to take up his position with Derrington about thirty yards distant while the bushranger rifled the bags, taking from the letters all the notes, cheques and orders which they contained. He then took the mail-man's saddle, which he said he would return, and eased Derrington of some cheques and silver, but handed back the latter; after which he rode off, leading the second horse. As soon as he had disappeared Bowden rode back to Manilla for a saddle, and while there observed two horses on the upper side of the river, which he believed to be "Thunderbolt's." Having resumed his journey towards Tamworth he met Constables Norris, Shaw, and Doherty, who were returning to their stations from the sessions at Baraba. To these he told his story, and then pushed on to Tamworth to acquaint the police there. After robbing the mail, the bushranger crossed the Namoi to Mr. Hill's public house, and while he was there McKinnon, the superintendent of Manilla Station, rode up. "Thunderbolt" saw him coming and at once went out, and mounting his horse sat in the saddle awaiting his approach. Thinking that the stranger was some traveller McKinnon paid no attention to him, and having finished his business at Hill's crossed the river to Veness' public house, where he saw several persons in excited conversation, and learned from them that the mail had been robbed. Before the narration concluded there was an interruption. Hearing Mrs. Veness utter a scream, McKinnon turned his head and saw the supposed traveller whom he had met at Hill's standing behind him and presenting a revolver at his head. "Thunderbolt" ordered him to dismount and take his place with the other people, whom he also commanded to "bail up." After overhauling the superintendent and making an exchange of saddles, he entered into conversation with his prisoners and partook of some grog, for which he paid. After an hour had elapsed, McKinnon begged to be allowed to proceed on his journey to Tamworth, saying he was on his way to the doctor's, and having obtained permission was fixing the saddle on his horse preparatory to making a start, when all were startled by hearing the bushranger ejaculate "What's that?" and looking down the road they saw Constable Norris approaching. "Thunderbolt" at once mounted his horse and rode leisurely round the corner and along a fence towards the river, leaving the pack horse at the hotel. As Norris rode up the people at the hotel cried out to him "Bushranger! after him!" and the constable at once let the pack-horse he was leading go, pulled the revolver out of its pouch, and followed. But the chase was short and ineffectual, for Norris was soon back at the hotel, and "Thunderbolt" was seen on the opposite bank of the river. As Norris returned to the hotel, Constable Shaw drove up in a buggy, and after a consultation the two policemen got into the buggy and drove towards the river. As they ascended the opposite bank they caught sight of the bushranger, who had evidently been waiting for them, for when they came within hailing distance he called upon them to stand. Shaw replied with a shot from his revolver, but his aim was defective and "Thunderbolt" put spurs to his horse and disappeared. The two policemen then drove up to Hill's house, and while Shaw proceeded to take the horse out of the buggy Norris ran back to Veness' for the horse he had left, to find that the bushranger had crossed the river and ridden down the road, picking up as he went the pack-horse which the constable had been leading. Sergeant Doherty at this juncture appeared on the scene, and Norris having joined him the two started in pursuit of the bushranger, who they were informed was more than half drunk and might be easily captured if they were smart. Before they had proceeded very far they caught sight of "Thunderbolt," and getting within range they fired, but without effect; and finding that the chase was getting too warm the bushranger abandoned Norris' pack-horse and soon out-paced his pursuers, who returned to the hotel to report another failure. Attention was then directed to the pack-horse which "Thunderbolt" had left at the hotel, and in the saddle-bags were found the cheques and orders that had been taken from the mailbags, amounting in all to £427; but the more easily negotiable bank-notes that had been taken were not there, the bushranger having doubtless considered his own pockets the safest place for them.

Shortly after this "Thunderbolt" made his appearance on the road with a boy as his robber companion, and the queerly-assorted pair committed many depredations on the road, her Majesty's mails still forming the chief attraction. The boy's name was Mason, and it was not long before he established a reputation for reckless daring equal to that of his chief. In many instance they abstained from robbing the passengers or the driver, and contented themselves with rifling the bags and "sorting" the letters, in which work they became quite proficient. Together they held the road, defying all the efforts of the police to capture them, for they took care to be always provided with the fleetest horses, well-known racers having to leave their owners' stables and do duty as hacks for them. How they managed to evade the police for such a length of time was a mystery, for credit must be given to the latter for putting forth every effort to take them. All attempts to discover their camps or hiding places while occupied were fruitless, although the baffled officials would now and then succeed in following a trail leading to a deserted retreat, the "birds" having flown to some other locality before their arrival.

But while so frequently levying blackmail upon the post in its transit from one place to another, "Thunderbolt" and his boy-mate were not particular as to the victims. The money they stole from the mailbags was not spent in the purchase of stores, although some of it may have gone into the pockets of active sympathisers and assistants, who, themselves not bold enough to "take the bush," kept the bushranger posted in the movements of the police. If stores were wanted they were generally obtained in sufficient quantities by a sudden descent upon some roadside pub-store (in those days the publican generally served in the double capacity of grog-seller and grocer), from the stock in which a good choice of needful articles could be made. "Thunderbolt" and his boy would present themselves at the establishment, each leading a pack-horse—not the heavy animal usually led by the traveller, and whose chronic pace was a slow jog-trot, but a well-bred, fleet-footed beast, equal to the task of a break-the-record pace if necessity arose—which they would load with flour, tea, sugar, potted fish, and anything else that the unfortunate storekeeper might have in stock, not forgetting a bottle or two or spirits. When fully loaded they would ride off as suddenly as they appeared. If there did not happen to be a general store near when provisions ran short, a visit would be paid to the house of a well-to-do settler, and if nothing more than provisions were taken the latter would count himself remarkably fortunate.

Shortly after "Thunderbolt" had committed a series of depredations, ending with the robbery of the Tamworth-Singleton mail, the Government awoke to the necessity of offering further inducements to the police and others to effect his capture, and the following notice was published in the "Gazette" and newspapers :—

Colonial Secretary's Office.

£200 REWARD

FOR THE APPREHENSION OF FREDERICK WARD (OTHERWISE KNOWN AS "THUNDERBOLT") AND £50 EACH FOR ACCOMPLICES.

Whereas, the abovenamed convict, who effected his escape from the Penal Establishment, Cockatoo Island, on the 11th September, 1863, is still at large, and is further charged with the commission of divers other serious crimes: And whereas, by notice dated the 4th December, 1865, a reward of £100 was offered by the Government for the capture of this offender: Notice is hereby given that an increased reward of £200 will be paid by the Government for the apprehension of the abovenamed offender, or, if effected upon information received, then one half the reward to the person giving such information, and the other moiety to the person or persons effecting the capture; and, further, that the Government will pay a reward of £50, to be similarly divided, for the apprehension of any accomplice of the said Frederick Ward, arrested in his company, or associated with him in the commission of crime.

The above reward to be in lieu of all other rewards payable by the Government under previous notice for the apprehension or conviction of this offender.

HENRY PARKES.

But still the depredations continued. As month followed month, and as report after report was published of highway robberies by one man whose immunity from arrest caused men to marvel, only those who were compelled to do so travelled through the infested district; and these resorted to every imaginable device for secreting the money and valuables they were compelled to carry with them, in the hope that they would be able to pass scathless. A serious block to business was caused by this state of things, and the residents of the northern district fretted under it. Business people were afraid to forward money through the post; when they were compelled to do so they sent it in the form of cheques. But even these were not allowed to pass by "Thunderbolt," who invariably took them away with him, and either concealed them in the bush or destroyed them, uttering many complaints about the "infernal" custom which had sprung up of paying for everything with "paper" which in a bushranger's hands was not negotiable.

For some time after Mason joined him, the two worked together, and occasionally the older ruffian would stand aside and allow the younger to do the whole work, himself keeping a watchful eye upon the intercepted travellers, who were naturally indignant that they should have to submit to be robbed by a boy scarcely out of his teens. "Thunderbolt" was one of those men of the road who could boast with truth that he was always courteous, if not kind, to females, who might happen to be in the company of those "stuck up;" and he trained his bushranger apprentice to act courteously also. On one occasion when he had stopped the mail coach between Murrurundi and Wallabadah, there were two females among the passengers, and he ostentatiously instructed Mason to confine his attention solely to the mail bags, and not to molest the passengers in any way for fear of "hurting the ladies' feelings." The lad was armed with a gun, and seemed inclined to "show off" a little in front of the women,

grumbling not a little that his "boss" should allow the
men to escape for the sake of the women, especially as
the principal letters contained the objectionable
"paper" instead of money.

A little later some excitement was created by the
news spreading that the police had encountered
"Thunderbolt" on two occasions and had captured him
—nearly. The first part of the report was correct.
Senior-constables Dalton and Cantrill had been vigorously scouring the bush and had come across tracks
which they believed to be those of the bushranger and
which they concluded were leading to his camp in the
mountains. They followed these tracks to a point
which they knew would not admit of any turning, and
then dismounted. Leaving their horses they proceeded cautiously into the bush on foot in the direction
of the spot where they concluded the camp would be.
It was night when they began this march, and they
could not make much headway, but as day dawned on
the following morning they saw that for once they had
hit upon a good trail; at a distance of about sixty yards
they saw the bushranger, who was in the act of putting
on his boots preparatory to catching his horse, which
was grazing near. He had one boot on and the other
and a bridle in his hands, but a slight noise caused him
to look up, and catching sight of the police he dropped
the boot and bridle and dashed off into the scrubby
range close at hand, the police following as fast as they
could and firing as they ran. But neither their firing
nor their running proved effective. "Thunderbolt"
had an advantage over his pursuers in knowing the
course, and after a race of about a mile he succeeded in

getting away at a spot where the scrub was more than usually dense. Returning to the camp the police secured a boot and two horses, one of which was supposed to belong to the boy Mason, and returned with them in triumph to the station. At a later hour of the day another party of police came across "Thunderbolt" on the same range. They had been escorting the mail from Warialda to Tamworth, and had turned off the road on the return journey when they saw two horsemen talking to a woman on the range. At first they thought the man belonged to the police, as one of the horses looked like a "force" animal, but on nearer approach they saw that it was "Thunderbolt" and Mason, and that they were talking to the mistress of the former.. The police made a rush, and so did the bushrangers, each of whom held a spare horse, which was dropped as soon as the flight commenced. Shortly after starting "Thunderbolt" and the boy separated, each taking a different road through the bush, but the police continued to chase the larger game, being more anxious to catch the master than the apprentice. They fired several times, but the bullets did not hit the mark at which they were aimed, and the bushrangers again escaped, although the pursuers reported that they had seen blood on the track, as though either a man of a horse had been wounded. "Thunderbolt" was still minus one boot, the foot having a black cloth wrapped round it. When the police returned to pick up the two spare horses the woman whom they had at first seen had disappeared.

The separation between the master and his boy proved fatal to the latter. He made no effort to rejoin "Thunderbolt," believing that he had fallen into the hands of his pursuers, and at once started off for another part of the country. The encounter in which he and his master were separated took place on the Borah Ranges, and for some time the police concentrated their forces in this locality, imagining that "Thunderbolt" and the boy would endeavour to rejoin each other near the spot at which they had been driven apart. Mason was riding a good horse when he disappeared, but the hard riding took all the "go" out of it and before he had reached Dangar's station, about thirty miles from Millie, it had completely knocked up. Leaving the horse, Mason put away his arms and the saddle and bridle, and performed the rest of the journey on foot. Here word was conveyed to the police, and Senior-constable Connery and other members of the force started in pursuit from Narrabri, and captured Mason without any resistance on the latter's part. The youngster admitted that he was "Thunderbolt's" boy, and that he had with him committed several robberies. He had on his person when arrested, cheques amounting to about £100, which had been taken from the Merriwa mail. During his trip to Tamworth he became very communicative to the police, giving them an account of his life. Among other things he told them that he was apprenticed out of the Orphan School to a Mr. Shaw, in the employ of Messrs. Gilchrist, Watt, & Co., of Sydney, at the age of twelve years; that he remained with him for some time and then proceeded "up country," where he engaged with different persons; that he was doing a job of fencing when he fell in with "Thunderbolt," who represented himself as a squatter, and engaged him to assist in taking a mob of horses overland; that he soon ascertained "Thunderbolt's" real character, and did not hesitate to join him in the free but dangerous life that he was leading. Mason was at the time of his arrest only about sixteen years of age, of slight build, fair complexion, and not by any means a formidable-looking character.

In due course the youthful bandit was brought before the court and committed for trial, was tried and sentenced to a comparatively short term of imprisonment, which term he served only to be released and imprisoned again, a proceeding which was repeated several times, sentences of ten, fourteen, and twenty years following each other.

After the capture of his boy mate "Thunderbolt" continued his single-handed depredations, his extraordinary power of keeping out of the hands of the police still being the constant theme of conversation. Occasionally, however, the hunters and the hunted would come near each other, but the report made by the former after the event presented a monotonous sameness.

Towards the end of 1867 "Thunderbolt" made his appearance at the house of a settler on the Goulburn River, near Muswellbrook, and told the woman of the house a story which at once aroused her pity. His faithful mistress was sick unto death, and he desired to secure for her a little comfort during her declining hours. He had nursed her for some time in their secret camp; but the rough life which she had been compelled to lead and the constant anxious look-out

which she had kept had undermined her health, and she
was slowly dying. Would Mrs. Bradford take pity on
her, admit her to the shelter of the house, and permit
her to breath her last beneath a roof? It would not be
safe for him to attempt to bring the woman to the
house, but he would describe the place so that it could
be easily found if Mrs. Bradford would agree to perform this act of charity; otherwise, he would seek aid
from the clergyman (Rev. Mr. White), who happened
to be in the neighbourhood, and ask him to report her
condition to the police, and have her attended to, for
he must leave the district, which was getting too warm
for him, at once. Mrs. Bradford readily consented to
do as "Thunderbolt" desired, and herself proceeded to
the spot described by him, and found the poor half-
caste woman lying helpless and speechless in an ex-
temporised camp near a cave on the mountain side,
sheltered from the sun's rays by some boughs. Without delay a cart was procured, and "Yellow Long"—
that was the name by which she was commonly known
—was slowly carried to Mrs. Bradford's house.
"Thunderbolt" had stated correctly that she could not
live many hours. It was seen that she was dying, and
while one messenger went to inform the police another
was despatched for the clergyman. The latter arrived
shortly before the woman died, and the police immediately afterwards. It was only natural, of course, that
"Thunderbolt" should seek aid and shelter for his
faithful paramour in her dire extremity, and it was not
less natural that he should desire for her decent burial
after death. Yet, in comparison with some of the early
bushrangers, he was singular in this respect. The

reader may remember how Michael Howe turned upon
the woman who had served him so faithfully and in cold
blood shot her down when she was running by his side
endeavouring to escape from the police.   The sick
woman must have been a constant source of danger to
"Thunderbolt" during the month preceding her death,
yet he tended her carefully until all hope of recovery
had fled, and did not scruple to reveal his hiding-place
in order to secure for her an easy death-bed.   When
the police subsequently visited the camp they found
one of the bushranger's horses tied up near the place ;
but the bushranger himself had disappeared, and
search for him proved fruitless.

For several weeks nothing was heard of him, and
many persons concluded that he had carried out the
intention expressed to Mrs. Bradford, and left the district.   But all uncertainty on the point was set at rest
one morning by the report that he had been seen and
chased—ineffectually of course—by the police. Owing
to his frequent raids, police were told off to patrol the
roads between certain places, and while carrying out
that duty two troopers enexpectedly came across him
when shoeing his horse in the bed of the Namoi River,
near Manilla.   Not expecting to find him in that
locality they were proceeding leisurely on their way,
talking rather loudly as they rode, when they suddenly
espied a horseman in the river's bed.   There was a
mutual recognition, and simultaneous excited movements, the troopers on the bank, which at this spot
was very steep, riding at good speed towards a point
which they knew would afford the man below an opportunity of ascending to level ground with them, and

NN

the bushranger pressing forward at top speed, eagerly looking for a tolerably easy spot to climb. He discovered that spot before the troopers could close upon him, and facing his horse at the bank he scaled it within view and almost within range of his pursuers Then ensued a rather exciting chase for a couple of miles; but "Thunderbolt" was riding a very fine blood animal which he had stolen from Mr. Clift, of Breeza, and almost without effort he outpaced the horses ridden by the troopers, and disappeared in the bush, one of his pursuers firing a harmless shot after him.

For fully two years after this harmless encounter "Thunderbolt" remained at large, making occasional raids on travellers, coaches, and wayside stores, and then hastening back to some close retreat in the mountains. But in May, 1870, his long career was brought to a close, and in a manner as sudden as it was unexpected. He was at this time near the little town of Uralla, whose inhabitants were one afternoon about dusk thrown into a fever of excitement by the intelligence that the bushranger was at that moment engaged in sticking-up travellers and others at Blanche's inn, about three miles from the township. The news was brought in by a hawker who had himself been robbed by "Thunderbolt," but who had obtained permission to proceed on his journey, taking the road leading away from the town. At a convenient spot, however, he turned and made all haste to Uralla, where he made his errand known to the police, and Senior-constable Mulhall, the officer in charge of the station, at once started out for the scene of the operations, instructing Constable Walker, the lock-up keeper, to follow him as soon as he had changed his uniform for a private suit.

Approaching Blanche's place Mulhall saw two well-mounted men talking together near a garden at the end of the inn, and at once concluding that one of them was "Thunderbolt," he galloped forward and fired his revolver. His horse took fright at the sound of the shot, and made away; but it had not gone many

CONSTABLE WALKER

hundred yards back towards Uralla when Walker was met with.

Pointing to the men in the distance, Mulhall said to Walker, "There are the wretches—I have just exchanged shots with them." Walker advanced by himself, and the men at the same moment separated, one of them coming along the road and the other starting off at a gallop through the bush. Rightly concluding that the latter was the man he wanted, Walker put spurs to his horse and galloped after him, but coming into contact with a sapling where the bush was thick he "came a cropper," although he managed to stick to the reins. Just as he fell the bushranger turned in his saddle and fired, the ball whistling close to Walker's ear.

Quickly remounting, the constable resumed the chase, and then saw that his man was trying to double round the paddock which adjoined the garden with the object of getting back to the main road. Putting his horse to speed he managed to block the way in that direction, and forced the bushranger into a small gully and through some swampy ground up a hill on the other side. From this vantage point the bushranger again took aim and fired upon his pursuer, but without result; he then galloped up to some large granite rocks at the edge of a pool, plunged into the water, and swam over, leaving his horse on the other side. But Walker was "up to the dodge." He saw that the design of the bushranger was to "spell" his horse double round the hole to him if his pursuer followed, and thus have a clear escape back to the road again. He thereupon turned his attention for the moment to the horse, and riding up to him sent a revolver bullet through his brain. By this means he literally destroyed the enemy's boats, and forced him to an encounter.

Having destroyed the horse, the plucky constable then rode round, crossing a narrow slip of water by which the hole was connected with another of some-

what similar dimensions. "Thunderbolt," making another dash, got across the narrow strip, and had just
reached the top of the bank when his pursuer reached
the edge of the opposite side.   Here the two men
paused, facing each other, and the bushranger spoke.
"Who are you?" he asked.   Walker replied "Never
mind; surrender."   "Are you a policeman?" queried
the other.   "I am; you surrender," replied his opponent.   "What's your name?" again asked the bushranger.   "My name is Walker."   "Have you a wife
and family?" asked the man of the road.   Walker replied "I thought of that before I came here; you surrender."   "Thunderbolt" replied "No; I'll die first";
and then Walker stuck spurs into his horse, and crying
out "You and I for it!" sought to urge his animal
across the water separating him from his opponent.
But his haste nearly cost him his life.   As the horse
jumped forward under the spur-stabs he missed his
footing and plunged into the creek almost head first;
before he could recover the bushranger rushed forward
and endeavoured to pull the constable from the saddle
into the water, his object no doubt being to either dis-
able or kill his opponent, and then escape on his horse.
That he did not succeed in his object was not his fault,
for he was a strongly-built, muscular man, while
Walker had only just recovered from a long sickness,
and if it had been a mere test of strength between the
two men the constable must have gone under.   But
the latter was fortunate in having reserved one charge
in his revolver, and in having kept the weapon out of
the water.   At the critical moment he managed to
press the revolver against the bushranger's body and

pull the trigger. Simultaneously with the discharge
of the piece "Thunderbolt" uttered a cry of rage and
pain, and staggered back, but speedily recovering himself—although, as was afterwards seen, the bullet had
passed clean through his body, tearing his right lung
and coming out at the back—he made another clutch
at his opponent. Walker knew that he had fired his
last shot. He at once turned the revolver and used it
as a club, striking his assailant on the head and knocking him back into the water, which at this spot was
about four feet deep. He then jumped from his horse
and dragged his fallen foe to the bank, where, after two
or three gasps, "Thunderbolt" expired.

Night had now fallen, and the officer, leaving the
body of the bushranger on the bank of the lagoon,
rode back to Blanche's, near which place he again met
the man whom he had seen with "Thunderbolt" on his
arrival. Thinking he was an accomplice, Walker, who
was now without ammunition, boldly called upon him
to surrender, which he did. Explanations followed;
it turned out that the man, who was a drover, had some
horses in his charge, and had himself been "bailed up"
by the outlaw, and the horse the constable had shot
was one that "Thunderbolt" had taken from him and
was giving a trial to. This explained the attempt
made by the bushranger to double back to the inn,
where he had left his own horse—a splendid thorough-
bred; had he succeeded in doing this he would have
easily shown his pursuer a clean pair of heels.

Having informed the people at Blanche's inn of
what had taken place, Walker started with some of
them to remove the body, but owing to the darkness

of the night the exact spot where the body lay could not be found, and it was decided to abandon the search until the following morning. No difficulty was experienced in discovering the spot in daylight, and the body having been removed to Uralla a magisterial inquiry was held before Mr. Buchanan, J.P., and a verdict of justifiable homicide was returned.

"THUNDERBOLT" DEAD

Walker received the reward which the Government had offered for "Thunderbolt's" capture, and in due course was further rewarded by promotion in the ranks of the force of which he had proved himself so useful a member.

What "Thunderbolt" had done with all the money

he had taken during his bushranging career was a mystery which no person was able to solve, and to this day that mystery remains unsolved. Unlike many of the other "men of the road," he had very few friends in the district to which his depredations were confined, and his takings could not have been dissipated in gifts as hush-money or payments for services rendered as telegraphs. The general impression was that he had "planted" the bulk of the spoil in the bush, and that impression was strengthened by a discovery that was made twenty years afterwards in a cave which had been used by him and his half-caste paramour near the Goulburn River. A lad was hunting for birds' eggs at this spot in 1890 and found an oil-bottle containing a large number of £5 Commercial Bank notes. The notes were damp and mouldy, and it was only with difficulty that the numbers could be deciphered on some of them, the pulpy mass being neither good for ornament nor use. There can be very little doubt that the notes were hidden by the bushranger in readiness for the flight which he contemplated making with his dark-skinned companion, all hope of which had been destroyed by the latter's illness and death, and the tragic ending of his own career in the encounter with Constable Walker.

CHAPTER XVIII.

THE BROTHERS CLARKE.

The career of the Clarkes, who infested the Braidwood and neighbouring districts during the sixties, is one of the most fearful in the annals of Australian crime. They illustrated tribal lawlessness in a civilised land, for the family, root and branch, was steeped in viciousness. John Clarke, the father of the family, died in Goulburn Gaol, while under a charge of having murdered a black tracker. His wife, whose maiden name was Connell, had four brothers. One of them was charged with being accessory to the murder of a party of policemen; another was serving ten years in Darlinghurst Gaol, having previously served five years for highway robbery; and his wife was in the same place for receiving stolen property. A third brother was shot dead by the police; a fourth had sentence of death passed upon him for highway robbery and wounding. Two of John Clarke's sons—Thomas and John—were executed for highway robbery and murder, and a third was imprisoned for three years for receiving bank-notes stolen from the Queanbeyan mail by Thomas Clarke, his brother, and a brother of Mrs. John Connell's. Thus the three families combined in a strong confederacy of violence, robbery and murder.

It is with the two Clarke brothers, Thomas and John, however, that I purpose here particularly to deal.

If the brothers commenced their bushranging career in company they did so in a very quiet way, for only Thomas was sought after by the police when public attention was first directed to the family. Thomas was caught by the police and placed in Braidwood

ESCAPE OF THOMAS CLARKE.

gaol on a charge of robbery under arms; he made a successful effort to escape, and on October 3rd, 1865, was posted as missing. From that day he kept the whole police force of that and the neighbouring districts in full cry after him for eighteen months, while he perpetrated outrages which at last became abominable. His record reads thus:—Stole a horse from Dransfield, at Jembaicumbene, October 27; stole a horse from Mulligan, at same place, December 1; stole a horse from Mallon, at Mericumbene, December 13; robbery of Mr. Hosking's, at Foxlow, December 29; of Summer's store, at Jembaicumbene, January 13, 1866; of Frazer and Mathison, on Major's Creek Mountain, January 15; of the Post-office at Michelago, February 3; of John McElroy, Manar, February 10; of Edward Eaton, of Crown Flat, February 13; of Morris' store at Mudmelong, February 23; of Cullen and Harnett, near Cooma, March 22; of the Nerrigundah mail, when a Mr. Emmett was seriously wounded, April 9; murder of Miles O'Grady—for which offence he was outlawed —April 9; robbery of Armstrong's store at Araluen, May 22.

From this point Thomas Clarke was associated with his brother John, and the exploits of the pair may be thus summarised:—Robbery of Levy and others, at Michelago, June 1st, 1866; of Thomas Well, at Jindera, June 4; of the Moruya mail (mailboy's horse taken), July 16; of King and Morris' stores at Mudmelong, July 16; fired at the Ballalaba police, July 17; of F. H. Wilson, at Manar Station, July 24; robbery of the Yass mail, July 27; of the Queanbeyan mail, July 30; of Hoskings, at Foxlow, August 22, also September 10; of Myers and Badgery, at Jembaicumbene, August 27; of a Chinaman, on the Araluen Mountain, October 9; of a Chinaman, at Jembaicumbene, November 20; of a number of Chinamen, at Major's Creek, same day; of the Yass mail, at Razorback, December 7; of a Chinaman, at Mudmelong, December 31; of James Hyland, at Crown Flat, same date; suspected of murdering four special constables, at Jindera, January 9, 1867; robbery of John Hornby, on Araluen Mountain, January 13; of Chowry and Lamb, at Mongarlo, January 14; of the Yass mail, January 22; of James Myers, at Jembaicumbene, January 26; of the Goulburn mail, February 22; of Frazer's store at Gundaroo, March 7; feloniously wounding Constable Walsh and Sir Watkin, the black tracker, when being captured at Jindera, April 27; tried at Central Criminal Court, Sydney, May 29; executed at Darlinghurst, June 25, 1867.

The list is not quite complete; but it is long enough and black enough, surely, to satisfy anyone that no more remarkable confederacy of robbery, violence and murder has ever been known to exist in any civilised community. The details of some only of the more serious of the offences above recorded need be given, for this story is not written for the purpose of satisfying morbid curiosity or pandering to the vitiated tastes of those who delight to hear or read of deeds of violence and blood; but simply in order that the Australian citizen of to-day may know something of the strange vicissitudes through which the settlers of earlier days had to pass—a knowledge to which they could not attain without a record of this kind being placed before them.

Mention has only been made of two brothers, but they were associated with others of the family, Connell being prominent in several cases, and a man named Fletcher being also with them. The four were together when the attack was made upon Nerrigundah township in April, 1866. Towards dusk on the evening of the 9th they rode into the town, two abreast, and while two of them stopped at Wallis' hotel, the other two rode on to Pollock's store. The two at Wallis' made all the persons at the hotel deliver up their cash and valuables, and were standing guard over them when Thomas Clarke brought in Mrs. Pollock and placed her with the other prisoners, at the same time taking from her about £7 in money and the key of the safe. Standing with the key in his hand near the door, Clarke was suddenly surprised at feeling it snatched from him by Mrs. Pollock, and he rather angrily demanded that it should be at once returned; but the plucky woman threw the key over his head into the street, and though he searched for it with a lamp from the hotel, he could not find it. Shortly after other residents of the town were brought in. Mr. Pollock about this time returned from the upper town, and as he turned the corner at Wallis' he was told to dismount. He at first thought it some practical joking, and refused, but the bushrangers pulled him from the horse and walked him into the bar. As he resisted, one of them put down his gun and struck him on the face, the others keeping him covered, and Clarke threatened to blow his head off. Seeing that resistance was useless, Pollock became quiet. The number of victims had by this time swelled to about forty, as the bushrangers forced every individual that came near to stand with the others in the house, where they were kept under cover of the revolvers.

By this time the news had spread among the inhabitants, and they either hid away with their money or ran down to the hotel to see what was there going on, only to find themselves ordered to take up their positions with the other victims. The leading butcher of the town, Drew, foolishly carried his money with him to the hotel, and was immediately commanded to take his place with the others. He hesitated a good deal when he was commanded to "fork out your cash," and when passing the door of a side room suddenly threw his roll of notes inside the tap-room through the door. One of the bushrangers observed his action and at once called for a light in order to ascertain what it was that Drew had thrown away; but before the light was furnished there was an interruption. Constable O'Grady and another constable, who at the time had sole charge of the town, had received word of the bushrangers' presence, and bravely determined to tackle them at the hotel. Coming to the place, O'Grady saw the four bushrangers inside, and raising his revolver took aim and fired. The shot told and Fletcher fell, upon which Thomas Clarke at once rushed out with the others and commenced firing. The constables retreated down the street, but before they had proceeded far, O'Grady fell, mortally wounded. The bushrangers then galloped away in the direction of Deep Creek, a village about three miles from the Gulf, threatening to come back and shoot every person in Nerrigundah.

O'Grady's death was followed by a proclamation against Thomas Clarke and Connell under the Felon's Apprehension Act. A summons was issued against them under the hand of the Chief Justice, calling upon them to surrender to the Governor of Braidwood Gaol by the 4th May, and the period of grace allowed having expired they were formally outlawed. A few days after the outrage the police and some volunteers came across the bushrangers near Boralo Range, leading a pack-horse, and fired upon them, but Clarke and his companions escaped, although "Tommy" was supposed to have been disabled by a spent revolver bullet striking him in the knee.

On several occasions the police had "brushes" with the bushrangers, and came near arresting one or other of them more than once. But their failure to capture the band formed the subject of much debate. Those who were unacquainted with the difficulties under which this special class of police duty had to be performed could not understand how it was that a small band of men could so successfully, and for such a length of time, evade capture, when every available man in the police force was engaged in the hunt for them, and power had been placed in the hands of any person to shoot them down as outlaws. But it was the old story of strong sympathetic aid from numerous friends—harbourers, scouts and "telegraphs." Several of the more prominent settlers and squatters in the wild locality in which they chiefly sought refuge were pronounced friends of the outlaws; but although it was known that they harboured the criminals, and in their interests watched every police movement, from the nature of the country and the confederation that existed it was not possible to bring home effective proof. The Government had been recommended to cancel the lease of the run upon which these people had settled, and had adopted that recommendation, but in a weak moment had subsequently revoked the order at the re-

quest of a member of Parliament who had suffered
himself to be misled.   Thus the nest of robbers remained undisturbed, and the State contributed to the
defeat of its own officers.

Towards the close of 1866 a party of secret police
—under the command of a man named Flynn—was
organised for the special purpose of breaking up this
gang, but after a short period of ineffective service, in-
ternal disagreements arose and the party was discharged from duty.   But the idea of a secret police was
not abandoned, and an effort was made by the authorities in Sydney to form a second party, stronger than
the first and more fitted for the peculiarly difficult and
dangerous work.   A senior warder in Darlinghurst
gaol, named Carroll, who had been in the police force,
volunteered for the service, and undertook to get certain other reliable men to join him.   Carroll was a
singularly efficient warder, and was remarkable as a
man of great activity and physical strength, of un-
daunted courage, of wary caution, of determined will,
and with an intelligence superior to his station.   He
offered to go after Clarke's gang, having some special
reason for believing that he could get on the track of
the outlaw.   The conditions were that if he failed he
was to receive no recompense for his trouble, but that
if he succeeded he was to have suitable promotion in
the public service.   His offer was accepted, and he
was allowed to choose his own party.   Two of the
men he chose—Patrick Kennagh and Eneas McDonnell—had been warders, and the other—John Phegan
—had been in some connection with Clarke's gang,
knew the country, and had served his sentence.

Each member of the party was furnished with Tranter's revolvers, and the leader carried with him as an introduction to the chief magistrates of the district an interesting document under the hand of the late Sir Henry Parkes, who was then Premier of the colony. That document read as follows:—

The Colonial Secretary to Mr. John Carroll.
[Strictly secret.]

Colonial Secretary's Office, 22nd September, 1866.

Sir,—You are hereby authorised by the Government to proceed, by steamer, to Braidwood, in charge of a secret expedition for the capture of the bushranger Thomas Clarke and his associates.

The Government approves of your engaging the services of the three men, named Patrick Kennagh, Eneas McDonnell, and John Phegan, to act under you in this expedition, and agrees to the terms of engagement with you and them, as specified below.

In respect to yourself, your remuneration is to depend entirely on your success. If you fail, you are not to receive any compensation whatever. If you succeed in capturing Clarke, dead or alive, or in performing any similar service equal in importance to the protection of society, you shall receive pay for your time, at the rate of 12s 6d per diem, from the day you leave Sydney until the day on which you return to Sydney, and you shall be appointed to an office in the public service superior to any you have hitherto held.

In respect to the persons acting under you:—If as a party you fail in the objects of the expedition, they shall be entitled to receive 7s per diem from the day they leave Sydney until the day on which they return, but shall have no other claim on the Government. If as a party you succeed in capturing Clarke, dead or alive, or in performing any equal service, they shall receive 10s per diem, calculated in the same manner, and shall be further entitled to be employed in the public service, in any situation for which they are properly qualified.

These terms are irrespective of any reward or rewards that have been or may be offered for the capture of the bushrangers.

On arriving in Braidwood, you will all be sworn in as special constables for the district by Messrs. Rodd and Bennison, Justices of the Peace.

Your obedient servant,
HENRY PARKES.

Thus equipped and authorised, Carroll and his companions were sworn in as special constables, disguised themselves as surveyors, and proceeded to measure out a flat near the residence of Clarke's father, near Jingera. While so engaged they were subjected to an unexpected night attack, and narrowly escaped being shot down round their camp fire before they had well entered upon their work.

After finishing some bogus surveying they returned to their camp and had tea. They were standing round the fire conversing, when suddenly they were startled by the report of a rifle, and the "ping" of the bullet as it struck the tree against which the fire had been made. They rushed for their arms, but before they could use them they were again fired upon from opposite directions. The night was very dark, and Carroll's party could not see their assailants, but they fired in the direction from which the shots had proceeded, and several volleys were exchanged, but without injury to either side.

After this murderous attack, disguise was at an end, and Carroll set himself openly to work to root out the harbourers. Some of Clarke's acquaintances, including two of his sisters, were brought up before the magistrates and committed for trial. When in court in connection with these trials Carroll complained that the police rather hindered than helped him. In a report to the Government he repeated that charge, and even implicated some magistrates in winking at the conduct of the bushrangers from a regard to their own property. Accusations of this sort could not, however, be acted upon by the Government in the absence of more specific information; and it is possible that Carroll, baffled in his first attempt, may have laid more blame on others than they deserved. So far as the police were concerned, it was clear that Carroll operated among the harbourers to an extent that had not been previously practised. Yet it had to be confessed that all the special expeditions sent out against the bushrangers had failed, and that whatever may have been the shortcoming of the police in capturing bushrangers, no other set of men had done what they had left undone.

Having abandoned the pretence of performing surveying work, Carroll and his men now openly hunted the bushrangers from the same level as the police, whose efforts were not in any degree relaxed, jealous though the subordinate members of the force may have been of the party whose movements were untrammelled by red-tape regulations or official mandates. But the bushrangers defied alike police and "specials," and still pursued their course of open robbery. There was no conclusive evidence, of course, that Clarke and his mates had been the assailants in the attack recorded; but no one doubted that the shots had been fired by them.

For a time Carroll's party were more cautious in their movements. They decided never to camp in a tent, which favoured a surprise by the bushrangers, who could approach them unseen and unheard. They also adopted the plan of rapid movements from one place to another, and succeeded in keeping the hunted men in a state of suspense and constant watchfulness. Failing by direct pursuit to accomplish their purpose, they tried what bribery could do among some of the many friends of the outlaws, and by this means they learned who were the chief harbourers of the gang and who kept them supplied with the munitions of war. In this way they were enabled to make several arrests, the most important being that of Michael Connell, a relative of the outlaws, and postmaster and storekeeper at Oremmeir, and that of another relative named Berry. It was during the hearing of the charges against them that Carroll charged some of the police with having actually partaken of the plunder of the Foxlow robberies, and with having been unduly familiar with some of the female members of the bushrangers' families.

On the night of the 8th January, 1867, Carroll and his companions started on foot from Jinden at about eight o'clock, intending to visit the house of a man named Guinnes, about four miles distant, which they believed to be a favourite resort for the Clarkes and their companions. To reach Guinnes's house they had to pass through a very dense scrub, about half a mile from Smith's place. That scrub proved their grave. The sound of firing was heard at Smith's house about half an hour after the party had started; then there was silence, broken some time afterwards by the sound of another volley. Yet no one appears to have thought the occurrence sufficiently serious to call for immediate inquiry, and the inmates of the house retired to rest, in blissful ignorance of the fact that Carroll, McDonnell, Phegan, and Kennagh lay in the bush stark and stiff.

The position of the bodies when found on the following day indicated pretty clearly that the men had been taken by surprise and shot down as they walked through an open space in the bush.   Some stockmen, the first to learn that any outrage had been committed, came across the bodies of Phegan and McDonnell

KENNAGH

PHEGAN

M'DONNELL

CARROLL

THE FOUR CONSTABLES MURDERED BY THE CLARKE GANG.

riddled with bullets.   The latter had apparently been first shot in the thigh, and his leg was twisted under his body, which was lying in a pool of blood, having several other bullet holes in it also.   Phegan's body was fairly riddled with bullets, and the two men had evidently fallen together. The bodies of Carroll and Kennagh were discovered by a party of police shortly afterwards, about half a mile from the spot where those of their two companions lay. The former had been shot through the temple and the latter through the throat; it was conjectured that they escaped the first volley, ran for cover, were followed, called on to surrender, and then deliberately shot as they faced their murderers. Carroll was lying on his back with a handkerchief neatly folded across his breast, and a one-pound note pinned to it. That the object of the murder had been revenge and not robbery was clearly proved by the fact that in the pockets of the leader there was a large sum of money left untouched, as also was the money in the possession of his companions. Mr. Smith immediately informed the authorities at the nearest station, and the bodies were conveyed to Jinden, where an inquiry was held before a magistrate, after which the bodies were hurriedly buried, sheets of bark being made to do the double duty of winding sheets and coffins. Some days afterwards the bodies were exhumed in order that a public funeral might be accorded them, that being the wish of the Government.

The news created a great sensation throughout the whole colony. Never before had an outrage like this been committed, and never before was such general anxiety manifested to hunt down the murderers. Carroll's party had probably been led into this trap by the Clarkes, and every detail of the murder had been carefully planned by the outlaws.

Shortly after the news reached Sydney the following proclamation was issued in a "Gazette" Extraordinary:—

To the Magistrates, Freeholders, and other of her Majesty's subjects resident in the Police Districts of Braidwood, Broulee, Queanbeyan, Eden, Bega, and Cooma. Whereas the notorious outlaw, Thomas Clarke, whose life is forfeit to the laws of his country, and certain other lawless men associated with the said outlaw, have committed numerous depredations on the property, and by repeated acts of murder have taken the lives of her Majesty's subjects: And whereas the said outlaw and his lawless associates, from the physical character of the district which they infest, and the facilities which it is believed are afforded them by evilly-disposed persons, possess unusual means of escape and concealment: And whereas the existence of this gang of murderers is incompatible with a settled state of civil society and that security which ought to be everywhere maintained under British law, and cannot be suffered without public disgrace: Now, I, Sir John Young, the Governor aforesaid, do call upon you, the Magistrates, Freeholders, and other of her Majesty's subjects resident in the several Police Districts aforesaid, individually and collectively, by the allegiance which you owe to law and authority, to set aside for the public good all reasons of profit and convenience, and employing every means within your power to support and assist the officers of police, and other servants of her Majesty, in arresting the aforesaid outlaw, Thomas Clarke, and his associates in crime, and in bringing to speedy justice all abettors, harbourers, and receivers in anywise unlawfully connected with the said offenders.

FIVE THOUSAND POUNDS REWARD.—MURDER.—Whereas the undermentioned persons, John Carroll, Patrick Kennagh, Eneas McDonnell, and John Phegan, whilst engaged in the service of her Majesty the Queen, were murdered near the Jinden Station, in the Police District of Braidwood, on the 9th January instant, by some person or persons unknown, under circumstances of great atrocity: Notice is hereby given that the Government will pay a reward of five thousand pounds for the apprehension of all the parties concerned in the murder; or a reward of one thousand pounds will be paid for the apprehension of any one of the murderers; or should the capture be effected by information supplied to the police, then one-half the said rewards will be paid to the informant, and the remainder to the person or persons who may effect the capture. It is also further notified that, in addition to the above rewards, the Government will recommend that her Majesty's free pardon be extended to any accessory to the said crime, not being one of the persons who were actually present assisting in the commission of the said murders, who will first give such information as will lead to the capture of the murderers, or any of them. And all parties are cautioned that by harbouring, assisting, or maintaining the murderers, they will make themselves accessories to the crime of murder, and render themselves liable to prosecution accordingly.

HENRY PARKES.

The Government also decided to equip a special force, composed of picked men and under the command of a selected officer, and despatch it without delay to scour the district; and a hope was expressed that, with the law-abiding residents of the district roused to activity, the career of the lawless gang would be speedily brought to a close. But from this point the gang appears to have assumed a more generally aggressive character. Within a week after the murders they were out again on the road, "bailing up" all the mails and robbing every traveller that passed along the highways; and from the fact that such robberies occurred in different places in the district simultaneously the authorities rightly concluded that the party had divided, each section "holding" particular portions of the district. On January 15th, the two Clarkes and another stuck up the coaches between Braidwood and Araluen, and robbed the passengers of every penny they possessed. On the following Tuesday morning they robbed the Araluen coach at Reidsdale and secured about £40 from the passengers; and simultaneously another coach was robbed on another road and between £70 and £80 taken from the passengers; while the people of Braidwood were startled by the circulation of a rumour that ten armed men were on the Major's Creek mountain on the look out for the Araluen escort, but the escort subsequently passed without molestation and the report was then believed to have been spread by some of the bushrangers' friends for the purpose of drawing the whole of the police away from the town.

Meanwhile the local police were not inactive, although, do their utmost, they could not catch sight of the outlaws or their companions. But they gained information which led them to arrest Michael Connell, James Griffin, and a man named Guinness, family connections, on a charge of being concerned in the murder of the special constables. They were brought before the court and not a little sensation was created by the former being admitted by the magistrate to bail. The public of Araluen rose in a body in protest, and a monster public meeting was held at which the conduct of the magistrate was condemned and resolutions praying the Government to protect them from judicial acts of wrong as well as from the bushrangers were passed. Shortly after this a commission was appointed and sent up from Sydney to inquire into the condition of affairs in the district; and on the very day they arrived in Braidwood other distinguished gentlemen visited the place, in the persons of Sub-inspector Stephenson and a company of picked men, and Sub-inspector Brennan and a black tracker of high repute in the police force. A third party of police from Sydney also arrived on the following day. The Commission had gone to look after the magistrates, who had been openly charged by the public with favouring the bushrangers' friends in order to curry favour with the bushrangers, and thus save

PP

their own persons and property from injury. The police had gone to look after the outlaws.

At this time there were about forty mounted troopers scouring the bush in the Braidwood district, and one would have thought that with such a force menacing them day and night the outlaws would have experienced great difficulty, even in hiding. But they did not attempt to hide, and, in fact, appeared to grow bolder in open movements, although they were always on the watch against a surprise, and always prepared for a fight. Evidently they had no thought of seeking safety in flight, and were determined to fill their cup of guilt to overflowing. While the police were hunting for them on the mountains they would visit the plains and seek victims on the roads, or at the wayside inns. On one occasion it was reported that they had actually been seen drinking publicly at a bar in the heart of Araluen, passing right before the noses of the town constables when making their exit.

The gang was reduced about this time by the accidental death of a member named Doran, and by the capture and conviction of Thomas Connell for wounding one Thomas Emmett and stealing from him twenty-five ounces of gold-dust and some money. Emmett had been stopped on the Moruya-road, and on attempting to gallop off was fired at and shot in the thigh, his horse being killed under him by a rifle bullet at the same time. In this attack five bushrangers were engaged, the Clarkes leading the party, and Connell forming one of them. Found guilty by the jury, sentence of death was pronounced upon him; but the death sentence was not carried out, it being subsequently commuted to imprisonment for life, "without mitigation," the first three years in irons.

The Commission of Inquiry exhausted all evidence procurable in the district concerning the relation of the magistracy to bushranging, sitting for several days and furnishing a most voluminous report, based upon the evidence given, no less than forty witnesses having been examined. Shortly after that report was handed in to the Government, an official announcement was made that a certain prominent magistrate of the district had been superseded—or, in other words, dismissed. Beyond securing the removal from the Bench of an occupant adjudged to have been unfaithful to the trust reposed in him, the labours of the Commission were not fruitful of much good; but its presence in the disturbed districts served as an assurance to the people that some regard was being paid to their complaints, and that there was a disposition to correct the evils to which they were so frequently calling attention.

Still the Clarkes held the road, the army of visiting police being as powerless to arrest them or to check their outrages as the few who resided in the district had been. Cases of "sticking up" were of weekly, if not daily, occurrence, and it really seemed as if the outlaws were possessed of charmed lives, so easily and often did they appear and disappear without leaving their pursuers a trace that they could follow.

It was about this time (April, 1867) that Goulburn was adorned with the presence of one of the Clarke family, as the following letter will show:—

It was to be expected that with so many important criminals, some of whom had been closely mixed up with bushrangers, we should have a dilution of the Braidwood notorieties. We have had no male Clarkes nor Connells, and I should be very sorry to refer to any of their relatives, had there not been a conspicuousness that rendered it almost impossible for me to shut my eyes or leave my pen still. I daresay that you have not forgotten what has been reported about Annie Clarke, sister of the outlaws, and one of the police, who, if I recollect rightly, got into bad bread on the occasion referred to. Well, Annie Clarke is in Goulburn, and it is supposed that her presence here is one of sympathy. I can't say about that. She is, however, here, and would no doubt have passed without notice, had she not apparently coveted distinction. Let me afford her vanity scope. She is really not a bad-looking girl, about twenty years of age, fully the proper height for a woman, with a figure that would pass anywhere. But she strives for observation. I only saw her during one day, and then—mimicking the ladies of the land— she changed her dress four times—possibly more than that, because I did not see her "full-dressed for the evening." There was something quiet in the first two costumes, but in the afternoon she came out in a "blood-red" one, with hat and feather, and nether pendants well ankled; presently, out she appeared in blue silk, with white shawl, ankled as before, but without that finish as to hose that lends its particular charms to criticising eyes. I would not have dwelt on the subject had it not been my impression that the Protean change of costume appeared to be as if in bravado—as if to show the less aspiring of her sex how much value there was in being connected with the most worthless of the "manly" sex. Such an example does more harm than fifty revolvers. I have nothing to say against the girl herself, except to condemn her want of judgment and womanly taste.

But the end of this lawless career was drawing very near. The police were working with a diligence that indicated their anxiety to come to close quarters with the desperadoes, who within the past few months had been three only—Thomas Clarke, John Clarke, and Scott. On one occasion they pressed the trio very closely, and having done so they strained every nerve to get to closer quarters with them. Just here the value of an experienced bush policeman in such a place and under such circumstances was made very apparent. Senior-constable Wright, whose character for efficiency in such service stood very high with his superior officers, had been sent to the district specially to hunt down the outlaws, and with four men, and a skilful black tracker, he at last succeeded.

It was on Saturday, April 27th, 1867, that the "running down" took place. The party of police had been camped at Fairfield, about twenty miles from Ballalaba, on the road from Jinden and Cooma, and lying on one side of the Jingeras, in the fastnesses of which the bushrangers had for such a length of time defied all efforts to capture them.

The police, consisting of Senior-constable William Wright, the officer in charge, Constables Walsh, Egan, Lenehan, James Wright, and a black tracker named Sir Watkin, picked up the tracks of the bushrangers at about one o'clock in the afternoon and followed them, the party being all on foot, until darkness and heavy rain prevented further movement for the time. They had their suspicions that the bushrangers were making for the house of a settler about two miles away, and concluding that they would there seek temporary shelter, they cautiously pushed forward. Reaching the hut, they saw sufficient to convince them that the men of whom they were in search were inside, and they at once made arrangements for spending the night on watch in the open—a not by any means pleasant task, owing to the heavy rain and dense darkness. Seeking shelter behind a small haystack some distance from the dwelling they waited until the moon rose, and then they observed a couple of horses grazing in the paddock, which upon closer inspection they saw were the "bloods" which were known to be in the possession of

the Clarkes. Having driven the horses to the far end
of the paddock so that they could not be easily reached
by the bushrangers, Senior-constable Wright and his
men waited patiently behind the haystack until daybreak, when they saw the two brothers emerge from
the hut with bridles on their arms, intending to bring
up the horses. Before reaching the animals, however,
one of the brothers called out, "Look out, there's someone at the stack," and the pair immediately turned and
commenced to run back to the hut. The police party
at once left their hiding place, called upon the bushrangers to stand, and fired at them, but the shots did
not take effect, and the fire was returned by the
brothers as they ran, they having their revolvers with
them. Several shots were thus exchanged, but the
brothers succeeded in regaining the hut, apparently un-
scathed, although it was afterwards found that Johnny
Clarke had been wounded, a rifle ball having struck
him in the breast near the socket of his right arm, and
in a most remarkable manner passed clean through his
body without touching a bone or vital part. Having
gained the shelter of the hut, which was of slabs, the
bushrangers seized their rifles and fired at their pursuers through the interstices, compelling them to retire behind whatever shelter they could find in the yard.
For some time an irregular fire was kept up, and two
of the attacking party—Constable Walsh and Sir
Watkin—were wounded, the former in the thigh and
the latter in the arm. Meanwhile reinforcements had
been sent for to the nearest police station, Ballalaba,
and when Sergeant Byrne and six additional troopers
appeared on the scene, the bushrangers, seeing that

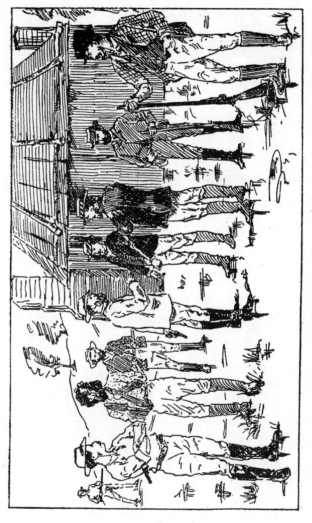

SURRENDER OF THE CLARKES.

further resistance would be useless, called out that they would surrender. Opening the hut door they came out, unarmed, and submitted to be handcuffed. Having been secured they were taken to Ballalaba, where they were met by another posse of police under Superintendent Orridge and Dr. Patterson, the services of the latter being called into requisition to dress the wounds of Johnny Clarke and the black tracker.

The value of the services rendered by the black tracker was greater than many persons imagined. As has been seen, Sir Watkin, who was looked upon as one of the best of trackers, not only conducted the party under Senior-constable Wright to the retreat of the bushrangers, but took an active part in the assault upon the hut, and was, during the encounter, more seriously wounded than any of the party. From the first it was seen that his arm had been wounded so severely by the bullet from Tommy Clarke's Tranter rifle that amputation would be necessary; and shortly after his arrival in Braidwood he was admitted as a patient in the local hospital. A few days after his admission Dr. Patterson performed the operation, taking off the arm above the elbow. With the stoical indifference to bodily pain for which the aborigines—equally with the Red Indians of America—were celebrated, Sir Watkin bore the painful operation without a murmur. He coolly walked from the upstairs' ward down to the dissecting room below, and after the operation unconcernedly walked back again, as if he merely had had a finger punctured. The old fellow—he had seen fifty-one summers—was not inclined to bear his honours meekly, and with pardonable pride strutted about exhibiting the stripes which had been attached to his ordinary uniform by the Superintendent of Police, declaring that he had been promoted to the rank of "sergeant-major." It may be remarked here that Sir Watkin did service as a tracker on many subsequent occasions, and was always treated by his comrades as an "officer" who had "won his spurs."

The prisoners underwent a private examination in Braidwood Gaol on the Thursday after their capture before the Visiting Justice and one or two other magistrates; but prior to its commencement their mother and sister were permitted an interview. In due course, they were committed for trial at Sydney, and were sent thither by one of the Clyde River boats, the escort consisting of Superintendent Orridge, Sub-inspector Wright (he had been promoted from senior-constable after the capture), and Constable Walsh. When it became known in Sydney that the notorious bushrangers of Braidwood were in the harbour, crowds of people assembled at the different wharfs in expectation that the landing would be effected at one or other of them. But in order to avoid the mob the police authorities sent out the official boat and intercepted the steamer as she was coming up the harbour, received the prisoners, and conveyed them to the Circular Quay, which was bare of spectators. An expectant crowd which had assembled at Mrs. Macquarie's Chair caught sight of them, however, and at once rushed down to the wharf, and had the satisfaction of witnessing the landing. A good deal of disappointment was expressed at the appearance of the two men. Instead of seeing two strong-bearded, villainous-looking desperadoes, they saw two sheepish-looking, overgrown native youths, and they could scarcely bring themselves to think that these were the ferocious, bloodthirsty bushrangers who had robbed and murdered people in the Braidwood district, and frustrated every effort of the police to capture them for such a long period. Both men were heavily ironed, and immediately upon landing were conveyed in a cart to Darlinghurst Gaol, where they were kept entirely separate from the other prisoners, pending the preliminary enquiry, which was conducted privately. A committal followed, of course, and the public looked forward somewhat anxiously to the opening of the Central Criminal Court in Sydney, at which the fate of the two bushrangers was to be decided.

That court opened on May 28th, 1867, before his Honour, Sir Alfred Stephen, Chief Justice, and the two prisoners were jointly charged with having wounded Constable William Walsh with intent to murder him. Mr. Isaacs, Solicitor-General, prosecuted for the Crown, and Messrs. Dalley and Blake appeared for the defence. His Honour, at the commencement of the proceedings, directed the strictest order to be maintained in Court, and announced that the constables had been ordered to arrest anyone attempting to contravene that command. He was determined that a repetition of the display of public sympathy which had taken place on the occasion when the Eugowra Escort robbers and Gardiner were tried in Sydney should not occur.

A question was raised by prisoners' counsel concerning the legality of the proclamation by which

Thomas Clarke was made an outlaw, for the first summons calling upon him to surrender before a given date, having been discovered to be faulty, had been supplemented by a second summons. The point was argued at great length before the evidence closed, but it did not affect the issue.

Both Mr. Blake and Mr. Dalley delivered powerful addresses to the jury. Their contention was that it had not been satisfactorily proved that the shot that wounded Walsh was fired by either of the prisoners, and that even if it had been, no felonious intent had been shown in the firing, the men having simply sought to defend themselves from a sudden attack, at the time not knowing that their assailants were police.

The Crown Solicitor addressed the jury in reply, and the Chief Justice having summed up, the jury returned a verdict of guilty.

Asked if they had anything to say why sentence of death should not be passed upon them, the brothers simply replied "No," and then his Honour addressed them thus :—

Prisoners Thomas and John Clarke, if in the opinion of most of those who hear me, and of a large portion of the community, it should be thought that you are about to receive a just retribution for your crimes, it will be proper for me to say that no such feeling influences this court, or is known to our laws. You are not to receive sentence of death as retribution—which belongs not to mortals—but the taking of your life is believed to be necessary for the peace and good order, for the safety as well as the welfare of the community; because of the example and warning that a capital execution may hold out to others to restrain them from committing similar crimes to those for which you stand convicted. This is the principle upon which all our punishment—certainly the punishment of death—rests, or it has no justification whatever. Now, I told the jury that they were to believe you innocent of those various crimes in respect to which the effort was made to apprehend you, and for which you were finally apprehended; and of course the jury took it for granted that you were innocent. But now I am not restricted by any such necessity or duty; on the contrary, without wishing to wound your feelings or add any sense of shame or humiliation, I must address you for the good of the community, and also to show what really is the extent of the crime committed by, or reasonably supposed to be committed by you, in respect to which the Executive will have to pronounce whether they can with propriety, or with any sense of decency, commute the sentence about to be passed upon you. Thomas Clarke, I hold in my hand a list of the offences on which you stand charged within the last two years. They amount in the whole, exclusive of the murders of which you are suspected, to nine robberies of mails and thirty-six robberies of individuals. Among those individuals robbed were all classes of persons—Chinamen, labouring men, publicans, storekeepers, tradesmen, and settlers. With respect to you, John Clarke, I find that offences are charged upon you, committed within the last year, most of them in company with your brother, numbering twenty-six. Now this is the result, you see, of a long career of bushranging. You have had many abettors; you must have had a large number of them in the district from which you have come. I believe that not only those but others—violent and infamous as they are—sympathise with you in your crimes—I hope not in the murders of which you are suspected. I shall not waste words in respect to such people. The community is disgraced by such crimes, but I would ask others—not you—and possibly it will be well for you to reflect before you die—what is the value of this course of violence and outrage that you have been pursuing for so long a time? In all cases—and I have tried many—of robbery, it has been a question with me, as with others, where is the money they have gained—where are the results? You have not one shilling in the world to call your own, and therefore you have not profited by it in the way of money. I never knew a bushranger, except one, who is now suffering a sentence of thirty-two years' hard labour, who made any money by it. Well, if you have not made anything by it, what could have induced you to pursue it? Crimes must end eventually in murder. Human life taken, life imperilled, misery inflicted upon hard-working men, and all this for no earthly good to any one of you! And yet you, young men, might have been happy—happy fathers of families, living happily with your wives—happy, because happiness is confined to the virtuous. Instead of which you are to die a dishonoured death on the gallows. Another consideration; all along from the beginning you must have had the idea of the gallows hanging over you. You must have known that the result of all this must be death, shocking and infamous to think of. I hope all those who ever think of pursuing such a course will only reflect that there is this horrible feeling of a public execution hanging over you for years or months that they can never escape from. You must have been constantly in terror; always in a state of alarm lest the police should track you out in your haunts. I have no wish to harrow your feelings—God forbid; I am saying this that it may sink into the hearts of others, and that it may restrain them from entering on a career so fatal. I say that during all this time men like you must have been dreading the intrusion of the police in your hiding places. Hunted about like wild beasts, you must actually have undergone an amount of labour and fatigue greater than you would had you been working on the roads—an amount of fatigue which, through honest labour, might have resulted in happiness, with a consciousness of virtue, and finally competence and honour. I say the amount of fatigue and want of comforts of all kinds surrounding you must be taken into consideration. The balance is all against you. I have said I never knew a man, or heard of one, who through a course of bushranging, gained a shilling's worth of property that he could call his own, or could gain it if let loose tomorrow morning. Where is there one flourishing in any single respect? I will read you a list of bushangers, many of whom have come to the gallows within the last four and a half years. I believe they are all caught but one. Many of these were young men, capable of better things; but died violent deaths:—Piesley, executed; Davis, sentenced to death; Gardiner, sentenced to thirty-two years' hard labour; Gilbert, shot dead; Hall, shot dead; Bow and Fordyce, sentenced to death, but sentences commuted to imprisonment for life; Manns, executed; O'Meally, shot dead; Burke, shot dead; Gordon, sentenced to death; Dunleavy, sentenced to death; Dunn, executed; Lowrie, shot dead; Vane, a long sentence; Foley, a long sentence; Morgan, shot dead; yourselves, Thomas and John Clarke, about to be sentenced to death; Fletcher, shot dead; Patrick Connell, shot dead; Tom Connell, sentenced to death but sentence commuted to imprisonment for life; Bill Scott, a companion of your own, believed to be murdered—by you. There is a list! The murders believed to have been committed by you bushrangers are appalling to think of. How many wives made widows, and children made orphans! What loss of property, what sorrow have you bushrangers caused! I have a list here of persons killed or wounded in the perpetration of robberies since August, 1863—six killed and ten wounded. Unfortunately, of the police seven have been killed and sixteen wounded in three years. I say this is horrible. Much as I dread crime, and much as I have had to do with the punishment of criminals, I don't know anything in the world that could furnish such a long list of horrors as that which I have laid before this crowded court to-night. And yet these bushrangers, the scum of the earth, the lowest of the low, the most wicked of the wicked, are occasionally held up for our admiration! But better days are coming. It is the old leaven of convictism not yet worked out, but brighter days are coming. You will not live to see them, but others will. Others who may think of commencing a course of crime like yours may rely on it that better days are coming, and that there will be no longer that expression of sympathy with crime which sometime since disgraced the country, and sunk it so low in the estimation of the world. Though the people among whom I move are much above those who sympathise with crime, it humiliates me to think that in this very court in which I am now sitting, one of the greatest ruffians of bushrangers, who was the very head and front of offenders, stood in the dock and was acquitted—and, I say it, acquitted wrongly—and when that verdict was announced there were expressions of rejoicing in the court, such as would disgrace any community on earth. I am happy to think that those days are gone at last. There. may be some here who were guilty of participation in that most abominable and most scandalous exhibition. You, young men, have now to receive the last sentence of the law. You will pass from the country which you might have helped to raise in the estimation of the world. You will pass out of the world felons, convicts, bushrangers, and, I very much fear, murderers.

Sentence of death was then passed on the prisoners in the usual form, and in the most solemn manner, and immediately afterwards they were removed from the dock. Both prisoners fixed their eyes on the Chief Justice while he was addressing them, and appeared to be listening attentively, but there was scarcely any emotion perceptible from their manner. As soon as his Honour had ceased speaking, John Clarke turned to his brother and made some remark with a smile on his countenance. The police removed the prisoners from the dock, and the immense crowd of persons who had thronged the court, and who had preserved the utmost silence, began slowly to disperse.

The condemned criminals were then removed to Darlinghurst Gaol, and after a week of suspense in their cells—although neither of them expressed any hope of the sentence being commuted—they were officially informed that the Executive had fixed the day for their execution, and that they would be hanged on the 25th June. On the Friday following their condemnation they were allowed to receive as visitors their mother and sister, and a very affecting scene took place as they parted from each other, never again in this world to look upon each others' faces. The brother, who was then serving a sentence on Cockatoo Island, was also permitted to visit them, and they strongly advised him to pursue an honest calling upon his release from custody. The two men appeared to be very attentive to the ministrations of Rev. Father Dwyer, Roman Catholic chaplain of the gaol, and the Sisters of Mercy, who were constant in their attendance at the gaol.

But if they were reconciled to their fate the lawyers who had defended them at the trial were not. They moved the Full Court for an arrest of judgment, and a new trial in the case, on the ground that there had been a non-direction of the jury upon a point of law. The alleged omission was that the jury were not directed by the Chief Justice as to their right to acquit the prisoners of the capital offence (wounding Constable Walsh with intent to murder him) and to convict them only of the minor offence of unlawfully wounding, if they thought that the evidence warranted and necessitated such a course. The answer given to this objection was in effect that as the jury had already on their oaths pronounced both prisoners guilty of the capital offence, the prisoners had no right to complain of the omission referred to; for assuming the finding of the jury to be correct, no question arose or could have arisen as to the prisoners' guilt of any minor offence. Their Honours upheld this view of the case and ruled that the judgment should stand.

There were some persons—prominent public men amongst the number—who considered that the Government did not exercise a wise discretion in putting the two Clarkes upon trial for their last offence, seeing that no life had actually been taken, and that many even more serious offences were understood to have been committed by the prisoners. But although they were suspected of having murdered the four constables and several other persons, including one of their own mates, it must be remembered that the Crown could not hope for conviction in any one case or a number of cases upon mere suspicion, and they had nothing but suspicion to go upon in any of those cases. The shooting at Constable Walsh with intent was, on the other hand, very easily proved; and perhaps it was just as well that the bushranging fraternity and those who sympathised with them should learn that there was danger in firing at a policeman even in resisting arrest. To hear some persons speak during the bushranging era, one might imagine that the members of the police force were under a social ban—that they were engaged in a conspiracy against the happiness of mankind—and that whatever happened to them "served them right." To give confidence to the police, and to intimidate those who were arrayed against their lawful authority, was, therefore, a matter of great moment at that period; and in enforcing upon the Clarkes so awful a penalty, the administrators of justice gave everyone to understand that a policeman's life was just as valuable as that of any other man. And judging from the fact that bushranging received about this time a temporary check—only a few cases of lawlessness occurring—the lesson inculcated by the conviction and hanging of the Clarkes was not altogether thrown away upon those for whom it was chiefly intended.

The remarks made by the Chief Justice when sentencing the two brothers had one good result—it secured for the services of the police a fairer and higher appreciation than that generally accorded. The public had simply expected marvels of them. It complained of them not being good marksmen when it had not taken the trouble to teach them to shoot; of their not riding down lighter men better mounted; of their not knowing by instinct the entire topography of a district they had never so much as ridden over. The public had continually ignored what they had done, while taunting them with what they had failed to do. And yet, to take the annals of one crime alone, the number of bushrangers whom they had taken or slain formed a very respectable list, attesting their efficiency, while the number of those who had lost their lives in defence of the law afforded melancholy proof of their zeal and courage. So much it is right that I should say concerning a body of men who, under many disadvantages —some of which have already been touched upon— efficiently performed a public duty that was both difficult and dangerous.

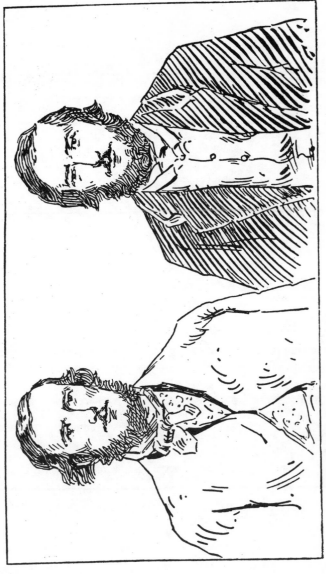

THOMAS CLARKE

JOHN CLARKE

And this brings me back to the murder of the four special constables—Carroll, Phegan, Kennagh, and McDonnell—concerning which something more remains to be said. Although the impression prevailed generally that Thomas and John Clarke had committed those murders, it was known that they must have been assisted by others, a few facts connected with the mysterious affair that the police were able to gather up pointing to the conclusion that at least four men had engaged together in the bloody deed. The reader has seen that the Clarkes were not charged with this murder—there was no necessity for that; but the police had arrested one man, a connection of the Clarke family, and against him they preferred the charge of murdering Carroll. The name of the accused was James Griffin, a young man of about 21 years of age, and who resided on a farm about twenty-five miles from Jinden, near which place the murder was committed.

Griffin was placed upon his trial at the same sittings of the court in Sydney as that at which the charge against the Clarkes had been heard, and he also was defended by Mr. Dalley. The case occupied a very long time, and created quite as much sensation as the trial of the Clarkes, the court being inconveniently crowded during the hearing.

After evidence had been produced supporting the account of the murder already given, and showing how the bodies of the four men had been found lying dead in the bush—two in one place and two in another, with gunshot wounds in different parts of their bodies—witnesses were called to connect the prisoner with the crime. Their evidence was of a character so extra-

ordinary that I make no excuse for the extensive quo
tations, taken from the published report of the trial,
which follow :—

Edward Smith deposed: On the 8th January last I was
managing the Jinden station, about forty miles from Bra d-
wood; I remember some dead bodies being found about a
mile and a half from Jinden House; the dead bodies were
those of Carroll, Phegan, McDonnell, and Kennagh; I saw
the prisoner at my place on the evening of the 8th of January
last. He did not remain there more than a quarter or half
an hour; he came to me and said that Carroll and his party
were on the road—that they were at the Dirty Swamp as he
passed them; prisoner was riding a bay horse, and when he
left my house he rode away towards Braidwood in the direction in which he had said Carroll and his party were coming;
on the same night a young man named Dempsey—who was
subsequently arrested—came to my house and stayed about
half an hour, and about sundown Carroll and his party arrived
and remained at my house all night; they left on the following
morning about seven o'clock, going towards the farm of a
man named Guinnes, a free selector; the prisoner came to my
house on that morning, about half an hour after Carroll's
party left; prisoner told me that he had seen Carroll and his
party going towards Guinnes's place; Carroll and his party left
my place on foot, having left their horses with me; prisoner
stayed about half an hour, and when he left he went as if he
were going to Guinnes's place: he was riding a grey horse;
he asked me to lend him my breech-loading rifle; I refused to
do so; I told him he should not have it; he told me not to
give it to Sergeant Byrnes or Carroll; I did not see any other
strangers about my place on the 8th January; I know
McEneny's place; it is about three-quarters of a mile beyond
Guinnes's; I was there about three days before; I did not see
any strangers about there or about Guinnes's; I next saw the
prisoner on the following Sunday at the house of Michael
O'Connell, a publican at Stoney Creek; some people call him
Connell; Stoney Creek is sixteen miles from my place; I had
some conversation there with the prisoner alone; I saw him
there on the following Sunday, the 13th; he said, "After leaving your place last night, I went towards Clarke's place;"
Clarke's place is between 20 and 25 miles from Jinden House;
prisoner said, "I brought the bushrangers up that night;" he
did not mention any name; he said, "Bill Scott and John
Clarke stood behind one tree, and Tommy Clarke stood be-

hind the other;" he did not mention any place; he said, "Carroll and his party advanced, and Tommy Clarke went out from behind the tree and called upon them to surrender;" those are the exact words; "Phegan and McDonnell fell; McDonnell fired one shot out of his revolving rifle and his leg was broken; they fired into the detectives; Kennagh and Carroll retreated down the flat; Kennagh took two balls from the tree behind which Bill Scott and Johnny Clarke were; Tommy Clarke ran round at the back of Kennagh and fired a shot at Kennagh, and the ball went into a sapling close alongside of him; Clarke called for a horse, and a horse was brought down." He did not tell me by whom the horse was brought down; that was after he told me Tommy Clarke got behind Kennagh; he did not tell me which took place first; Tommy Clarke fired a shot at Kennagh, and called upon Kennagh to surrender; Kennagh looked round and threw his rifle on his arm and surrendered; there was one shot in the revolving rifle when Kennagh surrendered; Tommy Clarke said to Carroll, "You are Carroll;" Carroll said that he was not Carroll, that Carroll was lying dead on the road; Tommy Clarke said "Make up you mind, you have not got many more minutes to live;" Carroll then said, "Mercy!" Tommy Clarke said, "You can't expect mercy, you did not show mercy to my sister;" that is all prisoner said; he said that Tommy Clarke shot Carroll, and that Bill Scott shot Kennagh; John Clarke did not shoot any of them; Tommy Clarke shot three out of the four; he did not tell me whereabouts the wounds were; he did not tell me what Tommy Clarke shot Carroll with, or what Bill Scott shot Kennagh with; he said all the money on them was only £1 2s 6d; that is all the prisoner said; he said nothing at all about Kennagh; he did not say on whom the money was found; he made some remark about Kennagh, but I do not remember what it was; prisoner said he held the horses; I remember that now; I don't remember anything more as to where he held them, how he held them, or anything else; he said that he held the horses; he did not tell me who took the horse down on the flat; he said Clarke called for a horse; prisoner expressed a wish to go with me to Gippsland; I told him that it looked very suspicious, and that he had better not go; he said Tommy Clarke had his boots off and was barefooted; Mick Connell, the landlord, was present, and asked Griffin if the gin had taken effect, and Griffin replied, "Only for the gin I could not have got 'em up to the pinch;" when prisoner came to the house on the 9th he had some gin in a square bottle; I was in the parlour when I heard the two talking, and Connell said, "Then you brought the horses there?" Griffin said that Tommy Clarke could not catch Carroll running down the hill barefooted.

The witness was subjected to a rigorous cross-examination by Mr. Dalley, who appeared for the accused, and admitted that he had sworn differently at the Police Court, but explained that he was then in fear of his life, some of the Clarkes' friends having declared that if he told anything against them he and all belonging to him would be shot down. In answer to the judge, Smith said that he had been previously fired at and his place burned down, and that after giving evidence at the Police Court he had sold out and left the district.

Catherine McEneny, who resided near Jinden at the time, identified the prisoner as one of four armed men who had called at her hut on the morning of the murder. She heard the firing in the bush after they left, and subsequently saw them returning across the bush. This witness also declared that she had been threatened and compelled to leave the district, her pigs and geese having been shot.

The jury returned a verdict of not guilty. There was some manifestation of feeling on the part of the crowd in the court; but the applause was almost instantly suppressed by the police.

The prisoner was then remanded to gaol to be subsequently tried with a brother for complicity with the bushrangers in other matters. In the charge preferred against them, however, the Crown failed to make good its case—in fact, circumstances redounding to the credit of one of the accused were brought to light in the court. He had frequently given information to the police regarding the movements of the bushrangers, and it was upon his information and by his guidance that the party of police under Wright surrounded the hut where the two Clarkes were staying the night preceding their capture. When discharging the two men —the jury having returned a verdict of not guilty—the Chief Justice said he thought the authorities might have shown them a little more consideration, in view of the services which they had rendered to the police.

But James Griffin was not yet out of the toils. In September following he was again placed upon his trial on the charge of being concerned in the Jinden Murders, Special Constable Kennagh being specifically named as the victim. He was ably defended by Mr. Dalley, but additional evidence was forthcoming which clearly established his complicity in the cowardly and bloodthirsty deed. One witness was called who declared that on the day preceding the murder the prisoner had asked him to join in the murder, while Smith repeated the evidence given by him on the former trial, concerning the conversation he had heard between the prisoner and Connell. Griffin was, on this occasion, found guilty and sentenced to death; but that sentence was subsequently commuted to imprisonment for life, the first three years in irons.

One more event in connection with the reign of the Clarkes remains to be recorded. At least one man of the many who had by sheltering and assisting them enabled the outlaws to successfully evade arrest for such a length of time, was brought to account. Shortly after the Griffins had been discharged, Michael Connell, brother of the bushranger of that name who was a member of Clarke's gang, and who had been shot by the police during one of their earliest encounters with the gang, was charged under the Outlawry Act with having harboured and assisted the Clarkes. Connell at the time of his arrest was postmaster and publican in that part of the district forming the favourite resort of the Clarkes, and it was proved that he had repeatedly furnished the bushrangers with provisions and spirits, and even with ammunition. The principal witness against him was a man who was serving a long sentence for highway robbery, he having been captured when engaged with the Clarkes in "sticking up" a store. This man declared that his principal duty was to obtain provisions for the gang, and that he repeatedly visited Connell's house, sometimes with another member of the gang, and obtained supplies, Connell knowing at the time that they were for the outlaws.

Upon this evidence Connell was convicted and sentenced to a long term of imprisonment, his land and goods being confiscated at the same time to the Crown. His was the first case brought before the court under the provisions of the Felons' Apprehension Act bearing upon secondary offenders—aiders and abettors of the criminals outlawed, and it goes without saying that Connell's fate served as a salutary warning to others who had been guilty of similar offences, or who may have felt inclined to commit them. It will be readily understood that the complete break up of the Clarkes' gang and its large cordon of accomplices and active sympathisers, gave satisfaction to the people of Braidwood. The beginning of the end of bushranging had already been seen in that district, and henceforth bushranging in gangs, either in this or other districts of the colony, was to be looked upon as a thing of the past, for although the crime of bushranging in New South Wales was not completely stamped out, it was narrowed down until it became confined to individual cases, one man preying upon his fellows, generally for only a short time, until the now better-managed police force succeeded in arresting the offender.

It must not be imagined that the "old leaven" of which the Chief Justice spoke in his address to the Clarkes, had worked out of the social system of what were known as the infested districts. The youth who were inclined to bushranging had not been suddenly made virtuous by any moral awakening to the sinfulness of that sin. But fear kept them from indulgence —the fear of treachery on the part of trusted friends, or the fear of the better police service which had developed—very slowly, certainly—out of a system which had more than once, in Parliament and in the press, been frequently characterized as "rotten." These were the causes operating to the greater peace and safety of the dwellers in the bush who hitherto had been the victims of the lawlessness that had prevailed; and the reign of long-lived, daring bushranging gangs was, so far as New South Wales was concerned, brought to an end by the execution of the Clarkes and the death or imprisonment of their confederates and their principal aiders and abettors.

It was reserved for the neighbouring colony of Victoria, whose constant boast it had been that bushrangers could not live in her territory for as many days as they had reigned years in New South Wales, to furnish, some ten years afterwards, one of the most notorious of all notorious bushranging gangs that ever cursed Australian soil—more daring, more cool and determined, more skilled in bushcraft, more blood-thirsty than any that had preceded it, and whose capture cost the State no less a sum than £115,000. The story of bushranging in Australia would not be complete if the extraordinary exploits of the Kelly Gang were not given; and although they relate to a period not at all early in the history of the colonies, their narration here will not, I trust, be considered out of place.

CHAPTER XIX.

THE KELLY GANG.

HISTORY OF THE FAMILY.

As in New South Wales, so in Victoria, the last of the bushranging gangs was the worst. The leading members of the gang in each case were brothers, springing from a vicious stock. Each gang operated in a district where tribal ramifications were strong and numerous, and "telegraphs" and harbourers as plentiful as mushrooms on an old sheep station after autumn rain. The most sanguinary deed of each was the murder of a party of policemen, entrapped in a lonely part of the bush. But the Kellys were in every way better generals than the Clarkes—more systematic in their proceedings, having bolder conceptions, which they carried out in a more daring manner.

It will be remembered that the Chief Justice of New South Wales, when referring to the criminality of the Clarkes, spoke of it as the working of the old leaven of convictism. For this statement he was taken to task by not a few press writers, and was charged with vindictively recalling things which should be carefully buried and kept out of sight. But whatever was said concerning the Clarkes might have been said with absolute truth concerning the Kelly's, who appear to have lived in an atmosphere of crime and luxuriated in robbery and violence. The family was, root and branch, morally diseased. "Red Kelly," as the father was called, had been transported to Tasmania in 1841 for attempting to shoot his landlord, and arrived in Victoria early in the history of that colony, which received not a few of the worst of the Van Demonians. He was first heard of at Wallan, thirty miles from Melbourne, which was in those days considered quite an out-station. Here he became acquainted with a family named Quinn, who had settled in the same locality; and whatever else he may have been, there was no reason to doubt the statement then made that he possessed a violent temper and was given to frequent quarrels and brawls. This trait, according to the little that was known, did not predispose James Quinn in his favour, and Kelly's visits to the house were discountenanced by him as the head of the family, although one of the daughters, the third, became violently attached to him. The two were married; after the marriage the Quinns became reconciled to the inevitable, as is usually the case, and the two families lived in amity; and when Quinn moved north to a station between Mansfield and Beechworth, called Glenmore, the Kellys went with him. Finally, the whole party got as far as Greta, and there, and in that neighbourhood, Kellys, Quinns, and relations of other names were settled in such number as to form quite a formidable clan by themselves. As the younger members grew up it became thoroughly well known that they were engaged in an extensive system of cattle "duffing"—the colonial term for stealing. Squatters and others within a radius of many miles lost cattle and horses in great numbers, and were not slow to attribute the disappearance to the Quinns and their friends. Ned Kelly himself admitted that during his bushranging career he alone had stolen over two hundred and eighty horses; and he, be it remembered, was but one of a large gang. Numerous prosecutions were, not always successfully, instituted against various members of the confederation. It was generally known that the stolen stock was taken northwards, and disposed of mostly in New South Wales, but principally through the agency of the allies on the Border.

"Red" Kelly's offspring consisted of three sons—James, Edward, and Daniel—and four daughters, one of the latter being Mrs. Skillian. At the time of the bushranging trouble there were two unmarried daughters, Kate and Grace, and of the former some romantic stories have been told. When Mrs. Kelly got into "trouble," she had an infant in arms, and when the mother went to prison the baby had to go with her. "Red" Kelly himself died some time before his two sons, Ned and Dan, attained full development in the course of crime which was to end so disastrously to them and those with whom they were associated.

Ned Kelly commenced his criminal career when but a raw lad, and cattle "duffing" was the profession to which he was educated. When only about sixteen years of age he was arrested as an accomplice of a notorious bushranger named Power, for whose apprehension the Victorian Government had offered a large reward, and concerning whose exploits it is necessary that something should be said.

THE BUSHRANGER POWER.

Harry Power, before making the acquaintance of Ned Kelly, had "put up" a rather heavy criminal record, and had been convicted several times of various offences, chiefly horse and cattle stealing; but imprisonment apparently served only to whet his appetite for further wrong-doing, and he became known as a confirmed law-breaker. The police had reason to know that he was a remarkably "smart" man, a splendid rider, a skilful bush-man, and daring and reckless to a degree. When at liberty, he gave the police great trouble to catch him, and when caught, he gave his gaolers all they could do to keep him—in fact, more than they could do on one occasion, just prior to the commence-ment of his bushranging career, with which we have only now to deal.

He was undergoing a term of imprisonment in Pentridge Gaol, and was, with other prisoners, en-gaged during working hours in drawing rubbish in a small go-cart from the stockade outside the gaol. Power's work was to assist in "drawing" the go-cart. There was a large heap of rubbish where the cart-loads had to be tipped; and as one of the loads which he had helped to draw was being emptied, Power quickly and quietly—without the knowledge of the sentries, al-though some of his fellow prisoners must have ob-served his movements—slid under the rubbish as it was shot down, and at once became part of the heap. The other prisoners drew the cart back, leaving Power concealed beneath the rubbish, and as they moved off for another load the sentries solemnly escorted them, ignorant of the fact that one of the "beasts of burden" was missing from the team.   It was only when the men were being subsequently mustered that Power was missed, and immediate search was made for him, but without avail. He had seized a favourable opportunity, crept from his hiding place, and hurriedly made off.

The first concern of the escaped convict was to obtain a change of clothing, for he knew that such a thing as uninterrupted liberty while wearing gaol garb would be an impossibility. He stole a suit of clothes from the first farmhouse he came across, and at once decided to turn bushranger; but for this calling fire-arms as well as clothes were needed, and his next concern was to procure the requisite "shooting sticks." For some time, however, he was unable to find what he wanted, and he started his bushranging career without gun, pistol, or revolver. Arm himself he did, nevertheless, but his solitary weapon was such as modern bushrangers, at least, would not think re-markably effective, although it was formidable enough for his purpose. Finding the blade of an old sheep shear, Power fastened it on a long stick and made a kind of lance, and with this he operated with some success. Before long, however, he came across an old traveller who possessed a revolver, and from him he took the more effective and easily handled weapon, at the same time relieving the traveller of his money.

Thus equipped, he proceeded to raid the country in a systematic manner, and committed so many rob-

RR

beries on the highway or from settlers' houses that his name speedily became a terror to travellers and persons living in isolated localities in the Beechworth and other districts. He had secure hiding places in the mountains, and having secured some of the best horses procurable—of course, he did not buy one of them—he would go backward and forward, sometimes riding fully seventy miles in the day, and completely baffling the police.

Some very sensational stories were told concerning the bushranger's operations when in full work on the road. One of these stories is worth re-telling. On one occasion he had "stuck up" several carriers on the Seymour Road, and one of them refused to hand over his money, saying that nothing in the world would induce him to part with it. Power remonstrated with him, and said if he allowed him to pass without giving up his money, others might refuse to hand over theirs when bailed up, and his occupation would be gone, and the people would say he was afraid to shoot a man. "I will, therefore," said he, "give you five minutes to think over the matter, and if after that time you still refuse, I will have to shoot you." Power then went behind a tree, and said he prayed to God to soften the man's heart; at the end of the stipulated time he went forward and again demanded the money, when the man handed it over without a murmur. This story is given on the authority of Superintendent Hare, who declared that he heard it from the bushranger's lips.

Profiting by previous experiences, Power did not make a close confidant of any man or woman, and after his capture he attributed his immunity from arrest to his practice of working "on his own hook." Being a thorough bushman, and well acquainted with the district, he did not need any guide or assistant in his nefarious work. For nearly two years he "held the bush" unhindered, although the police maintained an untiring search for him. At last information was supplied to the head of the Victorian police which was considered reliable, and as it was made by a man who was known to be intimate with the bushranger's haunts, special arrangements were made for surprising Power. Who this man was is not to this day known to the public, for one of the conditions of the compact entered into by him to lead the hunters to Power's hiding-place was that absolute secrecy as to his identity should be preserved. In their reports the police called this man L——, and we shall refer to him as L—— in the future.

A squatter had been stuck up and robbed by Power, who took from him, in addition to other valuables, a much-prized gold watch. Subsequently the bushranger sent a message to the squatter to the effect that he could have the watch back for £15. Upon hearing of this offer the police officers who had command of the search parties in that locality determined to put the genuineness of the offer of help made by L—— to the test. The Victorian Government had offered a reward of £500 for Power's apprehension, and the police promised L—— that he should have the whole of this amount if he conducted them to the bushranger's hiding-place and enabled them to make the capture. After much demur, L—— con-

sented, and the party started from the squatter's
station into a lonely, mountainous part of the country, properly armed, and having the £15 which was
to redeem the stolen watch. The party consisted of
Superintendents Nicholson and Hare, one trooper,
a black-tracker, and the mysterious guide; and it is
just here that difficulty confronts the historian, whose
chief desire is to set down nothing but the truth. Two
accounts of the course taken and the things done by
the party during this expedition have been published
—one by Superintendent Hare and one by Superintendent Nicholson. In the narrative given by Superintendent Hare all the glory attaching to the expedition belonged to Superintendent Hare. In that given
by Superintendent Nicholson many of the statements,
pretensions and claims made by the first writer are dis-
puted, and whatever glory there was has been equally
divided, even the black-tracker receiving his fair share.
The reader will be interested in the story of Superintendent Nicholson, as he told it in a letter to one of the
leading Victorian papers so late as February, 1892. Mr.
Nicholson introduced his narrative by the following
letter to the editor:—"Sir,—I have endeavoured to
condense into the following narrative every fact of
importance connected with the capture of Power, the
bushranger, omitting nothing, exaggerating nothing,
and making no statement that is not capable of being
verified on oath if necessary. I deeply regret that
such a proceeding should have been forced upon me
by the erroneous and misleading statements put forth
by Mr. Hare in the third chapter of his 'Last of the
Bushrangers.' But to have allowed these to pass

without notification would have been to acquiesce in the falsification of history." And this is the story as told by him :—

The guide (L——), assisted by the sergeant, led us through the ranges, avoiding paths and traces of settlement as much as possible. Towards the end of the second day we camped in a secluded gully within six miles of the Quinn's place, and L—— was promptly despatched there with the view of visiting Power's hiding-place if possible. He was provided with £15 in bank notes, which were first initialled by Mr. Hare, and with which he was to obtain from Power a certain gold watch and chain. The following evening after dark L—— re-appeared in our camp and handed me the watch and chain, indicating thereby that he had been in Power's company. The same evening at Mr. Hare's special request I entrusted him with the watch, so that he might have the pleasure of returning it to the squatter. L——, who was a man of few words, laconically stated that he had lingered at the Quinn's both coming and going, lest he should awaken their suspicions, and had succeeded in being taken to Power's retreat on the range opposite their house, where he had an interview with the bushranger. We timed our start so as to pass through Quinn's place not earlier than 2 a.m. The Quinn's house was situated on the edge of the King River, and on a flat lying between it and a crescent-shaped range. Immediately under and along the range and between it and the flat, ran a lagoon which was connected with the river by anabranches and other channels. The first and largest portion of the flat which we had to traverse was covered with timber and scrub, and the lesser portion, upon which the house was situated, was fenced in and under cultivation. These people had also fenced across the Government cattle track along the river; and further, the bridge across the lagoon, giving access to the range, was enclosed within their horse and cattle yards. We started from a point near the river, and when we began to cross the first five miles of the flat we found that our difficulties were only commencing. Owing to the heavy rain the flat itself was almost covered with water; the channels across it were full, and in many places deep, and the river was in a roaring flood, so that we could scarcely hear each other speak; and we had the timber and scrub to get through in the intense darkness which prevailed. We failed, but extricated ourselves, although with difficulty, and finally we were compelled to retrace our steps to the point whence we had started. After a short rest and consultation I decided that as no further time could be lost we must take the river as our guide, and this we did, keeping as close to the bank as possible. After a severe struggle of over five miles we were at last rewarded by being brought up suddenly by Quinn's paddock fence. The portion of it I first recognised in the dark was that which projected over the bank into the river to keep the cattle out of the cultivation. This in my opinion, was the most trying work we had to perform during the expedition, and here Sergeant Montfort particularly was of great use. We dismounted, planted our horses in the scrub, and after getting over the fence we cautiously passed the Quinn's premises, crossing the bridge and reaching the foot of the range without causing any alarm. After proceeding along the base of the range, looking upwards for Power's camp fire, but without catching the faintest glimpse of it, our guide, old L——, who had for some time been showing signs of succumbing to cold, fatigue, and terror, now collapsed, and declared himself unable to proceed one step further, and equally unable to recognise the hill on which was situated the outlaw's lair. We also were then suffering from cold, fatigue, and want of food, and the night was still very dark and wet. I, therefore, proposed that all the party except myself should lie down and rest, and I undertook to watch, and to awaken them at daybreak. They lay down on the ground. After they had had a short sleep signs of approaching dawn appeared. I aroused them, and, although they had slept saturated with rain, they were all considerably refreshed, and one of them jocularly spoke of having dreamed of food. We resumed our search, silently and carefully scanning the shallow gullies on the side of the range from there upwards to where the gullies ended at the crest. Here I received just such valuable aid from the blackfellow as I had expected. The range was clothed lightly with timber and scrub towards the top boulders, and rock cropped up, whereas at the bottom, amongst the finer soil, were some very large trees. I was looking among these latter for a hollow tree stump which had been described to me as "Power's Watchbox" by young Ned Kelly, whom I had left behind me under the care of the police at Kyneton. (Old L——, I believe, also knew of this.) At last my attention was attracted by the stump of a large tree, the small branches and leaves apparently sprouting from it being brown, withered, and dead, offering a striking contrast to those of the other stumps, which were alive and green. Springing towards it, I found the withered branches came away in my hands, disclosing peep-holes cut in the hollow trunk, which they had served to mask. Inside was some dried grass strewn on the floor, but no bed, as Mr. Hare describes. At this time the blackfellow, who had been keeping near me, recognising that I had made a discovery, sprang towards me and looked at the tree. Without speaking I glanced back to old L——, who was feebly following us, and I pointed to the stump; he silently signalled with his head and outstretched arms an affirmative gesture and disappeared. I never saw him again. It was then just daylight, and the mist was rolling up the hills, rendering it almost impossible in some places to distinguish it from smoke; but Donald, after one look, pointed straight up the gully, and, with dilated eyes and nostrils, uttered in a suppressed tone "Moke! Moke!" Notwithstanding what Mr. Hare has asserted in his published narratives, he was certainly not present when the above occurred, and he had no opportunity of examining the hollow tree-trunk until after Power's arrest. Superintendent Hare and Sergeant Montfort were at that very time exploring a short distance off, and near a small swampy flat partially bordered with ti-tree, and on a lower level. I attracted their attention by a low hissing whistle. but knowing that there was not an instant to be lost, as Power might wake up at any moment, I did not wait for them, but commenced running up the gully, whilst Messrs. Hare and Montfort followed, making a short diagonal cut to get on my line, thereby leaving the tree-stump behind them, and at some distance on their left. As I ascended, a defined track became plain, and I then observed some distance above me a thin column of smoke rising among some boulders. A little more, and a few yards to the left of the line I was following, the small fire and a few cooking utensils around it appeared in view, close to a large boulder; and straight before me, what might have been taken for a small thicket of leafy green scrub, but the straightness of one or two of its outlines, as well as a foot in a clean worsted stocking projecting from the end next to the fire betrayed its artificial character. These were on a small plateau or shelf on the side of the range. With a twist of my shoulders, as I ran, I got rid of my loose peajacket, which was soaked and heavy with rain, and quickened my pace. The thicket was broadside to me, its entrance and the foot facing the fire. Apprehensive lest the owner of the foot should escape either by the rear or far side, I waved my right arm to Superintendent Hare and Sergeant Montfort, who were still behind and below me, to go round, whilst I made a dash at the entrance, and throwing myself into the gunyah upon the prostrate body of the occupant, I seized and held him securely by the wrists until the Superintendent and the Sergeant appeared almost immediately, the former catching the man by his legs and Sergeant Montfort by his ankles. With one simultaneous heave we swung our prisoner outside, and then the Sergeant quietly handcuffed him.

The little structure, although low and narrow, was well put together and comfortable. It consisted of a good tough frame covered with blankets, and these were skilfully covered and concealed by leafy twigs and branches. There was a neat floor of small saplings about six inches above the ground upon which straw and blankets were spread. When I entered Power, apparently asleep, was lying on his back, dressed excepting his coat and boots. His revolver was loose by his side, and his double-barrelled gun loaded and cocked was slung from the ridge pole, the trigger within easy reach of his hand, and the muzzle sweeping the entrance, and not the track up which we had come, as Mr. Hare inaccurately states—indeed the track was at right angles to the gunyah. If any member of our party had attempted to draw Power out of his retreat by the ankles, as Mr. Hare describes, the rash experimentalist would have been blown to pieces. Fortunately, Power was unconscious of our approach owing to the ground being saturated by days of heavy rain, and therefore our footfalls were noiseless. Had there been any touching or pulling of Power's legs before his wrists were secured —in short, had not the whole thing, after the blackfellow sighted the smoke, been done at a run, our party would have probably returned at least one short of its number. for although Power, after finding himself surprised and overpowered, did not behave to us like "a desperate ruffian," as Mr. Hare designates him at the commencement of his historical romance—on the contrary—yet he was certainly not a man to be trifled with. We all partook of some of his breakfast, and hurried away Sergeant Montfort and Donald to where we had planted the horses. More than once at this time, Superintendent Hare, very much elated, surprised me by seizing my hand and wringing it most effusively. Mr. Hare would have it believed that he undertook the duty of escorting Power past the Quinn's house, and armed with Power's double-barrelled gun. This is one of the many amusing occasions upon which Mr. Hare borrows his facts from his imagination. He carried a light single-barrelled rifle of the Lancaster pattern, and wore a revolver as well. Before marching Power off I examined his gun, and finding it in good order armed myself with it, carrying it at "the ready" and at half cock. I also had my revolver. I led the way, followed at from six to ten yards by Superintendent Hare, with Power close in front of him. When near the house I observed three men standing near the porch, and another man known as "Red George" outside. I halted, turned round, and addressed Superintendent Hare and Power in a firm and distinct tone of voice, as follows:—"Mr. Hare, if any attempt is made to rescue the prisoner, or if he attempts to escape, shoot him." Then turning towards the men about the porch I gave them to understand by my gestures how I was prepared to deal with them if necessary. We resumed our march, and for an instant a large bush intercepted our view, but when we cleared it and the porch came in sight again the men had disappeared, and in their places stood three rather tall women in black, who silently stared at us, but we caught sight of the men behind them, peeping over the women's shoulders and under their arms. We passed on without exchanging a word. Poor Power gave his friends an inquiring wistful look, to which came no response. We soon reached a spot outside the fence, where we were glad to find Sergeant Montfort, Donald, and the horses safe and sound and ready to proceed. I directed the sergeant to lead us to the selection of one W. Lally, from whom I hired a good horse and spring cart, and that evening we all reached Wangaratta with our prisoner, after another long dark ride; and although Sunday I was able to announce by telegram our success to the Chief Commissioner thus:—"Wangaratta, Sunday.—Power, alias Johnstone, was arrested this morning at 7.30, in the King River Ranges, on the Glenmore Run, by Superintendents Nicholson and Hare and Sergeant Montfort, and is now in the Wangaratta watch-house.—(Signed) C. H. Nicholson." This telegram was published by the Melbourne press next morning. On arrival we found that our clothes, as well as our hands, were turned one uniform colour, owing to the continued rain dripping upon us through the gum-trees for so many days. Whilst warming and drying ourselves before a blazing fire at the police quarters our plight became known to some of the inhabitants, who most kindly and considerately sent us clean, dry clothing, which we shared with Power. The latter, after being thoroughly dried, warmed, and refreshed, was provided with a comfortable bed in the watch-house. An armed sentry was placed on duty— and we all gladly went to rest. Subsequently, when Mr. Hare was confined to his room under the care of Dr. B. Hutchinson, then of Wangaratta, suffering from the effects of cold and exposure he had undergone, I drew up the official report of the affair by his bedside, and I directed him to append his signature next my own. In fact I could hardly refrain from asking Sergeant Montfort from doing likewise, only doing so would have been contrary to discipline. I here repeat that what was alluded to in my report and characterised in the press as "indistinct" and "vague" arose from my desire to avoid causing any invidious distinction being drawn between us three, as each had done his best, and each had contributed to the success of the expedition as far as his opportunities would allow, and again I was embarrassed by the necessity for avoiding any allusion which might lead to the discovery of the identity of our guide, L——, for this at that time would probably have cost him his life. After escorting our prisoner to Beechworth, I returned to Melbourne in company with

POWER AT TIME OF HIS RELEASE

Superintendent Hare. Soon after, on a vacancy occurring, I was transferred to the charge of the metropolitan district— not as promotion, but by right of seniority, and also through being deemed suitable for the office.

From Wangaratta, Power was removed to Beechworth, where he was placed upon his trial for highway robbery, convicted, and sentenced to fifteen years in Pentridge Gaol. And this time the authorities took particular care of their prisoner. He served about fourteen years of the sentence, and was then released. He had evidently been quite cured of his bushranging proclivities by prison diet, prison quiet, and prison work, for he did not again transgress in that particular direction. After his release he found employment, and earned an honest livelihood, although he did not manifest any desire to keep the past hidden from public gaze, as he frequently "fought his battles o'er again" when in the presence of those who sought to learn from his own lips the story of his bushranging experiences. About six years after his release he left Melbourne under engagement with the showmen speculators who had fitted up the old convict hulk "Success'" and floated her over to Sydney. Journeying overland he reached the Murray River, near Swan Hill, but he got no further, for one morning his dead body was found in the river.

HOW THE KELLY GANG WAS FORMED.

Mention has been made of the fact that Ned Kelly was at one time associated with Power in his horse-stealing and bushranging exploits; but in the latter he appears to have served only as a scout and occasional assistant, merely holding Power's horse during the time he was overhauling his victims on the road. As a horse "lifter," however, he had even a greater reputation than Power; horse-stealing was the calling to which he had devoted his life, and he followed that calling with untiring assiduity. He commenced his career by removing carriers' and travellers' horses during the night to a safe "plant," where he would keep them until a reward was offered for their recovery, and then he would hand them over in the most innocent manner and claim the reward. Naturally, the next step was to horse-stealing pure and simple, any stray animal worth picking up being appropriated and kept in a secure place until an opportunity presented itself of turning it into money. Before he had fully grown a beard he became acquainted with prison life, and served several short sentences for horse-stealing, being recognised as a confirmed criminal by the authorities while yet in his teens—a circumstance which is not to be considered wonderful when the nature of his surroundings is taken into account. Although he was known to be connected with the escaped convict and bushranger who was causing such trouble, he was not called to account for any offence committed in Power's company; and it was generally believed that the police had obtained from him the information which enabled them to track Power to his hiding-place on the mountain—Power himself at one time entertaining that opinion—but the arresting Superintendents invariably denied any statement to that effect.

Power had been in gaol for about eight years, however, before what is known as the Kelly Gang of bushrangers was formed and began to operate openly, and although the influence and example of the older bushranger may have had something to do with shaping the subsequent career of the leader of that gang, it cannot be said that the one was the direct outcome of the other.

But before proceeding to narrate the extraordinary doings of the gang, it is necessary that I should give a brief sketch of the earlier life of the different members.

I have already mentioned that Ned Kelly had two brothers and four sisters—Dan, Jim, Mrs. Gunn, Mrs. Skillian, Kate, and Grace. Dan Kelly was seven years younger than Ned, having been born in 1861, but from the time he was able to sit upon a horse he was more or less associated with his elder brother in criminal pursuits. The boy "lifters" were the terror of carriers and drovers who had to pass through the district in which they resided, and it is said that persons in charge of stock not infrequently went many miles out of the direct course in order to avoid Greta, fearing that some of their cattle would miss their proper destination if they attempted to pass through the "Kelly Country." Night and day young Dan would prowl about looking for "game," and knowing the bush intimately, he could at any time get away with that "game" when he found it, to some spot where it would be beyond reach of the proper owners. It will thus be seen that he was well qualified to act as his brother's lieutenant, and, indeed, it was through him that the outbreak occurred.

The third member of the gang was a young fellow named Steve Hart, a native of Wangaratta, who had also made a name for himself as a horse thief, indulging in night prowling in search of stray animals. He was born in 1860, and was therefore a year older than Dan Kelly, who was his closest "chum" during the campaign, and his companion in death when it closed, the two falling together in the conflict with the police.

The fourth member of the gang was Joe Byrne, who was born at the Woolshed, near Beechworth, in 1857. He was a splendid sample of a young Australian, and had received a fairly good education, but abandoning himself to criminal pursuits had joined the Kelly boys in several of their horse-stealing raids. He had served one sentence of six months in Beechworth Gaol before joining the gang. Byrne acted as scribe to the party, reducing to writing the plans for the attacks upon banks and other contemplated robberies, which were rigidly adhered to.

These four formed the gang, but there were others associated with them as scouts and "telegraphs" and harbourers, whose names will appear as occasion arises for mentioning the service rendered by them. Aaron Sherritt was one of the most active of these assistants during one part of the campaign. He had attended the same school as Joe Byrne, and the intimacy that had grown up there was continued after school days were over, the two engaging in horse-stealing raids together, and forming close criminal business relationships with the Kellys. Sherritt was a native of Beechworth, his parents being most respectable people.

In March, 1878, a warrant was issued for the arrest of Dan Kelly on a charge of cattle stealing; and as it became known that he was at his mother's house at Greta, a constable named Fitzpatrick, stationed at Benalla, proceeded thither to arrest him. Fitzpatrick's version of what took place was that when he got to the house he found Dan Kelly there, and arrested him in the presence of his mother and sisters. He was proceeding to take his prisoner to Benalla, when he was asked to permit him first to take a meal, with which request he complied. While the meal was in progress, Ned Kelly, with Skillian, his brother-in-law, and a man named Williamson, came in, and Ned at once demanded if Fitzpatrick had a warrant for the arrest of Dan. The constable replied in the negative, and then Ned drew a revolver and declared that his brother should not be taken without one. Fitzpatrick pulled out his revolver to protect himself, and ensure the safe custody of his prisoner, when Ned Kelly fired and wounded him in the wrist, the result being that the revolver fell out of his hand and was secured by the Kellys. Fitzpatrick was then, according to his account, secured, and it was proposed to shoot him; but upon his solemnly promising to say nothing of the affair, he was allowed to go. The wound in his wrist was very trivial, and the bullet had been picked out with a knife before he reached Benalla. His promise of silence was not kept, and warrants were immediately issued against Ned Kelly for shooting with intent to murder, and against Dan Kelly, Skillian, Williamson, and Mrs. Kelly for aiding and abetting. When it was attempted to enforce these warrants, it was found that the brothers Kelly had disappeared; but the others named were arrested, tried, and sentenced each to lengthy terms of imprisonment, Fitzpatrick's version of the occurrence at the house being accepted as correct.

But the Kellys and their friends gave altogether different versions of the story; they emphatically denied the truth of Fitzpatrick's statements, and complained very bitterly that their relations were unjustly cast into prison on his unsupported evidence.   One version was that no shooting at all took place, but that Fitzpatrick had concocted the whole affair in a spirit of revenge, because certain improper advances which he had made to one of the female members of the family had been rejected with considerable warmth; another was that Fitzpatrick never had Dan Kelly in charge, and that the arrest was resisted because of the absence of a warrant, and in a scuffle Fitzpatrick slightly wounded himself with his own revolver; and a third was that Mrs. Kelly took no part whatever in the affair, not being in the house at the time—that Skillian and Williamson were miles away at the time, and that Dan and Ned Kelly were alone concerned in what took place.

After the disappearance of Ned and Dan from the home at Greta, nothing more was heard of them for some months, although the Government offered £100 reward for their apprehension, and every effort was made by the police to capture them.   It was then known that they had "taken to the bush," and there was a general impression that they were concerned in several cases of road robbery that took place about that time in remote portions of the district; but, reckless and daring though they were known to be, it was never for a moment thought that they were capable of the fearful crimes by which they were shortly to make themselves notorious.

THE MURDERS IN THE WOMBAT RANGES.

Fully five months elapsed before the police managed to obtain any reliable information concerning the whereabouts of the two brothers, although every imaginable device was adopted to discover their hiding-place, which was supposed to be somewhere in the almost impenetrable ranges forming the watershed of the King and Broken Rivers. That they had made this their retreat was subsequently discovered, as was also the fact that they had not been idle during the time of their hiding. In the month of October the police received private information upon which some reliance could be placed that the Kellys were in the ranges at the head of the King River, that they had been joined by two confederates, and that the four had raided several selectors' huts at the points of settlement nearest their impenetrable retreat; further, that they were well mounted, and carried arms in the shape of rifles and revolvers. The names of the two confederates were not disclosed, and the police did not know them until some time after.

Acting upon the information supplied, the police authorities of the district organised two parties of troopers and secretly despatched them in the direction of the Wombat Ranges—one party starting from Greta and one from Mansfield, the two townships being about fifty miles apart. The Greta party consisted of five men, with Sergeant Steele in command, and the Mansfield party of four men—Sergeant Kennedy (in charge), and Constables Scanlan, Lonerigan, and McIntyre. Though the movements of the Mansfield party were supposed to be kept "dark," it is thought that the mission and its object leaked out and was "telegraphed" to Ned Kelly and his mates by one of his numerous relatives—for the ranges were infested with a brotherhood of Kellys, Lloyds, Quinns, etc.,

NED KELLY

who were always on the look out. It was broadly hinted at a later period that the man who had given information to the police had done so with an ulterior motive, and that as soon as the police began to move he caused the Kellys to be apprised of the fact. Be that as it may, however, it is beyond dispute that the Kellys knew when the party started out from Mansfield and that they waited for them, intending to take them by surprise when far beyond the reach of assistance, and remove them effectually out of their path.

Sergeant Kennedy and his men started out on their mission on the morning of 25th October, equipped with revolvers, one Spencer rifle, and a double-barrel gun (the two latter weapons having been lent to the police by a resident of the township, who had recognised the poverty of the equipment); also, a tent and sufficient provisions to last for a week. They reached Stringy Bark Creek, about twenty miles from Mansfield, that evening and camped on an open space on the creek, pitching their tent near the ruins of two diggers' huts, for the place had at one time been worked for gold. No special precautions were taken, as the party considered that they were still a good distance from the retreat of the bushrangers. The ranges round about were almost uninhabited, and the party were not quite sure whether they were on the watershed of the King or the Broken River; but both Kennedy and Scanlan knew the locality intimately. It was Kennedy's intention to camp for a few days, patrol backwards into the ranges, and then shift the camp in.

About 6 a.m. next day Kennedy and Scanlan went down the creek to explore, and they stayed away nearly all day. It was McIntyre's duty to cook, and he attended closely to camp work. During the forenoon some noise was heard, and McIntyre went out to have a look, but found nothing. He fired two shots out of his gun at a pair of parrots, and these were heard by Kelly, who must have been on the look-out. About 5 p.m. McIntyre was at the fire making the afternoon tea, and Lonerigan by him, when they were suddenly surprised with the cry, "Bail up! Throw up your arms!" They looked up and saw four armed men close to them. Three carried guns and Ned Kelly two rifles. Two of the men they did not know, but the fourth was the younger Kelly. The four were on foot. They had approached up the rises, and some flags or rushes had provided them with excellent cover until they got into the camp. McIntyre had left his revolver at the tent door, and was totally unarmed. He, therefore, held up his hands as directed, and faced round. Lonerigan started for shelter behind a tree, and at the same time put his hand upon his revolver; but before he had moved two paces Ned Kelly shot him in the temple. He fell at once, and as he lay on the ground cried out, "Oh, Christ, I am shot!" He died in a few seconds.

Kelly then had McIntyre searched; when they found he was unarmed they let him drop his hands, and at once took possession of the police revolvers. Kelly remarked when he saw Lonerigan had been killed, "Dear, dear, what a pity that man tried to get away." They then sat down to wait for the absentees. One of them told McIntyre to take some tea, and asked for tobacco. He supplied tobacco to two or three, and had a smoke himself. Dan Kelly suggested that he should be handcuffed, but Ned pointed to his rifle and said, "I have got something better here. Don't you attempt to go; if you do I'll track you to Mansfield, and shoot you at the police station." Ned Kelly said he had never heard of Kennedy, but Scanlan was "a flash ——." McIntyre asked whether he was to be shot. Kelly replied, "No, why should I want to shoot you? Could I not have done it half an hour ago if I had wanted?" He added, "At first I thought you were Constable Flood. If you had been, I would have roasted you in the fire. I suppose you came out to shoot me?" "No," replied McIntyre, "we came to apprehend you." "What," said Kelly, "brings you here at all? It is a shame to see fine big strapping fellows like you in a lazy loafing billet like policemen." Subsequently he told McIntyre if he was let go he must leave the police, and McIntyre said he would; it was then suggested that the best thing McIntyre could do was to get his comrades to surrender, for if they escaped he would be shot. "If you attempt to let them know we are here, you shall be shot at once," said Kelly. "If you get them to surrender I will allow you all to go in the morning; but you will have to go on foot; for we want your horses. We will handcuff you at night, as we want to sleep." McIntyre asked Kelly if he would promise faithfully not to shoot them if they surrendered, nor let his mates fire. Kelly said, "I won't shoot them, but the rest can please themselves." Kelly also stated that Fitzpatrick, the man who tried to arrest his brother in April, was the cause of all this; that his (Kelly's) mother and the rest had been unjustly "lagged" at Beechworth.

Meanwhile they had been anxiously listening for

Kennedy and Scanlan. At last sounds of their approach were heard, and the four bushrangers concealed themselves, three behind logs and one in the tent. They made McIntyre sit on a log, and Kelly said "Mind, I have a rifle for you if you give any alarm." Kennedy and Scanlan shortly afterwards rode into the camp, and McIntyre went forward and said, "Sergeant, I think you had better dismount and surrender, as you are surrounded." Kelly at the same time called out "Put up your hands!" Kennedy, thinking a jest was intended, smiled and put his hand on his revolver case; but he was speedily undeceived, for he was instantly fired at, but not hit. He then realised the hopelessness of his position, jumped off his horse, and cried out, "It's all right! Stop it! Stop it!" Scanlan, who carried the Spencer rifle, jumped off also and tried to make for a tree; but before he could unsling his rifle he was shot down and never spoke again, dying where he fell.

Seizing a favourable moment while the gang were occupied with Kennedy, McIntyre jumped on Kennedy's horse and galloped full speed down the creek, receiving as he rode the fire of the bushrangers, but without injury, although one shot struck the horse. As he rode away he heard shots exchanged between Kennedy and his assailants, but he did not wait to learn the issue of the fight. He galloped through the scrub for about two miles at full speed, and then met with a severe fall through the horse stumbling; but remounting he resumed his flight until the horse fell exhausted. With true bushman's instinct he then took off the saddle and bridle, and sought a hiding-place some distance from the spot; and having found a large wombat hole in a dense part of the scrub he crept into it and decided to remain there until darkness set in, for he still feared pursuit. While lying in the hole he tore some leaves from his pocket-book and wrote a concise account of the tragedy of which he had been the witness, and then concealed the paper, his object being to leave a record that might at some future date clear up the mystery that would enshroud the fate of the whole party should the bushrangers succeed in overtaking and killing him. The account closed with the words "The Lord have mercy upon me!"

But daylight gave place to darkness, and the foes he feared had not come near. Then, having removed his boots to render his tracks less distinct should the Kellys search for him on the following morning, McIntyre left his hiding-place and set out on foot in the direction where safety lay. Walking steadily on, his mental agony outweighing his bodily suffering, at 3 o'clock next day he came in sight of a station; but to his horror he observed several horses standing near the place, one of which he felt sure was the animal that he had himself been using. He naturally concluded that the bushrangers had outstripped him, and were waiting at the station for him to come up; but seeing, on closer inspection, that the horses belonged to the place, he went up and told his news. With all speed the owner (McColl), drove the now thoroughly exhausted trooper into Mansfield, where he reported himself at headquarters and told his story.

Two hours or so later, Inspector Pewtress with

several troopers and seven or eight civilian volunteers started for the scene of the murders, McIntyre and a guide being with the party, most of whom were provisioned for three or four days. The police had only four rifles between them, and two of these supplied by a civilian, but of regulation revolvers there was no lack, although McIntyre told the authorities that for an expedition against men like the Kellys, revolvers were comparatively useless, and that the police ought to be furnished with breechloaders. They reached the camp at two o'clock in the morning, and found the bodies of Scanlan and Lonerigan lying where they had fallen. The tent had been burned down, and everything removable had been taken away. There were four bullet wounds on Scanlan's body and five on Lonerigan's, three of the latter having evidently been fired into the dead body. Many months afterwards, Ned Kelly admitted that the extra shots had been fired by those of the gang who had not actually shot the policeman, in order that all might be equally implicated. Kennedy's body was nowhere to be seen, although diligent search was made in every open spot, for the bush round the scene of the murder was made up of dense dead wattle saplings, so close together that a man could stand six feet off the track and not be seen. The search having proved unsuccessful, the bodies of the other two men were conveyed to Mansfield on the back of a pack horse, and on the following day they were interred after an inquest had been held. A monument was subsequently erected to their memory.

When reinforcements arrived from Melbourne,

a stronger search party was organised to discover
Kennedy's body, and to pick up the tracks of the
murderers and endeavour to run them down. On the
third day of the search, the body was found not more
than a quarter of a mile from the camp. Kelly afterwards declared that Kennedy fought determinedly
and bravely, and did not fall until he had exhausted
all the shots in his revolver; as he fell they all ran up

MONUMENT AT MANSFIELD (VIC.) TO POLICE KILLED BY BUSHRANGERS

to him, when he begged them to spare his life for the
sake of his wife and children; but as they did not like
to leave him in the bush in such a state they fired at
and "finished" him. Aaron Sherritt—who was at
that time and for several months subsequently in
league with the murderers, but who afterwards sought
to betray them and was killed by them at the door of
his own hut—declared that Ned Kelly had told him

Kennedy was the bravest man he had ever met, and that out of respect for him he walked back to the camp after shooting him, got a cloak and carefully covered up his body. In all probability this story was correct, as the body was covered by a cloak when found by the search party.

To say that the news of this triple murder sent a thrill of horror through the whole community but feebly expresses the effect produced; and in the same breath the public of Victoria denounced the murderers and the authorities—the latter for sending out troopers inadequately armed upon a mission so dangerous. Members of the force had complained from the outset that the arms supplied to them—chiefly revolvers—were unsuitable, and that sufficient ammunition even was not supplied; but no attempt to remedy the deficiency was made until after the death of the three policemen named; and then proper arms could not be purchased, the most suitable procurable being breechloading shot-guns, which the Government bought from a Melbourne gunmaker at a cost of about £8 apiece.

THE SEARCH FOR THE MURDERERS.

Even before the bodies of the murdered men had been buried, all the available police of Victoria were being forwarded to the disturbed district, Superintendent Nicholson going thither to direct operations. The task of hunting down the murderers was evidently to be one of great difficulty, owing to the inaccessible nature of the country, which was mountain ranges densely covered with forests. The Government offered a reward of £200 a head for the murderers, and in a day or two increased this to £500 a head, the money to be paid whether the bushrangers were taken alive or dead; later still they doubled this amount. They also prepared and passed through Parliament an Outlawry Bill, under which any man charged with felony could be called upon by a judge to surrender, and to take his trial, and if he failed to surrender in due course, any person, without challenge, might "take such outlaw alive or dead." And any person sheltering such outlaw, or aiding him with information, or withholding information from the police, rendered himself liable to fifteen years' imprisonment. The Felons' Apprehension Act which had been passed by the New South Wales Legislature during the reign of Ben Hall's Gang had operated so beneficially that the Victorian Legislature did not scruple to pass one framed on similar lines.

At the instance of the Attorney-General an application was made by the Crown Solicitor to the Chief Justice on November 4th for orders requiring Edward and Daniel Kelly and their two associates to surrender themselves. The application was made under the Felons' Apprehension Act, passed a few days before, and the necessary formalities having been gone through, his Honour granted an order against each of the gang calling upon them to surrender at Mansfield on or before Tuesday, November 12th, to stand their trial for murder. The orders or summonses were published next morning, but the accused failing to comply with them, were declared outlaws. The police authorities in town at this date appeared to give credence to the report that the bushrangers were lurking about the Rats' Castle Ranges, near Indigo Creek, and reinforcements of police were sent to that district by special trains.

Although bulletins were received from different parts of the district day by day describing the proceedings of the search parties, no definite intelligence reached headquarters. The following despatch dated Benalla, November 5, is a fair sample of these daily accounts :—

A special party of men, who have been in reserve for several days, have just been ordered up the line. It is the impression of the police that the Kellys are still in the ranges north-east of this place. It has been ascertained that they have endeavoured to pass themselves off as police, with the assistance of the handcuffs and revolvers they got at the Wombat, but their youth and looks ought to be against them. One of Strahan's party arrived from Mansfield to-day. They worked the ranges from the Wombat to the head of the west branch of the King, going along the top of the range. They were out for four days, and had a good deal of wet weather, but Saturday was fine, and they got an extensive view of the valley of the King from the high ground. The tracks seen were not recent, and doubtless were left by horsemen connected with stations beyond Mansfield. On one night they stopped at an old hut on the Wombat range. They crossed the blazed track from Mansfield to Glenmore, but did not descend to Quinn's haunts. News was circulated in Benalla yesterday to the effect that the Kellys had stuck up a store on the King River, between Glenmore and Whitfield. The statement was found to be correct, but the occurrence took place three weeks ago. The owner of the store tried to shut Kelly out, but at night the marauder forced a road in, and told him that if he ever barricaded his doors in that way again he would be shot. This man was so frightened at the threats he heard that he made no complaints to the police, and his relatives only mentioned the matter privately in the course of a visit to Benalla yesterday, so for his sake the name of the locality must be withheld. This will show how effectively the scattered settlements have been held in terror. To show how extensive the Kelly connection is, it may be mentioned that scarcely a day passes that we do not hear that some relative has been in Benalla.

The following extract from the report of a special correspondent of one of the Melbourne daily papers, dated from Benalla, November 7th, will further and more fully illustrate the character of the work the men had in hand:—

The police have had information respecting the Kelly gang in their possession during the past day or two, but it was not considered desirable to make use of it, owing to its doubtful character, until yesterday, when corroborative reports were received, and it was then felt that there was every probability of securing the ruffians. Superintendents Nicholson and Sadleir, having this knowledge in their possession, had arranged for a strong party to proceed to the district indicated, which, it may now be said, was about midway between Beechworth and Eldorado, on what is known as Reed's Creek. Here are living two or three families who, if not directly connected with the Kelly gang by family ties, are known to be close friends of theirs, and the idea was to pay them a sudden domiciliary visit with the expectation of finding some of the gang with them. The matter was kept very secret. Captain Standish, the Chief Commissioner of Police, arrived at Benalla by the afternoon train yesterday to confer as to the best steps to be taken. As soon as Captain Standish arrived he was met by Mr. Nicholson, Mr. Sadleir having earlier in the day gone on to Beechworth to make the necessary arrangements, and as soon as the whole of the facts were laid before him he fully coincided with the views of his two officers, and it was arranged that the plan should be at once carried out. Unfortunately it has failed, but there can be no doubt that this is, in a great measure, due to the fact that the Kellys have their spies and sympathisers in all parts of the district, so that as soon as any information leaks out, or any movement is noticed, information is at once conveyed to them. For instance, when Captain Standish arrived by the train in the evening, two of the Lloyds and Isaiah Wright were seen on the platform, and again subsequently, as will be seen later on, the same party inopportunely put in an appearance and attempted—by cutting the railway telegraph wires—to frustrate the object of the expedition. About 2 p.m. notice was sent quickly round to all the troopers available in Benalla to report themselves, with arms and horses, at the railway station at midnight, arrangements being at the same time made with the Railway Department to have a special train in readiness shortly after that hour to proceed to Beechworth; but when an attempt was made to communicate with that township it was found that the wires were cut, or at any rate thrown out of circuit, and it was also found that the line on the Melbourne side of Benalla was interrupted. However, after some delay, the special train got away about 1.30 a.m., and rapid progress was made to Beechworth, which place, after a few minutes' stoppage at Wangaratta, was reached soon after three o'clock. The train consisted of two horse trucks and the guard's van. In the former were ten horses, and in the latter was the Chief Commissioner of Police, Superintendent Nicholson, nine troopers, and a black-tracker. Four of these men had been out in the ranges for several days previously, under the command of Sergeant Strachan, and had only returned to Benalla and gone to rest a few hours before they were again called upon to turn out for duty. The men were, however, on the alert, and not only ready but anxious for active duty again. It must be said that the appearance of the party in the van would not have given a stranger any idea of the usual smart appearance of the Victorian police force, for had such a crowd been met on a well-frequented thoroughfare there would have been a general desire to at once hand over any valuables that might be in the possession of the travellers without any cry of "Stand and deliver" being made. It should here be said that while the party was waiting on the platform for the train to get ready, three men were seen hanging about taking stock of the party. They were at once pounced upon, and being interrogated made some unsatisfactory replies, and were detained for the time. Beechworth was reached just as the cold grey dawn was showing over the eastern hills, and the party being here met by Superintendent Sadlier, quietly proceeded to the police camp, where they were reinforced by another strong body of police, until at last, when a departure was made, there were over thirty well-armed and determined men, together with two blacktrackers. Rapid progress was made for a few miles along the southern road, and then a divergence was made to the left entering the timber, the men at the same time dividing into three parties, so as not only to push forward more rapidly, but cover as much ground as possible. The ground was anything but suitable for rapid progress, as in places it was quite rotten, the horse sinking at times up to their knees, while in other places patches of granite cropped up out of the soil, and this being smooth and slippery from the recent rains, rendered it necessary for every man to keep a tight hand on his bridle, more especially as the gun or rifle carried by each man was loaded, and in readiness for use. After a few miles of such work a halt was called, just as a clearing with a large slab hut was seen in the valley below. A short consultation was held between the officers, and then the place was surrounded by a cordon, while some half-dozen, with Superintendent Nicholson and Sadlier, went to pay a morning call at the house, where it was hoped to find the Kellys. A reserve of about a dozen men was kept in hand by Captain Standish, in order to give chase should the desperadoes break through the cordon drawn around them.

A few minutes of intense anxiety, and then the report of a gun was heard. This was quite enough. No necessity for any order to advance. Each man of the party, from the Chief Commissioner to the junior trooper, instinctively drove his spurs home, and a rush was made for the house. Logs that would have been looked at twice before leaping on another occasion were taken recklessly, rotten ground was plunged through, and a sharp turn round a paddock fence showed a nasty-looking rivulet, swollen with the late rains, and with very bad ground on the taking-off side. None of these were noticed, but each man, keeping a tight grip on his weapon with one hand and on his bridle with the other, galloped forward, the only anxiety being who should be in first, so as to join in the melee. The pace was terrific while it lasted, but when all pulled up at the door of the hut and rushed it, they found, to their disgust, that the Kellys were not there, and that the report they heard had been caused by the accidental discharge of one of the guns in the anxiety of the advance party to make sure of their expected prey, whom they supposed to be in the house. This one incident very plainly shows me that the remarks that have been made about the police not desiring to come to close quarters with the Kelly gang have been quite uncalled for. What I think is, that the men want to be held more strongly in check, or some more valuable lives will be lost. That the men desire to meet the Kellys and their two confederates is very plain, and when the parties do meet I fancy the four ruffians will never be brought in alive.

The house to which such an unceremonious visit had been paid was that of a man named Sherritt, who is well known to have long been intimately connected with the Kellys, and whose eldest daughter was to be married to one of the party now wanted by the police. The house and immediate vicinity were closely searched, but with no success. The birds had evidently received warning, and had taken their departure. Of course, the man Sherritt put on a virtuously indignant air, and asked whether he ought to be suspected of harbouring such persons, after having been in the police at home. As it was evident that nothing could be got at this place, a push was made for another selection some distance off, belonging to Sherritt, junr., a son of the last-visited individual. Upon entering this hut young Sherritt was not to be found, and from the appearance of the squalid den, the sole furniture of which consisted of a large bunk, a rough table, and stool, it was evident that neither the proprietor nor any of his acquaintances had been there that night. No time was lost in speculating upon possibilities, but the party pushed on over the ranges, and descending a precipitous and dangerous gorge over eight hundred feet, came upon a green valley known as Sebastopol, having a creek running through it, and overshadowed on either side by the high ranges known as the Woolshed Ranges. A sharp turn to the left brought us in front of a slab hut, situated in a nicely-cleared piece of land. This was the hut of Mrs. Byrne, who is also known to be most friendly to the Kellys, and is further said to be connected with another of the gang. She appeared at first greatly scared at seeing such a large party surround her house, but finding that she was not required, she became very bold and impudent. She could not, or probably would not, give any information, and, in fact, denied all knowledge of the Kellys.

It was now plain that information had been already forwarded to the gang that this locality was not safe for them and that they had consequently shifted their quarters, for those who speak on authority are certain, from the information afforded them, but which unfortunately arrived too late, that the Kellys have been about this part within the last few days. That they have not crossed the Murray is quite certain; but at present there is some doubt which direction they have taken, the general opinion being that they are doubling back to their old position. Whichever way they do take, they must sooner or later show themselves to obtain provisions, and be pounced upon. In the meantime, the police officers and men are working their hardest to secure the ruffians. As nothing further could be done for the day, the whole of the men being pretty well tired with their last few days' work, the party dispersed at Byrne's hut, Captain Standish, his officers, and some of the men returning to Beechworth, while the others separated and went to the respective points where they are stationed, and from whence they were summoned. As showing the absurd character of the statements which are made to the police officers, it may be said that Dr. Cleary, of Beechworth, went to Superintendent Sadlier about half-past ten o'clock last night, and reported that while driving from Everton during the evening seven shots were fired at him, and he showed a small scratch as the effects of one of them. Of course, his extraordinary story was set down to the effect of imagination, but it shows how men who are supposed to be endowed with a little common sense may be carried away by the present scare. Captain Standish returned to town by the afternoon train. The men who were out to-day were greatly pleased to see him with them in the field.

Among the earlier police reports received were two intended to carry the impression that the outlaws had attempted to cross the Murray into New South Wales territory and then returned to find better shelter among their numerous relatives and friends among the Warby Ranges. The report ran that they had been traced to the Murray River, below Wodonga, about ninety miles from the scene of the murders, and had called at the house of a settler who knew them, having in use at the time the horses and arms belonging to the police. They tried to cross the river, but it was flooded, and after nearly getting drowned they made their way back. The police, it was said, received intelligence of these movements, but did not take action until too late. The whole country was in a state of flood at this time, and the next report was that the outlaws had been seen crossing the swollen creek at Wangaratta at daybreak. The police in this case also refused at first to believe the report that the four men who had been seen going through the flood were the Kellys, and when they did take up the tracks, which were plainly visible on the soft ground, they were more than a day "behind the fair." They followed the hoof-marks of the horses to the house of a well-known sympathiser, where they learned that the outlaws had breakfasted, and continuing the search into the Warby Ranges they came across poor Kennedy's horse, which had been almost ridden to death and then abandoned. Then, as though the leader of the pursuing force (a small one from Wangaratta) appeared to think that a nearer acquaintance

TT

with the Kellys would be dangerous, the party returned to the station, taking the crippled horse back with them as sufficient spoil recovered.

In the earlier days of the search for the outlaws after the murder of the three policemen, discoveries were made in the locality of the outrage which clearly indicated that Kennedy and his companions were on the right track when surprised and shot down; and furnished evidence also of the fact that Kelly and his mates had abandoned themselves absolutely to a career which they knew must result in death to themselves and others. The following extract from the letter of a press correspondent who subsequently visited the spot will prove of interest here:—

Leaving Melbourne one day last week, I took train to Longwood, and from thence coached it to Mansfield, the township which derived so much notoriety through the outbreak of the Kelly gang. Procuring a horse well used to rough country, and obtaining the services of a guide, who, I may state, was intimately connected with the Kellys and their friends, and had undertaken to conduct me to several of their haunts, I started early in the morning from Mansfield, and, so as to avoid observation, made a slight detour before finally getting on the direct track to the Wombat Ranges. Thence we made our way across country to the scene of the police murders, which, I was informed, was near to the fortified hut of the outlaws. Traces of the murders are still visible; on every side are bullet-marked trees, and a few old posts of Walter Lynch's hut can be noticed almost in the centre of the cleared space, which the Kellys and their confederates approached by creeping up under the shelter of the tufts of speargrass. Whether Kennedy was aware of it or not, all the time he was retreating and dodging from tree to tree, firing as best he could, and sternly contesting every inch of ground, he was making in almost a direct line for the hut in which the Kellys and their mates had lived for many months before they committed the crime which caused their outlawry.

A ride of about half a mile from the spot where Kennedy's body was found brought me and my companion to the stronghold of the Kellys, situated on a small rise in the midst of a basin, bounded on the east by Ryan's Creek, on the west by a very high and steep mountain, forming part of the Wombat Ranges, on the north by a small creek flowing down from between the hills, and on the south by a medium-sized ridge, which, however, is high enough to effectually conceal the hut from view in that direction. Reining in my horse on the crest of this ridge, and taking a glance at the scene which lay before me, I could not but be struck with wonderment that such a perfect settlement should have existed so long within half a dozen miles of selections without its existence being discovered. A farmer named Jebb lives within four, and another named Harrison within six miles of it, and yet neither—at least so they assert—were even aware that the Kellys were in the locality, although the latter must have lived on this spot many months, or they could never have got matters into such an improved state. The plateau contains altogether, I should say, about seventy acres, and this is fenced in on three sides (north, south, and east) by a sapling, dogleg, and brush fence, the west side requiring no fencing owing to the steepness of the hill which constitutes its boundary.

Immediately surrounding the hut some twenty acres have been cleared, the trees ringed, and the timber—principally swamp gum and peppermint—placed in heaps ready for burning. The ground had even been raked, so as to give every chance for the grass to grow, and the aspect of the whole place denotes that the Kellys had lived in this secluded retreat many a long day before the Wombat murders took place; and as a proof that someone knew of their existence, I may mention that on a large peppermint tree within a short distance from the hut the name of "J. Martain" has been carved in the sapwood of the tree after the sheet of bark had been taken off to put on the roof of the hut. In the creek flowing to the north of the hut a considerable amount of gold-digging has been done, sluicing being the principal means employed, and from appearances gold has been got in payable quantities, and the workings are of such an extent that it would be utterly impossible for any four men to carry them on under a period of several months.

Perhaps, however, the most startling sight of all is the appearance of the hut and its immediate surroundings. Imagine a house erected of bullet-proof logs, fully two feet in diameter, one on the top of the other, crossed at the ends after the fashion of a chock and log fence, and with a door six feet high by two feet six inches wide, made of stiff slabs and plated with iron nearly a quarter of an inch in thickness, which was loopholed to fire through. The door is on the north side, opposite the gold workings in the creek, and a well-built log chimney occupies the greater part of the west end of the hut. Such was the home of the Kelly gang for some months before the police murders. Its interior was fitted up just as substantially as its exterior, and in a manner calculated to stand a long siege, there having been every provision made for the storage of flour, beef, tea, sugar, and other necessaries of life; and to show that in fresh meat, at least, they were not wanting, we discovered portions of several carcases, together with seven or eight heads of cattle, with bullet holes in the centre of the forehead, lying outside the hut, which may have belonged to either "scrubbers" out of the ranges, or the fat bullock of some not far distant squatter or farmer, but most probably the latter. Empty jam and sardine tins, old powder flasks, cap boxes, broken shovels, old billy cans, glass bottles, door hinges, and a great variety of other articles were to be seen all round the hut. But the crowning wonder of all was the evident pains taken by the Kellys to improve themselves as marksmen. In every direction—taking the hut as a standing-point—we saw trees which were marked with bullets, from five to fifty having been fired into each, at ranges varying from twenty to four hundred yards. The bullets, being afterwards chopped out, were melted down and converted again into their former state. On one small tree a circle of charcoal six inches in diameter had been traced, and into this two or three revolver bullets had been fired, one striking the black dot meant to represent the bullseye in the centre, and the other two being close to it. Some of the bullets had gone to a depth of four inches in the trees, and consequently a great deal of chopping had to be done to get them out; and there was abundant evidence, too, to prove that, the more practice the outlaws had, the more they improved in the use of the rifle and revolver, the shooting at some marks on the trees being very wide, and on others remarkably straight and dead into the bullseye.

I did not attempt to inspect the country in the vicinity of this stronghold of the outlaws. By the time I had taken a hurried sketch and picked up a few interesting relics, it became time to think of turning homewards; so, only waiting a few moments to inspect the track which led from the hut across the creek and over the gap towards Greta, my guide and I turned our horses' heads southwards, and after a rather rough ride reached Mansfield late at night, from whence I took coach to Longwood next day, reaching Melbourne the same night, none the worse for my trip in the Kelly country.

THE RAID UPON EUROA.

More than a month passed away in fruitless search, all that was returned to the public for the money expended in the wearisome hunt for the outlaws being "report" upon "report," each of which conveyed intelligence of non-success, disheartened men, and knocked-up Government steeds. But the time had arrived for fresh interest to be created in the gang, for a greater display of police ingenuity and energy, and for public patience to be further exercised. Leaving their mountain fastnesses, Ned Kelly and his companions made a bold raid upon the township of Euroa, a small settlement on the main road between Melbourne and Sydney, and deliberately, in open day, "stuck up" the National Bank, emptying its coffers of all the gold and notes that were stored therein. Their plan of operations was cleverly arranged and carried out to the last detail in a remarkably cool and systematic manner.

The town at this time contained about three hundred inhabitants, and could boast of a police station, two or three hotels, and a number of other business places; it was the centre of a flourishing agricultural district, and the main line of railway between Melbourne and the Murray ran partly through the town. The Strathbogie Ranges, covered with thick scrub, lay at the back of the settlement, extending as far as Mansfield; but only experienced bushmen could easily cross the rugged, heavily-timbered belt.

About three miles from the township was a station owned by a settler named Younghusband, and it was here that the quartette first made their appearance, at noon on December 18th, 1878. One of the station hands named Fitzgerald was quietly eating his dinner in the men's hut, when a man, apparently an ordinary bush hand, appeared at the door, and in a matter-of-fact tone of voice enquired if the manager was in. Fitzgerald replied in the negative, and suggested that if the stranger's business was not very particular he might do instead of the manager. The stranger replied that it was of no consequence, and sauntered away. Fitzgerald continued eating his dinner, but upon looking up a few minutes after the man had left he saw that there were now three rough-looking bushmen instead of one, that they were leading four very fine horses, and were on their way to the homestead, which was not far from the hut. Mrs. Fitzgerald happened to be at the homestead, and was rather surprised when two of the men walked in without invitation. In reply to her inquiry as to who they were, and what they wanted, one of them replied that he was Ned Kelly, and that he wanted refreshment for himself and his mates, and food for their horses, adding at the same time that there was no occasion for fear, as they would do no harm. At once Mrs. Fitzgerald called to her husband, who left his dinner and came over, to find himself face to face with his former visitor, and learn that the men were notorious bushrangers. Having learned from his wife that the bushrangers had demanded refreshment, and observing a revolver in Ned Kelly's hand, Fitzgerald ordered dinner to be provided, at the same indicating where the horse-feed was to be found to Dan Kelly, who at once proceeded to bait the animals.

In the meantime the fourth outlaw had appeared on the scene, and while Joe Byrne stood outside the door as guard, Ned Kelly and Steve Hart interviewed the station hands as they came up for their dinner and made prisoners of them all, converting a detached storeroom into a temporary prison, in which all the "hands" belonging to the station, with Fitzgerald at their head, were marched one by one, the door being locked, and the prisoners told that they would not receive injury unless they interfered or attempted to escape.

Mr. Macauley, manager of the station, was greatly surprised as he approached the homestead on his return during the afternoon, at the quiet that reigned; and his surprise was increased when he learned the cause of it. Fitzgerald called out to him from the storeroom that the Kellys were in possession; at the same instant Ned Kelly came out of the house, and told the manager to bail up, informing him that they were not going to take anything, but had called at the station to get food and rest for their horses and sleep for themselves. Submitting to the inevitable, Macauley said they all might make themselves as comfortable as possible; and tea having been made, they partook of it together, although only two of the outlaws would sit down at a time, relieving each other in couples in keeping a look-out. They also made some of the prisoners taste the food before them— with what object may be easily understood.

Before nightfall another prisoner was made, a travelling hawker named Gloster, who called at the station to obtain water for his tea, after having unharnessed his horses and fixed his camp near the homestead. When told by Ned Kelly to bail up, Gloster

at first took the command as a joke, but was speedily
undeceived by a threat from Dan Kelly to shoot him
where he stood; and after a little parleying he consented to take his place in the storeroom with the
other prisoners.   The four robbers then proceeded
to the hawker's cart and chose each for himself a new
suit of clothes, also taking some firearms that were
in the cart; then they returned to the homestead and
prepared to make themselves comfortable for the
night, which they did by taking turns, two by two, at
sleeping and watching.

On the following morning they were astir early,
and told Macauley that they intended to stick up the
Euroa Bank during the day: and that in order that
intelligence of their presence at the station should not
reach the township they must keep all parties close
prisoners, with any others who might call at the homestead. At this time there were over twenty prisoners
in the storeroom under lock and key, and four more
were added before many hours had passed. About
two o'clock in the afternoon a farmer named Casement drove up to the gate in his spring cart, with
three other persons, Messrs. McDougal, Jennant, and
Dudley.   One of the visitors was in the act of opening
the gate when the party were startled at an order to
"bail up" from Ned Kelly and Byrne, the former
being on horseback and the latter on foot.   After
some demur they complied, and found themselves in
the company of the other prisoners, who, although
weary of their enforced confinement, appeared rather
pleased than otherwise at the addition to their numbers. Having seen their latest prisoners safely located,

two of the bushrangers overhauled the cart and appropriated a rifle, a gun, and some bullets, powder and caps that Casement happened to have there.

Leaving Joe Byrne in charge of the prisoners (the women folk at the station were allowed to move about freely, but were closely watched), the other members of the gang procured axes and proceeded to cut down some of the telegraph posts on the railway; then they tore down a considerable length of the line, chopping away the wire for a good length so that it could not be easily or quickly repaired. While thus engaged they made another capture—four railway fettlers who had seen them destroying the line and gone forward to ascertain the reason, being enlightened and made prisoners at the same time. These men were marched up to the station and placed with the other captives, and then the gang made arrangements for visiting Euroa.

First getting Mr. Macauley to draw out a cheque for a small amount, they made Gloster's lad hitch up the horse in the hawker's covered cart; Ned Kelly drove that, Dan Kelly got into Casement's vehicle, Hart mounted one of the saddle horses, and the expedition started for the township, leaving Byrne in charge of the prisoners, with a rifle in his hand, revolvers in his belt, and two other rifles within easy reach.

Shortly after the party had started, a train stopped opposite the station, and a telegraph line repairer alighted. A glance at the broken line was sufficient to show him that the break had not been caused accidentally and that he would be unable to repair it unaided, and he at once walked towards the homestead to procure assistance. Here he was challenged by Byrne, and speedily found himself under lock and key in the already overcrowded storeroom.

Meanwhile the bushrangers with the carts were approaching Euroa, and Hart had already reached the township, where he entered the hotel and had a meal without attracting attention. When the two Kellys drove up he joined them, and the three went direct to the National Bank. Ned Kelly drove up to the front door of the bank in one of the carts, jumped out, and fastened up the horse. At the same moment Dan Kelly drove the other cart in to the back yard of the bank, and Hart rode into the same place. Although after bank hours, the bank doors were open, as the station-master was frequently in the habit of getting drafts for Melbourne late in the day. Ned Kelly entered the front door of the bank, and at the same moment Dan Kelly and Hart entered by the back door. It so happened that all Mr. Scott's (the manager's) family were at the moment in one of the rooms of the house, as they were just preparing to go for a walk, while Mr. Scott himself was about to attend a funeral. On entering, Ned Kelly presented the cheque signed by Mr. Macauley; but as soon as the other two made their appearance he pulled out a revolver, announced himself as Kelly, and ordered Mr. Scott, Mr. Bradley (the accountant), and the two clerks to "bail up" and "put up their hands." He then demanded the money from Mr. Bradley, who appealed to Mr. Scott whether he was to comply. Mr. Scott replied that he supposed they could not prevent the bushrangers from taking the money, but they

would not give them anything.   Kelly then helped
himself to all the cash in use, amounting in all to
£300 in specie and notes.   They then prepared to
visit the other part of the premises, leaving Hart to
keep guard over the prisoners in the banking room

DAN KELLY

They conducted themselves quietly enough.   The
ladies acted bravely, and there was no noise, which
would have perhaps resulted in loss of life.   As soon
as Mrs. Scott discovered who her visitor was she told
him that he was a better-looking man than she fancied

he would be; but Ned Kelly passed over the compliment without remark, and told her to get herself and children and servants ready for a drive, as he was going to take them over to Younghusband's station. He then returned to the banking room and said he knew very well they had not all the money; in spite of Mr. Scott's protest he got the keys of the strong room, and proceeded to appropriate the reserve cash. This he packed up in a neat parcel with the other, also examining some of the bank notes and letters, and took one or two deeds of trifling importance, but left the bulk of the bills and securities untouched. The total sum taken was £1942, besides thirty ounces of gold.

All this time Mr. Scott's family and the bank officials were under guard, and of course, as everything was very quietly conducted, and it was after bank hours, no alarm was given. The party then started, Dan Kelly in the hawker's cart with the clerks and one of the female servants leading the way. Then followed Mrs. Scott with her mother and seven children (the eldest of whom was thirteen years of age) in Mr. Scott's buggy, which Ned Kelly had pressed into the service; Mrs. Scott acting as driver and being cautioned not to indulge in any "larks" on the road. After this came Ned Kelly with Mr. Scott and another servant, while Hart, on horseback, brought up the rear. The money was in the cart at the feet of Kelly. In this way the cavalcade went out of the town without attracting much attention. The total number of persons carried off was fifteen. The object of carrying them bodily away was to prevent the alarm being given at once, and as a matter of fact it was not known in Euroa what had occurred at the bank until after eleven o'clock that night, and then the direction taken by the bushrangers was a matter of mystery. Before leaving the bank Kelly secured the two revolvers on the premises, and also demanded and secured two other revolvers and two bags of cartridges, in all about eighty rounds.

At the station the manager and his clerks were placed in the storeroom, and the females joined those belonging to the homestead, the bushrangers shortly afterwards taking tea with them. After the horses had been saddled and brought round, Ned Kelly announced to those in the storeroom that they were about to leave, declaring at the same time that if any of the prisoners moved from the spot until three hours had passed he would afterwards hunt them out and shoot them; and he specially commanded Macauley to see that this injunction was carried out faithfully on pain of losing his life. The outlaws then mounted their horses and rode away at a rapid pace in the direction of Strathbogie Ranges, it being observed that Ned Kelly carried all the spoil. It was then past eight o'clock, and quite dark, and as it was thought probable that one of the gang would be on the watch, Mr. Macauley decided that no person should move from the station until the allotted time had passed. Shortly after eleven o'clock Mr. Scott and his charge started on the return journey to Euroa, reaching the place in safety and finding that no suspicion of the startling events that had occurred under their very noses had been entertained by his fellow-townsmen.

The other parties remained at the station during that night, and left early next morning for their several homes; but not before the police had commenced to move, for they were at work near the station at daylight endeavouring to pick up the tracks of the outlaws, hoping to get upon them while still fresh, and to follow them until they came up with the bushrangers themselves. In this, however, they were disappointed, for they found tracks leading in every direction; and then it became plain that the Kelly sympathisers had been at work before them, riding over the ground, first in one direction and then in another, in order to baffle the pursuers and throw them off the scent.

The raid was one of the boldest that had yet been made in Victoria by any bushranging gang, and the colonists were prepared to hear of other outrages of a like character at any moment. The bankers in the country towns were specially concerned, and revolvers became prominent articles of furniture in the managers' rooms and under the serving counters. The police became wretchedly restive under the monotonous round of unsuccessful search journeys, and the unmerited abuse heaped upon them by civilians who thought failure to take the outlaws, or even to catch sight of them, was the result of inefficiency. And just at this time the Victorians passed through the very experience that had so worried New South Welshmen during the reign of Hall's gang and the Clarkes. That four young fellows should set at defiance every effort of that mighty Engine of Civilisation—the police force—was one of the most extraordinary things of the age—as ridiculous as it was reproachful; and in the eyes of a large section of the public the police appeared greater offenders than the outlaws. But the police were not altogether to blame. They did their utmost to follow and capture, but were always at a disadvantage, having to carry on their work in places to which they had hitherto been total strangers, while the outlaws enjoyed the advantage of knowing every turning in the sombre fastnesses, and having scores of friends to serve them in a double capacity—informing them of every movement of their pursuers, and at the same time hiding the tracks they had made, and giving the police wrong information, or misleading them in a thousand and one different ways.

To stimulate the police to even greater exertions, and at the same time place a strong inducement before the Kelly sympathisers to turn informers and betray the outlaws, the Victorian Government increased the reward for their apprehension to £4000— or £1000 for each one taken. It was a big bait, but it was not so readily taken as the authorities appeared to anticipate. And still the fruitless search went on— days growing into weeks and weeks growing into months without any nearer approach being made to the accomplishment of the end desired. The press, which had boasted during the reign of the Hall gang that no bushranger could actively exist in Victoria, found its weapon turned against itself by contemporaries in New South Wales, and sought to ease the pain of its humiliation by "slating" the police of its own territory   And didn't the Force in New South

Wales chuckle over this turning of the tables! Even the blacktrackers of the elder colony made sport of the men who had boasted and failed.

At last a hope sprang up in the breasts of that section of the police which had set itself specially to work to bribe some of the Kelly sympathisers. One man, who was supposed to be a bosom friend of Ned Kelly, appeared inclined to "turn dog" on his former mate. This was Aaron Sherritt, who lived near Beechworth, and was known to have been one of the most active "telegraphs" of the gang, supplying them with information concerning the movements of the police and furnishing them with food. Sherritt was carefully approached by one of the leaders of the search parties, and after much persuasion consented to put the police on their track, the promise being made that he should receive the whole of the £4000 which the Government had offered for their capture if the information supplied by him resulted in their being taken.

The first piece of information supplied by Sherritt was that the gang had decided to cross the Border into New South Wales, and there "stick up" one of the banks—at Goulburn, he believed. He said that they had asked him to accompany them, but he had declined, and they had then set off without him. Subsequent inquiries proved that there was truth in Sherritt's statement, for Byrne and Dan Kelly were reported to have been seen going in the direction of the Murray River, and to have called for provisions at a shanty where they were known. This information was conveyed to the police on the New South Wales side of the Murray, but although the river crossings were carefully guarded, no sign of the outlaws could be discovered; and the authorities decided that they had been deceived, and lived in daily expectation of hearing that an outrage had been committed at some place nearer what the bushrangers were pleased to call "home," for they knew that they would not keep quiet for any length of time, especially as their last raid had been so successful. And sure enough, before ten days had elapsed, New South Wales and Victoria were both ringing with the news that another successful raid upon a small town had been made, and that another bank had been robbed.

THE RAID UPON JERILDERIE.

Jerilderie was then a township with a population of about four hundred inhabitants, containing one bank, a police station, three or four hotels, and a telegraph office, in addition to the other ordinary business places of a bush village. It is about sixty miles from the Murray on the New South Wales side, and about ninety miles in a direct line from Mansfield.

At midnight on Saturday, the 9th of February, 1879, the four outlaws rode quietly into the town and surrounded the police station, which was occupied by Constables Devine and Richards, the former being in charge. The town was in darkness, and the constables, like the other inhabitants, were in bed asleep, when their slumbers were disturbed by hearing someone calling out that a murder had just been committed by a drunken man at Davidson's hotel, and that the presence of the police was urgently required. Both

uu

constables hurriedly ran out to learn fuller particulars,
when they were immediately secured, and, the key of
the cell having been produced, were locked up together.   Devine's wife and children were then
aroused and shut up in another part of the watch-
house, receiving an assurance that no harm would
come to them if they remained quiet, but if they raised
any alarm both the locked-up constables would be at
once shot by Hart, who had been placed over them
as sentry.   Having thus secured the inmates of the
lock-up the bushrangers brought their horses into the
stable and fed and bedded them, after which they settled down for the night, a constant watch being kept
by one or other of them over the prisoners.

During the Sunday nothing unusual occurred to
disturb the quiet of the town or of the four ruffians
who were already in possession of its custodians.   It
was the aim of the outlaws to make everything appear
natural, in case any person acquainted with the lock-
up people and their duties might call and notice that
there was either halt or hitch.   Hence, Dan Kelly,
Byrne, and Hart put on police uniform, and were prepared to act the part of policemen in charge.   Mrs.
Devine was permitted to move about freely during
the day, but a close watch was kept on her movements, and she was not allowed to leave the station,
except on one occasion, and that furnished its novel-
ty.   It appears she had undertaken the weekly task of
preparing the little church with which she was connected for service every morning; when this became
known to Ned Kelly he decided that she must perform
that duty, and the good lady went about it with Byrne

as her attendant and guard.   During the afternoon
Hart and Byrne made an excursion through the
town, taking Constable Richards along with them,
and as all three were dressed in police uniform they
did not attract any attention, those who saw them
doubtless concluding that Richards was simply showing two of his brethren from a distance the lions of
the place.   The object of the excursion was to enable
the bushrangers to learn exactly the position of the
different public-houses, bank, etc., with a view to
speedy and easy operations on the following day.
After perambulating the streets for about half an hour
the trio returned to the station, and Richards was
again placed under lock and key with Devine.   No
person called at the station during the day, and the
prisoners and their keepers prepared to spend another
quiet night at the station.

Early on Monday morning, Byrne, still dressed
in police uniform, took two of the horses to the local
farrier and had them shod.   Then the Kellys began
to think of business.   Having securely locked up
Constable Devine and his wife and children, they
pressed Richards into their service as decoy, and at
eleven o'clock started down town, Richards walking
with the brothers Kelly, all in police clothing, and
Hart and Byrne riding slowly on horseback behind
them.   The first place of call was the Royal Hotel,
where they saw Cox, the landlord.   Richards introduced Cox to Kelly, who said he wanted the rooms
in the Royal, as he intended to rob the bank, but
would not do anybody any harm.   The bushrangers
were then placed by Ned Kelly at the front part of

the hotel, and as people went in for a drink they were seized and placed in a room, where Dan Kelly acted as sentinel. In the meantime Byrne busied himself in collecting all the servants from the back part of the establishment, making prisoners of them also; and everything being in readiness, they proceeded to honour the Bank of New South Wales with a call.

The bank building was near the hotel, and there were three officers engaged therein—Mr. Tarleton (manager), Mr. Living (accountant), and Mr. Mackin sub-accountant), and Living's account is so clear and full that it may be quoted here:—

About ten minutes past twelve on Monday morning I was sitting at my desk in the bank, when I heard footsteps approaching me from the direction of the bank door. I at first took no notice, thinking it was the manager, Mr. Tarleton. The footsteps continued approaching, when I turned round on the office stool and noticed a man approaching from the back door. I immediately accosted the fellow, who already had a revolver levelled at me, and on asking who he was and what right he had to enter the bank by the back way, he answered that he was Kelly, and ordered me to bail up. The fellow, who afterwards turned out to be Byrne, ordered me to deliver up what firearms I had. I replied that I had none. Young Mackin, who was standing in front of the bank, then came in, when Byrne ordered me to jump over the counter, which I did. He then told me to come with him to Cox's hotel, and remarked that they had all the police stuck up. We went into the hotel, where we met Ned Kelly, who asked for Mr. Tarleton, and was told that he was in his room. They went back to the bank, but could not find the manager in his room. Ned Kelly said to me, "You had better go and find him." I then searched, and found the manager in his bath. I was at first a little alarmed at not finding the manager in his room, and at first thought that he had got some clue that the bushrangers were in the place, and cleared out. On finding the manager in his bath, I said to him, "We are stuck up; the Kellys are here, and the police are also stuck up." Byrne then got Hart, and left him in charge of the manager, who was subsequently taken over to the room where all the others were kept prisoners. After he had got out of the bath, Ned Kelly came and took me into the bank, and asked me what money we had in it. I replied that there was between £600 and £700, when Kelly said, "You must have £10,000 in the bank." I then handed him the teller's cash, amounting to about £691. Mr. Elliott, the schoolmaster, then came into the bank, and as soon as Kelly saw him he ordered him to jump over the counter. Mr. Elliott replied that he could not, but Kelly made him, and they then tried to put the money in a bag, but not having one sufficiently large, Ned Kelly went and brought a bag, and we put the money into it. Kelly asked if we had more money, and was answered "No." Kelly then obtained the teller's revolver, and again requested more money. He then went to the treasure drawer, and requested to know what was in it, and was told by me that it contained nothing of any value. Kelly insisted on its being opened, and one of the keys was given to him, but he could not open it, owing to the manager having the second key, which was required to open it. Byrne then wanted to break it open with a sledge hammer, but Kelly brought the manager from the Royal Hotel, and demanded the key, which was given to him, and the drawer was opened, when the sum of £1450 was taken out by Kelly and placed in a bag. Kelly then took down a large deed-box, and asked what it contained, and was told that the contents consisted of a few documents which were of no use. He replied that he would burn the contents, but Mr. Tarleton argued with him, and Kelly took one document and put it into the bag, and then expressed his intention of burning all the books in the office. He, however, left the rest of the papers, and said that he would come back and see if there were any deeds for town allotments. The whole party then went into the Royal Hotel. Daniel Kelly was in the hotel, and Ned Kelly took two of the party out to the back of the hotel, where he made a fire and burned three or four of the bank books. In the meantime Mr. Rankin (a merchant and justice of the peace) and Mr. Gill (the local newspaper proprietor), seeing the bank door open, went in, and were immediately followed by Kelly, who ordered them to bail up. Both gentlemen at once made off, Mr. Rankin running into the hotel, and Mr. Gill in some other direction. Ned Kelly ran after Rankin and caught him in the hotel. Kelly caught him by the collar, and asked him why he ran away, at the same time telling him to go into the passage, and that he intended to shoot him. He took Mr. Rankin into the passage, and, after straightening him against the wall, levelled his revolver at him. Several persons called out to Kelly not to fire, and he did not. He then called Hart by the name of "Revenge," and told him to shoot the first man that attempted any resistance, and told Rankin that if he attempted he would be the first shot. Kelly then asked for Gill, and took Richards and me with him to look for Gill. The policeman had his revolver with him, but Kelly had previously withdrawn the cartridges. They went up to Gill's house and saw Mrs. Gill. Kelly said to her, "I have a statement here which contains a little act of my life, and I want it published by Mr. Gill; will you take it?" She refused to do so. I then took the paper, and promised to have it published, and asked to get one. The party then went to McDougald's hotel, where Kelly took a blood mare out of the stable, and remarked that he would take the animal, but would return it in three weeks. The party then went to the telegraph office, where they met Byrne, who had cut the wires. Ned Kelly then broke the insulators at the office with his revolver, and after this he took the postmaster and his assistant to the Royal Hotel and left the party there. Kelly then returned to the bank and obtained a saddle and a pair of riding trousers belonging to Mr. Tarleton, and also a gold chain and a gold watch. The saddle was then put on the mare, and Dan Kelly, mounting it, rode away, but returned in five minutes. Dan Kelly and Hart then both kept guard at the hotel, and Ned Kelly then informed the postmaster that if he attempted to mend the wires before next day, or offered any resistance, he would be shot. He also told Mr. Jefferson that he intended to take him a few miles in the bush and liberate him. He informed those present that he intended sticking up the Urana coach that night, and would shoot any one who attempted to give warning. Byrne still rode in the direction of the Murray with the money, and in the meantime Mr. Tarleton had succeeded in despatching a messenger to Urana to warn the bank manager there. The remaining part of the gang then rode in the direction of the police camp, and the party were liberated, and I started for Deniliquin.

The bank manager, Tarleton, gave some further particulars. He stated that at the time of the occurrence he had not long returned from a ride of forty miles, and was having a bath, when the teller came rushing into the bathroom and exclaimed that they were stuck up. Mr. Tarleton at first thought it was rubbish; but on seeing two men with revolvers he believed such to be the case. As soon as he came out of the bath, Hart pointed the pistol at him, and then searched his clothes. Mr. Tarleton then made some inquiries as to the movements of the Kelly gang, but Hart, answering one or two questions, replied in an angry voice that he had better cease asking such questions. Hart then took him into the hotel, and as he was going in he noticed Byrne strike the Chinese cook. He was placed with some others in the bar-parlour, where he was kept until taken back to the bank. Hart stood the whole time at the door of the room with revolvers, and evinced a strong desire to shoot somebody occasionally, if there was a little too much talking in the room. During his confinement in the room he was placed in such a position that he thinks he could have knocked Hart down, but on asking the policeman if he would back him up, he replied that Dan Kelly had them covered with his revolver, and if he happened to miss them he would be sure to kill some of the others. The gang then prepared to go, but before doing so Ned Kelly made a speech with the evident intention of exciting pity.

During the day the outlaws paid periodical visits to the other hotels, having "soft" drinks, and treating everyone civilly. Hart took a new saddle from the saddler's, and several watches were taken, but afterwards returned. Two police horses were taken, and other horses wanted; but the residents begged, as they belonged to women, that they should be left, and Kelly did not take them. The telegraph operators, with a number of others, were taken prisoners to the lock-up, and were not let out until 7 p.m. Eight telegraph poles were cut, and Byrne took possession of the office. He overhauled all the telegrams sent that day.

In his harangue to the crowd before leaving the town, Ned Kelly referred to the affair which took place at his mother's hut when Constable Fitzpatrick was shot in the wrist. He declared that Fitzpatrick was the aggressor, and that he received his wound when Dan's arrest was being resented. The documents which he handed to Mr. Living, and which he said he wanted Mr. Gill to publish in his paper, purported to be a history of his life. They were subsequently handed over to the Victorian Government. In this so-called history (which was doubtless written by Byrne, the scribe of the gang) Kelly was made to pose as a martyr to police interference and persecution. He said his criminal career commenced when he was only fourteen years old, and received a sentence of three months' imprisonment for, as he put it, "using a neighbour's horse without his consent." Then other convictions followed rapidly, and "the police became a nuisance to the family." He declared that his brother Dan was innocent when Fitzpatrick came to arrest him, and that he was wounded by his own revolver going off in a scuffle with Dan. Referring to the murder of the constables in the Wombat Ranges, he admitted that the gang surprised them and showed them no mercy, but they shot the constables because they believed the constables had come out to shoot them.

The bushrangers did not all leave Jerilderie together. Byrne, as already stated, started first, leading a pack horse with the bank treasure strapped across the saddle. Shortly afterwards Ned Kelly started, also leading a spare horse, one of those taken from the police stables, but he returned to Cox's hotel and told the prisoners they were at liberty to leave, but that Constables Devine and Richards were not to be released from the lock-up for some hours. He told those at the public-house that none of the gang need have any fear of being shot, for if one of them fell the lives of every person in the town would be taken as revenge. Dan Kelly and Hart amused themselves before leaving by galloping up and down the street, brandishing their revolvers and shouting at the top of their voices, "Hurrah, for the good old times of Morgan and Ben Hall!"—a sentiment which appeared to please some of the persons who heard them, for they indulged in a feeble cheer. They then also left the town, of which they had held possession for two whole days.

From a threat Ned Kelly had made during the Monday that he would stick up the Urana coach before he left the district, the Jerilderites had concluded that the gang had gone to Urana, and that they would shortly hear of outrages having been committed there. But they were out in their reckoning, for Kelly and his mates appear to have made all haste to cross the border back into their own territory before the news of their outrage on the New South Wales side had been widely circulated. As soon as telegraphic communication had been restored the startling news of the raid was flashed along the wires, and the police at every centre in the south were quickly on the alert. At Wagga Wagga and Albury fears were entertained that the outlaws would pay the banks there a flying visit, and police were told off to guard those establishments, while other members of the force went out in search of the visitors who had so successfully evaded capture by the Victorian police. Word was sent to every station near the river, and a close watch was kept upon the several crossings; but the excite-

JOE BYRNE

ment waned as the days passed, and no news of the outlaws could be gained. Then all doubt was set at rest by a report from the Victorian police that at least one of the Kellys had been seen riding back in the mountains some fifteen miles from Beechworth.

It will be readily imagined that the news of the raid upon Jerilderie put the authorities and police of New South Wales in a ferment of excitement. The Inspector-General of Police in Sydney at once wired to all the frontier stations warning and instructing them, and at the same time dispatched a number of mounted men from Sydney to assist the local constabulary on the border. Unfortunately, however, the Murray waters were very low, and being crossable at almost any point along a distance of one hundred miles or so, the chances of intercepting the outlaws on their journey back were considered remarkably slight. The probabilities are that Ned Kelly and his mates had crossed the river before the river stations had heard of the outrage at Jerilderie; in any case, as we have seen, they got back into their old quarters near Beechworth without difficulty.

The Government of New South Wales also took action, and joined with that of Victoria in offering stronger inducements for the capture of the gang. Parliament happened to be sitting at the time, and shortly after the news of the Jerilderie outrage had reached Sydney, Sir Henry Parkes, Premier, enlightened the House concerning the steps he had taken on behalf of the Government. He read the following letter which he had forwarded to the Chief Secretary of Victoria:—

Colonial Secretary's Office,
Sydney, 14th February, 1879.

Sir,—I have the honour to inform you, in reference to the appearance in this colony of Edward Kelly and his associates recently outlawed under a law of Victoria, that the Government are about to decide on extreme measures, with the hope of arresting the course of these desperadoes. It appears to me that the two colonies should unite in their efforts to vindicate the law now that the crimes of the outlaws have become common to both; and with this view I venture to suggest that the reward for their apprehension should be a joint reward, and that the police in the Border districts should act in concert.

The banks in Sydney chiefly concerned in the Border trade, propose to contribute £1000 towards a reward, and the Government is prepared to contribute £3000, making a total of £4000. If a like sum was raised in Melbourne, the joint reward would amount to £8000, or £2000 for each of the four outlaws.

If the information of the next few days should confirm that which we at present possess as to the whereabouts of the outlaws, this Government will seek to obtain from Parliament under a suspension of the standing orders, special powers for dealing with these and any similar class of criminals, the object of which will be to secure the possession of them dead or alive.

I hope your Government will concur in these suggestions for united action; and in that case may I ask you to inform me of your concurrence by telegram, as I hope that by the time you receive this communication we shall be in a position to take decisive steps.

I think it will be best, for the present, to regard this communication as confidential.

In reply to this he received two telegrams, as follows :—

We cordially reciprocate your offer of co-operation, and agree to increase the reward to £8000—£2000 for each outlaw; the Victorian Government being responsible for £4000, concurs in the proposal that the police on the border should act in concert.

Have published increased reward in "Gazette" to-night, and also notified the intention of the New South Wales Government to add an equal amount.

The Assembly endorsed the action of the Premier, and next day the following notification was published in the "Government Gazette" :—

Whereas Edward Kelly, Daniel Kelly, Stephen Hart, and Joseph Byrne have been declared outlaws in the colony of Victoria: And whereas warrants have been issued by Mr. James Bambrick, J.P., at Wodonga, Victoria, charging Edward Kelly, Daniel Kelly, and two men whose names were then unknown, with the wilful murder of Michael Scanlan, police constable of the colony of Victoria, and the said warrants have been duly endorsed by Captain Brownrigg, Police Magistrate at Albury: and whereas Victorian warrants duly backed for execution in New South Wales, were subsequently granted for the apprehension of Joseph Byrne and Stephen Hart, charging them with the murder of the aforesaid Michael Scanlan: And whereas the above-named offenders are still at large, and have recently committed divers felonies in the colony of New South Wales: Now, therefore, I, Sir Hercules George Robert Robinson, the Governor aforesaid, do, by this my proclamation, issued with the advice of the Executive Council, hereby notify that a reward of £4000 will be paid—three-fourths by the Government of New South Wales, and one-fourth by certain banks trading in the colony — for the apprehension of the above-named four offenders, or a reward of £1000 for the apprehension of any one of them; and that in addition to the above reward a similar reward of £4000 has been offered by the Government of Victoria; and I further notify that the said reward will be equitably apportioned between any person giving information which shall lead to the apprehension of the offenders and any members of the police force or other persons who may actually effect such apprehension or assist thereat; and that if, in attempting to effect the capture of the said offenders, any member of the police force should be wounded. thereby incapacitating him from earning a livelihood, he will be pensioned; or in the event of any member of the police force losing his life in the execution of such duty, his widow or family depending upon him for support will be provided for by the Government.

There was thus a price of £8000 upon the heads of the Kelly gang, or £2000 upon the head of each; and it was thought that this was a large enough sum to tempt even the greatest friend of the Kellys, outside their immediate family circles, to betray them, should the opportunity for doing so present itself. But many months were yet to elapse before the course of the outlaws was brought to an end; and in the meantime they sought to strike terror into the heart of any friend who might think of betraying them by shooting—in a manner hereafter to be described—one whom they had good reason to suspect of treachery.

In addition to offering the reward stated above, the New South Wales Government introduced and carried through Parliament a Felons' Apprehension Act, similar to the temporary measure which had been passed during the reign of Ben Hall and his mates. This Act, however, was made permanent, and provided that any men outlawed in a neighbouring colony might be outlawed in New South Wales. Thus it was sought to hedge Ned Kelly and his mates about with difficulties insuperable. But neither the large reward on the one hand nor the double outlawry on the other appeared sufficient to bring the daring quartette or either of them within the reach of the "arm of the law."

FRUITLESS SEARCHING.

For fully sixteen months after the Governments of the two colonies had joined in offering this large reward the Kellys remained passive, and all the efforts put forth by the Victorian police, whose energies were devoted almost exclusively to the work, were futile. So silent were the outlaws, so skilfully did they evade observation, and so "close" were their friends, that many persons believed they must have escaped from the district, if not the colony. To tell the full story of unsuccessful searching would take some time, and the telling would serve no good purpose, save, perhaps, to illustrate the absence of the proper man-hunting instincts in the leaders of the police forces; but some portions of it may be told, as they serve to illustrate the hardships of the life which the majority of the subordinate members of the force were subjected to.

One of the first things done after the return of the gang from Jerilderie was to arrest a number of those who were known or suspected to be their friends and sympathisers and assistants; but although they were kept in custody for some time, being repeatedly remanded for that purpose, nothing definite could be proved against them, and they were eventually released. Long excursions were made into the bush where the outlaws were supposed to be in hiding, tedious night watches were set over the houses of their relatives, the services of experienced black-trackers from Queensland were called into requisition, and—what was thought to be the best movement of all—the man Sherritt was induced to place himself at the command of the leader of one of the search parties, the whole of the reward of £4,000 offered by the Victorian Government being promised him if the outlaws were captured through his instrumentality. But neither watching nor tracking were of any avail; and the search parties were literally worn down to a condition of despair.

Aaron Sherritt appears to have kept faith with the men to whom he had undertaken to betray his former comrades, and besides conducting them to retreats which were evidently used by the outlaws in the mountain fastnesses, he watched with them, while still keeping on friendly terms with the relatives of the gang, particularly with Joe Byrne's mother and sister, at whose house he was a frequent visitor, being the accepted lover of the girl. He was playing a very dangerous game, and was well aware that he carried his life in his hands, but he trusted to his native cunning to keep the knowledge of his treachery from the people who still trusted in him. How he failed in his endeavour, and the fate that befel him when the outlaws became aware of his unfaithfulness to them and the sale of his services to the police, will be told later on.

The following brief narrative of the efforts Sherritt put forth in assisting one of the police parties will show conclusively that he was not playing a "double game" as far as the police were concerned. Shortly after the Jerilderie outrage, Superintendent Hare sought Sherritt out and an arrangement was made for him to conduct the police to a favourite camp of the bushrangers in the mountains at the back of Mrs. Byrne's house, he having expressed an opinion that Kelly and his mates would hasten thither from the Murray. He declared that this spot was known only to the bushrangers, and suggested that hiding in the mountain by day and watching Mrs. Byrne's house by night would be the surest means of catching the outlaws, who were sure to visit Joe's mother sooner or later. The police took blankets and provisions with them, and prepared for a lengthy watch. Lying securely hidden in the mountain retreat during the day, alternately sleeping and watching, after dusk they would, one by one, creep down to Mrs. Byrne's stockyard, take up positions behind trees, and lie there watching until daybreak next morning, when they would again steal back to the camp. Sherritt was with them a great part of the time, and spent most of his evenings in the house with the old lady and her daughter, the information gleaned during his stay there being at a later hour given to the superintendent; but occasionally he would leave the camp and go to his hut in the ranges or to his father's house, which was between the camp and Beechworth.

The position of the police was not by any means a pleasant one. The weather was very cold, but they dare not make a fire at the camp for fear of the smoke being seen by the Byrnes or the bushrangers, if they were in the locality; and as they could not cook their food they were compelled to live upon monotonous fare of water, bread, and preserved beef. And added to these discomforts there was an ever-present fear that the outlaws or some of their scouts might unexpectedly come upon them when in camp or watching near the house, in which case they knew what to expect.

For nearly a month the watchers stayed at this place, hoping that the expected visitors would put in an appearance. But their hopes grew fainter as the weeks went by, and they were at last rudely destroyed by the discovery of their hiding-place by Mrs. Byrne. Here is Superintendent Hare's account of the occurrence :—

On the last morning of my stay thère, Aaron, who had been watching with us all the night, came into camp with us. It was a Sunday morning. After we had a meal, each of us lay down in the spots we had selected and fell asleep. I was the highest up the hill, and could look down upon all the others. Near me sat the sentry, and Aaron had lain down the furthest down the hill in a hollow below a large rock. At about eight o'clock in the morning, the sentry, without moving from his post, called me and said the old woman, meaning Mrs. Byrne, was in the camp. I sat up in my cave and looked out, and saw her stealing up. She stood up for a few moments, saw articles lying about the camp, then came

vv

a few steps further on, looked down in the direction of where one of the men was lying, then halted for a moment, and retreated. The camp was so situated that unless a person got within a yard or two of it he could not be seen. I watched her, and did not even let her know that we had seen her. Directly she left I jumped up and went to see who it was she had seen, and to my horror I found it to be poor Aaron. I called him up. He was lying partly on his side, and I was not certain she could have recognised who it was. I told Aaron what had happened, and he turned deadly pale, and huge drops of perspiration broke out on his face. He could scarcely speak, and said, "Now I am a dead man." I told him the best thing he could do now was to be off as hard as he could, and go and show himself to some of his friends, so that if Mrs. Byrne had recognised him he could prove an alibi, and convince her she was mistaken.

Aaron always wore a peculiar dress, and would have been known by anyone at a distance. His dress consisted of a white shirt, a pair of trousers, and long boots, with his trousers tucked inside. The first thing I did before I let him leave the camp was to send the sentry over the hill to see if anything could be seen of the old woman. He returned in a few minutes and pointed her out on a hill opposite to us.

I should here describe the formation of the country we were hidden in to make myself understood. We were on the one side of a deep gully, with high hills, quite impassable to horsemen, in front and behind us. A road or track ran at the foot of the gully, and on one side of the track, about a hundred yards from the bottom of this gully, was our watching-place, about half a mile from Mrs. Byrne's house. We remained quite quiet, and watched her go up the opposite hill to something white that was on a rock. This was her shawl, which she had left behind. It afterwards turned out that she was searching for the police in the mountains, and when she got to the spot where we saw her pick up her shawl she had noticed a sardine tin on the rock in our camp shining in the sun. This had been inadvertently left there after breakfast. When she saw this shining thing, she left her shawl and went to see what it was, and after being in our camp, she returned and picked up the shawl (this she afterwards told Aaron). I put a watch over her, and saw her come down the hill again.

When she was out of sight I put my hat and great-coat on Aaron, and started him off over the back of our camp, so that if the old woman had seen him walking away she could not recognise him. When he was gone, we set ourselves to watch the old woman closely, as she was bent on finding out how many men we had there. She was evidently under the impression that she had not been seen by anyone in the camp. She descended the hill and commenced ascending the hill behind us. We could see her crawling down the hill upon her hands and knees, evidently with the object of looking into our camp to see what she could. I told Senior-constable Mills to go up the hill and give her a good fright and drive her off. He ascended the hill in the direction he saw her coming down, unobserved by her, and lay behind a rock with his rifle in his hand. The old woman came down to the very rock he had taken shelter behind, and just as she was going to take a good observation of our camp the senior-constable sprang upon her and roared out. She almost died of fright. She had not the slightest idea anyone was near her. For a moment she shook from head to foot, but soon recovered herself, and began to slang the senior-constable, and told him she would get her son with the Kellys to shoot the lot of us, as he did Kennedy's party. After some conversation she left and went back to her home.

Nothing transpired that day until dusk, when Aaron re-appeared as usual. I asked him what he had done with himself after leaving me that morning. He said that he had gone to an intimate friend of his and shown himself, and some time afterwards had drawn attention to the early hour at which he had called. I asked him what he intended doing —if he meant to go that evening to see his young woman. He said, "Oh yes; I must go and see if the old woman recognised me this morning." I said, "Don't you funk it?" He replied artfully, "But I must find out if she knows it was me." He went on, "I have brought a penny whistle, and I will commence playing it within a hundred yards from the house, and perhaps my girl may come out to meet me, and I can find out from her whether the old woman has said anything about me."

He left us just as we were going to the watching-place, and about twelve o'clock came as usual and sat down beside me. He told me that he went with his whistle straight to the door of the house, but his young woman did not come out to meet him. He walked inside and continued playing. When he got inside there was a strange man (a neighbour) in the room. The old woman said nothing to him, but he said, "I watched her countenance, and I felt sure she had not recognised me." After a little while the old woman went outside, and he followed her. She said, "A nice trick you have been playing on me." He said, "What do you mean?" She said, "Who could have put the police into that camp in the mountains but you?" He replied, "I don't know what you mean." She told him how she had discovered our camp, and said there were thirty men in it. He pleaded ignorance, but she said she felt certain that he knew all about it. She asked him how it was that she could find us out and he could not. He replied he could not tell, and she said, "Well, you go there to-morrow and see for yourself."

From that time I thought it was useless my remaining there any longer, but all my men begged me to stay, and so did Aaron. I stayed for two nights longer, but two old women discovered our watching-place. My men and Aaron pleaded that Mrs. Byrne had no means of communicating with the outlaws, as she did not know where they were to be found, and they were sure to seek Aaron out before going to her place. However, I could not see the use of staying any longer, so I left, though the men remained for two or three weeks longer. I was not sorry to leave the spot.

Other search parties and watchers were equally unsuccessful, and yet, as was proved subsequently, the outlaws were not at any time far distant from the district in which their numerous friends resided. Other "agents" supposed to be in the confidence of the Kellys, either directly or indirectly, were employed by the police, but although some of these furnished information of their movements occasionally—information that was evidently reliable — the police appeared unable to make use of it in time, and they could never do more than obtain "traces." On one occasion word was received by Sherritt in a letter which he had declared had come from Byrne, but which the police could not decipher, that the gang would be at certain races to be held in the district, that Byrne would run a favourite black steeplechase mare in one of the events, and requesting Sherritt to meet them at the back of the course in order that he might ride the horse. Picked members of the force were sent to the races in disguise, and Sherritt also attended, but not in their company. The bushrangers did not "turn up," however, and it is more than probable that they had sent this letter to test whether

Aaron was true to them, they having, no doubt, heard by this time that he had been of late suspiciously friendly with the police. One of the disguised policemen rode in the race for which the black mare was supposed to have been entered and won it; but Aaron had no "seat," except on the animal upon which he had ridden to the course, and he had to content himself with watching the running. Byrne's brother was on the course, however, if Joe himself was absent, and although he and Aaron were much together nothing was said about the outlaws having arranged to be present. The probabilities are that they had learned from their friends that the police had gone to the races disguised, and if the letter to Aaron had been intended as a test the senders no doubt concluded that their former companion had really "turned dog."

As a matter of course, the house of the Kelly's at Greta, near Glenrowan, was made even a greater centre of secret observation by the police, the movements of Kate Kelly and her sister, Mrs. Skillian, being watched very closely. The sisters were splendid horsewomen, and were almost as well acquainted with the ranges as their brothers; and despite the watchfulness of the police they managed to hold communication with the outlaws and supply them with necessaries. A couple of instances illustrative of the "cuteness" of the sisters may here be given. They knew that the police were watching the house from hiding-places in the bush, and nearly every night before retiring they would let their dogs loose and hunt round the house for a distance of several hundred yards, and if any of the watchers were anywhere near, the barking of the dogs would soon reveal their hiding-place. Efforts were made by the police to poison the dogs, but they were frustrated by muzzles being placed on the animals so that they should not pick up any poisoned baits that might have been placed for them.

On one occasion Mrs. Skillian perpetrated a very clever hoax upon a party of watchers, of whose proximity she had by some means become aware. The party had located themselves near her house during the darkness, and knowing that her movements would be observed, at about four o'clock in the morning she went out into the paddock, caught and saddled her horse, and having tied a rather bulky bundle on her saddle, she mounted and set off in the direction of the Warby Ranges, which were immediately behind the residence. Without hesitation the policemen who were on the watch followed her on foot, congratulating themselves on having at last succeeded in catching the woman on one of her relief expeditions to the outlaws' retreat. Pushing after her as speedily as they could, they saw her make for a steep gap in the mountains, and up this they toiled, fondly imagining that it would bring them somewhere near where the outlaws were in hiding. The reader may imagine their chagrin, however, when they reached the top and saw Mrs. Skillian seated on a log, calmly awaiting their approach with her thumb at her nose and her fingers spread out. The disappointed pursuers could not arrest her for any breach of the law; the most they could do was to examine the bundle on her saddle bow, and this turned out to be a harmless old tablecloth which she had made up into a parcel for the purpose of deceiving them.

Scores of reports of such wild-goose chases by one party and another of the police found their way into the press, and a running fire of contemptuous ridicule and angry reproach was kept up against the force, the heads of which were most unmercifully "slated" in newspaper articles and letters. It was about this time that the famed blacktrackers connected with the Queensland force were brought over and distributed among the different sections of searchers; but even these keen-eyed hunters could not bring the troopers and the outlaws together, although they on several occasions came upon tracks which had undoubtedly only recently been made by the latter. These dusky hunters were not looked upon altogether with favour by the Victorian police, and after they had been at work a little time reports that jealousy was interfering with efficient work began to be freely circulated. The subordinates, rather than the officers, appeared to be the disaffected parties in this case, however, for some of the latter were loud in their praises of the skill and energy of the blackfellows, and did not refrain from openly endorsing the action of the Government in having applied to the Queensland authorities for a loan of them.

The fact that the movements of the black-trackers were hampered in many instances by the men with whom they had been deputed to work at last reached the ears of the Queensland authorities, and as success had not attended, and was not likely to attend, their efforts in the Kelly country, a request was forwarded

to the Victorian Government that they might be sent
back to Queensland, where there services were in request.   Shortly after this, therefore, they were withdrawn from active service, and were on the eve of their
departure for Queensland when an event occurred
which caused the Victorian Government to hurriedly
call upon them again.   But as the sequel will show no
further tracking was required from that point—the
outlaws having fallen into a trap of their own making;
a trap from which death formed the only door of
escape.

THE MURDER OF AARON SHERRITT.

As I have already intimated, the outlaws had by
some means become suspicious of Sherritt, and as
soon as they had made sure of the fact that their
former sympathiser had sold himself to the police for
the purpose of selling them, they proceeded to work
out a cold-blooded plan of revenge.   After the discovery by Mrs. Byrne of the party of police spies in
the mountains, the old lady gave Sherritt clearly to
understand that his visits to the house were not wel-
come, and the attachment between him and Joe's
sister was consequently broken off.   That the thiev-
ing instinct was still strong upon Sherritt was proved
by his stealing a horse from Mrs. Byrne.

This theft took place just previous to the rupture,
and through that piece of knavery his services were
very nearly lost to the police.   For some time after
the disappointed watchers had left the mountain retreat near Mrs. Byrne's house, Sherritt remained in
touch with Superintendent Hare, but that gentleman
having gone to another part of the district for a time,

a break was made in the connection, and before it was resumed Aaron had found another sweetheart, and had become a benedict, settling down as a married man about a mile from Mrs. Byrne's residence.

It was still thought advisable to keep watch upon Mrs. Byrne's house, and as no more convenient place for doing this was available than Sherritt's house, the police became frequent visitors there—secret visitors, of course, although the Byrne family must have known that they were under constant surveillance, and that Aaron was lending himself to the hated members of the force. The plan adopted was for a party of three of four troopers to be hidden in Sherritt's house during the day and creep out under shelter of the darkness and watch Byrne's house from different positions during the night. But the work grew so monotonous that the police on watch grew very weary of their work, and evaded duty occasionally; and at last they made application to be allowed to visit Benalla for a time to recruit their health, the constant exposure during the wet nights having completely knocked them up. They were allowed to leave the place for a short time. They had only resumed duty a few days when they were brought into contact with the gang in a manner they had never anticipated. Whether the hour had arrived for the nightly visit to Mrs. Byrne's house or not does not appear, but it was dark and the constables were still in Sherritt's hut, when on the Saturday night about eight o'clock the inmates were visited by a "surprise party" of a very objectionable kind. Aaron, his wife, his mother-in-law, and four police were in the hut

(which consisted of two rooms) at the time, the three
former being in the back room and the latter in a
room at the front; when suddenly a voice was heard
calling from outside the back door. Sherritt asked,

AARON SHERRITT

"Who is there?" and the reply came, "Antonio Wicks,
I have lost my way," or something to that effect.
Aaron recognised the voice as that of Wicks, who had
a farm in the neighbourhood, and without any hesi-

tation he opened the door and stood on the threshold
to talk to the caller. There was a bright fire burning
in the hut at the time, and standing as he did Aaron
was in full view of anyone outside. Before
he could distinguish anything in the darkness, a shot
was fired and he was struck in the face. He staggered
back into the centre of the room, and at once his
assailant jumped to the doorway and fired a second
shot, which struck him in the chest, and he fell dead
upon the floor. Then one of the women in the place
recognised the murderer as Joe Byrne, and shortly
afterwards saw and recognised Dan Kelly standing
near the doorway with his rifle on his arm. The man
Wicks was standing trembling near him, securely
handcuffed; and it subsequently transpired that he
had been secured and forced by Byrne and Dan Kelly
to go to Aaron's hut and call out to him, they knowing that when he heard Wick's voice their intended
victim would not apprehend any danger of a surprise,
and they would then be able to dispose of him quickly
and without any trouble. The murdered man never
spoke after the shots were fired.

There was naturally great consternation in the
hut when this tragedy happened. The attack completely paralysed the constables, who made no attempt
to engage the men for whom they had been specially
waiting for so many weary nights. They did not
move from their hiding-place in the back room, and
did not even fire a shot from their hiding-place, although an opportunity must have presented itself
when Byrne jumped to the doorway to fire the second
shot. Having finished Sherritt, the outlaws showed

that they knew the police were in the house by calling upon them to come out, at the same time firing a volley into that part of the dwelling (it was a slab hut) in which they supposed the police were located. This they repeated several times, but as no answering fire was returned they threatened to burn the house down and roast the timid hunters who were there hidden. They did not carry out this threat, however, and although they stayed about the place until 6.30 next morning, giving the occupants an occasional hint that they were awake and active, they then quietly left and, as was afterwards discovered, rode off to Glenrowan to join Ned Kelly and Hart. When the constables had assured themselves that the outlaws had left the locality of Sherritt's hut, one of their number stole out and made what haste he could to Beechworth to give information to his superior officer at the station there, and thus the whole army of police was once more set in motion.

Sherritt had very few friends to lament his death. He was known and feared by not a few of the residents of the Beechworth district, where he was looked upon as a most dangerous character, and up to the time when his treachery became known his only friends were the outlaws and their sympathisers. Naturally the latter rejoiced exceedingly that he had been so effectually "put out of the way" by Joe Byrne, for they themselves were in danger of being convicted under the Outlawry Act, should the arrest of the bushrangers remove the necessity for secret movements on Sherritt's part; and there can be no doubt that he would have "peached" upon them as readily as he had upon the Kellys if the latter had been in safe custody. And the police did not look upon him altogether with favour, as witness the following statement of Superintendent Hare:—"It was doubtless *a most fortunate occurrence that Aaron was shot by the outlaws;* it was impossible to have reclaimed him, and the Government of the colony would not have assisted him in any way, and he would have gone back to his old course of life, and probably have spent his days in gaol; or he might have turned bushranger himself, when he would have been quite as dangerous a man as Edward Kelly himself." And when mentioning that the Government had given the widow a comfortable allowance, the same officer laconically observed "she was much better off without him."

THE LAST EXPLOIT OF THE OUTLAWS.

A few days before the visit to Sherritt's hut Mrs. Byrne had boasted to one of her friends (who repeated the boast to the police) that "her boy" and his mates would shortly do something that should astonish, not only the people of Victoria, but of the world. We are about to see how that boast was fulfilled.

Having determined that Sherritt should die, with great cunning the gang planned to make his death and the manner of it the instrument of their further designs. They knew the police were in his house before the arrangement was made for the visit, and while the two told off for the murder were engaged in their work, the other two were proceeding to Glenrowan. Believing that the police would hasten away after the murder to give information, and that there would be a hurried and heavy outrush of police with the blacktrackers from Benalla to Beechworth, they planned to destroy the train with its living freight by tearing up the lines at Glenrowan, and having accomplished this and slaughtered those of their pursuers who might not be killed by the wrecking of the train, to obtain a fresh supply of arms and ammunition from the carriages, and then ride on to Benalla—a distance of about fifteen miles—set fire to the courthouse, release the prisoners in the gaol, rob the banks and the stores, and then make back to their haunts in the Strathbogie ranges. It will thus be seen how it was that they did not interfere with the telegraph lines when Sherritt was shot, as they had done when committing the raids upon Euroa and Jerilderie. They wanted the information to be sent to the more important stations, and they wanted the police to come along the line as fast as special trains could carry them.

The sole object of the bushrangers' visit to Glenrowan appears to have been to murder the blacktrackers. The hatred which the leader of the gang had for them was very great, and it is certain that the fear of them had kept the gang quiet so long. Ned Kelly knew that the trackers had returned to Melbourne, and he correctly formed the opinion that as soon as the intelligence of the murder reached headquarters they would be sent on with the police to the scene by special train.

Ned Kelly and Hart arrived at Glenrowan during the Saturday night, and at once commenced operations. The town was a very unpretentious place, containing only a few score inhabitants, two bush hotels, a police station, and a railway station. On the outskirts of the town lived a line-repairer named Reardon, and he was the first person to be made aware of the presence of the two outlaws. At about midnight he was awakened by a violent knocking at the door, and he at once jumped out of bed and inquired who wanted him at that hour of the night. The answer was the glint of a revolver barrel in his face and the voice of Ned Kelly saying, "Come with me, old fellow; I have a job for you," at the same time making himself known to the startled man, and saying he and his mates had been at Beechworth and killed several people, and were now going to kill the police and black-trackers, who they knew would shortly arrive from Benalla. Reardon begged Kelly not to force him to assist in such a bloody work, but the outlaw said that if he did not come at once he would shoot him. Reardon then hurriedly dressed himself and prepared to follow Kelly, but immediately after starting his custodian told him to go back and tell the "missus and kids" to dress too and accompany them, as they might be away for some time, and during their absence the woman might raise an alarm. This Reardon did, and the whole family prepared to follow Kelly up to the railway station, whither he said he was bound.

In the meantime Steve Hart had been on the same mission as Kelly, and had succeeded in rousing up two or three other line-repairers (Reardon being the ganger), and when Kelly arrived with his batch he immediately gave the women and children into the custody of Hart, and leading the men away (under threats of immediate death if they did not obey his orders) made them open the tool-box, get the necessary tools, and march in front of him till they came to a spot half a mile from the station. Here he superintended the pulling up of two lengths of rails. The spot was admirably situated for the purpose for which the villain intended it. At the extreme end of a large cutting the line took a very sharp curve, crossing a deep ravine, over which was erected a sort of culvert. It was on the top of the embankment over this ravine that the rails were torn up.

After two hours' work a huge gap was made in the line, and the men were marched by Kelly into Glenrowan. Hart had marched with those under his charge to the house of the stationmaster (John Stanistreet), situate at the gates about a hundred yards from the station; and having roused the stationmaster he enlightened him as to their mission, and made a convenience of his house as a prison, there being several men who had been called up on the road, together with the women and children under Hart's care. When Ned Kelly returned he made some inquiries concerning the signalling of trains, and particularly how the train was stopped by the signal lamps. Stanistreet enlightened him so far as to say, "White means right, and red wrong, and green generally come along." "There is a train coming," said Kelly, "and you will give no signal"; at the same time saying to Hart, "Watch his face, and if he gives any signal shoot him." After daylight on Sunday morning every passer-by was hailed and sent into the stationmaster's house to keep the other prisoners company, even little children on their way to Sunday-school having to share the common fate. During the Sunday no less than seventeen persons were compul-

STEVE HART

sorily lodged in Stanistreet's house, and until darkness set in no further movement was made.

The exact hour of Dan Kelly's and Byrne's

ww

arrival at Glenrowan was not known, but they must have reached the place early in the morning, and immediately joined their companions, and relieved each other in standing guard over the prisoners, who were allowed to go outside occasionally, but were every moment kept under the strictest surveillance by one member or other of the gang. They did not treat their prisoners harshly, although they gave them to understand that any attempt to escape or raise an alarm would be attended by instant death.

The outlaws evidently anticipated that the special train would arrive during the Sunday, and they grew very anxious as the hours went by without any signs of its coming.   At about midday all the male prisoners except the stationmaster were removed from Stanistreet's house to the hotel kept by a Mrs. Jones, about one hundred yards from the house; here the bailing-up process continued, all persons coming near being compelled to enter and take their places with the other prisoners. The only constable of the township, named Bracken, became a prisoner soon after the arrival of Byrne and Dan Kelly on the scene, his capture having been effected in a very simple manner. Taking with him one of the lads who had been intercepted and detained, and who was well known to the constable, Ned Kelly proceeded to Bracken's house, and told the lad to call out that his father wanted to see the constable. At once the door was opened, and Bracken stood on the threshold, but only to find himself covered with a revolver, and to hear Ned Kelly commanding him to come at once with him. Being unarmed and taken completely by surprise, the constable had no choice in the matter, and having warned Mrs. Bracken that her husband would be shot if she left the station or raised any alarm, Kelly conducted his prisoner to Jones' hotel, which was already more than comfortably full, there being no less than sixty-two persons there, including some whom Bracken recognised as well-known sympathisers of the outlaws.

Confident of their power over their prisoners, and knowing that any attempt to arrange a rush upon them would speedily be communicated to them by one or other of their friends in the crowd, the outlaws did not keep them under lock and key, but allowed them during the day to wander about between the hotel and the station; but they were always on the alert and ready for any emergency. The male prisoners could get as much grog as they wished at the hotel, and Ned Kelly gave them to understand that he wished them to make themselves as comfortable as possible, and during the afternoon one or two of the gang joined them in some jumping contests in the yard. Ned Kelly prided himself upon his ability in this class of athletics, and made his jumps with weights in the shape of a revolver in each hand; but one of the prisoners covered a distance which the leader of the gang could not beat, although he tried to do so three or four times. At last he took off his coat, and failing then also, Byrne remarked, "You seem a bit off to-day, Ned." "Yes," replied Kelly, "I'm a bit handicapped; these fellows are a little too good for me." It was then seen that he wore a plate of armour under his waistcoat, covering his front and back—the plate being of wrought iron about a quarter of an inch in thickness. It was subsequently discovered that each of the outlaws was provided with similar coats of mail, and that they had head coverings made of the same material, ready to put on when the time for fighting came.

One of the prisoners was Mr. Curnow, the Glenrowan schoolmaster, and as he is the hero of the whole series of subsequent events, his account is worth giving in full. The following is his statement:—

On Sunday morning, 27th of June, 1880, I determined to take my wife, sister, and child out for a drive along the road from Glenrowan to Greta. We left the school in a buggy about eleven o'clock in the morning, accompanied by David Mortimer, my brother-in-law, who rode on horseback. When we got in sight of Mrs. Jones' hotel, and opposite the railway crossing, through which we intended to pass, we noticed a number of people about the hotel, and at the crossing. I said, "Mrs. Jones must be dead; she has been very ill." As we got near the hotel a man ran out of it towards Mrs. Jones' stable, distant about twenty yards from the hotel. I drove past the hotel to the crossing, and, seeing Mr. Stanistreet, asked him, "What's the matter?" He replied, "The Kellys are here; you can't go through." I thought he was joking, and made a motion to drive through the gates, when a man on horseback, who blocked up the crossing, and was talking to a young man whom I knew to be named Delaney, wheeled round his horse and said to me, "Who are you?" I then saw that he had revolvers in his belt, and was convinced of the truth of Mr. Stanistreet's statement that the Kellys were there. I replied that I was the teacher at Glenrowan. He said, "Oh, you are the schoolmaster here, are you? And who are those?"—pointing to my wife, sister, and brother-in-law. I told him. He then said, "Where are you going?" I answered, "Out for a drive." He then said, "I am sorry, but I must detain you," and directed us to get out of the buggy, which we did. He then turned to Delaney again and resumed his conversation with him. I afterwards found that the man who addressed me was Ned Kelly, the outlaw. I noticed another armed man near Kelly, and I afterwards found out that he was Byrne.

When we got out of the buggy I led the horse off the crossing, and tied him to the railway fence alongside, directing Mrs. and Miss Curnow to go into Mr. Stanistreet's house, which they did. As soon as I had fastened the horse I joined

Mr. and Mrs. Stanistreet and others, who, I was told, had been taken prisoners by the gang, and was informed by them that Glenrowan had been stuck up since three o'clock that morning, and that the gang had forced Reardon and others to tear up part of the railway line beyond the station for the purpose of wrecking a special train of police and black-trackers which, the outlaws said, would pass through Glenrowan. Some person—I believe it was one of the boys who had been bailed up by the gang—then told me that the Kellys had been at Beechworth during the previous night, and had shot several policemen.

After some further conversation we all listened to what Ned Kelly was saying to Delaney. The outlaw was accusing Delaney of having, some short time previously, ridden a horse from Greta into Wangaratta to oblige a policeman, and of having sought admission into the police force. He threatened to shoot Delaney for this, and pointed a revolver at him several times. Ned Kelly declared to all of us who were listening to him that he would have the life of anyone who aided the police in any way, or who even showed a friendly feeling for them, and declared that he could and would find them out. He said that a law was made rendering it a crime for anyone to help them (the outlaws), and that he would make it a crime for anyone to aid the police against the Kelly gang. The women who were listening to what Kelly was saying asked him to let Delaney off. After keeping Delaney in a state of extreme terror for about half an hour the outlaw made him promise never again to seek admission into the police force, and finally said, "I forgive you this time; but mind you be careful for the future." Byrne then produced a bottle of brandy, and offered some in a tumbler to all adults there. Some accepted it. Byrne drank some himself, and gave Delaney two-thirds of a bottle, which he drank. Ned Kelly refused to take any, and directed some of his boy prisoners to take my horse and buggy into Mrs. Jones' yard, which they did.

Ned Kelly and Byrne then went from the railway crossing to Mrs. Jones' hotel, preceded by the majority of their male prisoners, and I was with them. When we reached Mrs. Jones' there were, including those who had just been taken over, about fifty persons in and about the hotel, all of whom appeared to be prisoners of the gang. We were allowed to go about in the hotel, except in one room, which the outlaws used, and of which they kept the key, and we were allowed outside, but were forbidden to leave the premises. Dan Kelly, a short time after I entered the hotel, asked me to have a drink, and I drank with him at the bar. I said to him that I had been told they had been at Beechworth during the previous night and had shot several police. I asked him whether it was true. He replied that they had been near Beechworth last night and had done some shooting, and that they had "turned the devils out," alluding to the police. Byrne came to the bar, and, looking at Dan Kelly's glass, said, "Be careful, old man." Dan replied, "All right," and poured water into his brandy. While talking with Byrne and Dan Kelly I expressed surprise at Glenrowan being stuck up by them, and they said they had come to Glenrowan in order to wreck a special train of inspectors, police, and black-trackers which would pass through Glenrowan to Beechworth to take up their trail from there. They said that they had ridden hard across country, often being up to the saddle-girths in water, to get to Glenrowan, and that they had had the line taken up at a dangerous part, and were going to send the train and its occupants to h—l.

About one o'clock I was standing in the yard of Jones' hotel, thinking of the intentions of the gang, and I keenly felt that it was my duty to do anything that I could to prevent the outrage which the outlaws had planned from being accomplished, and I determined that I would try to do so. While standing in the yard Dan Kelly came out of the hotel and asked me to go inside and have a dance. I said that I could not dance in the boots I had on. Ned Kelly then came out of the hotel, and hearing me object to dance because of my boots, said, "Come on, never mind your boots." I said to him that it was awkward to me to dance in those boots, as I was lame, but that I would dance with pleasure if he would go to the school with me to get a pair of dancing boots. It flashed across my mind that, in passing the Glenrowan barracks to reach my house, Bracken, the trooper stationed there, might see us, and be able to give an alarm. I knew that Bracken had been stationed at Greta, and felt sure that he would recognise Ned Kelly. He (Ned Kelly) said that he would go, and we were getting ready, when Dan Kelly interfered, and said that Ned had better stay behind and let him and Byrne go with me. Someone else also urged Ned Kelly not to go away, and said that my house was near the police barracks. Ned Kelly turned to me, and asked if it was. I said, "Yes, we shall have to pass the barracks; I had forgotten that." He then said that he would not go, and I went into the hotel, and danced with Dan Kelly.

After we had finished dancing Ned Kelly said that he would go down to the police barracks and bring Bracken, and Reynolds the postmaster, up to Jones'. I laughed at him, and said that I would rather he did it than I, and asked to be allowed to accompany him when he went, and to take home my wife, sister, and child. He gave me no reply. The intention to do something to baffle the murderous designs of the gang grew on me, and I resolved to do my utmost to gain the confidence of the outlaws, and to make them believe me to be a sympathiser with them. I saw clearly that unless I succeeded in doing this I should not be able to get their permission to go home with my wife, child, and sister, and consequently should not be able to do anything to prevent the destruction of the special train and its occupants by giving information to the police at Benalla, which I purposed doing if I could induce the outlaws to allow me and mine to go home. The outlaws kept a very sharp watch on their prisoners without seeming to do so.

About three o'clock in the afternoon Ned Kelly and Dan caused several of their prisoners to engage in jumping, and in the hop, step, and jump Ned Kelly joined with them, using a revolver in each hand as weights. After the jumping was concluded I left Jones' and went to Mrs. Stanistreet's house to see my wife and sister. They came out to see me, and, noticing the red llama scarf wrapped round my sister caused me to think, "What a splendid danger-signal that would make!" The idea of stopping the train by means of it then entered my mind, and made me still more anxious for liberty. I went in to my wife and sister into Stanistreet's house and saw Hart lying down on a sofa. He had three loaded guns by his side. He complained to me of having swollen and painful feet, caused, he said, by not having had his boots off for several days and nights. I advised him to bathe them in hot water, and asked for some for him. It was brought, and he followed my advice.

Shortly after, Mr. Stanistreet and I were walking about at the back of the house, and Mr. Stanistreet expressed a wish that an alarm could be given. Mrs. Stanistreet came out to us, and I asked them if they thought it would be wrong to break a promise given to the outlaws. They said it would not. I then asked Mr. Stanistreet if the outlaws had taken his revolver from him. He said they had not. I saw what use this fact could be made of by me in my efforts to gain the confidence of the outlaws, and to make them believe that they could safely allow me to go home. I said to Mr. and Mrs. Stanistreet that we had better go inside, for I was afraid of being suspected by the gang if they saw us in private conversation, and we did so. I do not know whether Mr. and Mrs. Stanistreet suspected the use I intended making of my liberty if I got it; but afterwards I heard Mrs. Stanistreet saying to Ned Kelly that he ought to allow me to take home my sister, who was in delicate health.

I was sitting in Mr. Stanistreet's when Dan Kelly came in inquiring for a small parcel in a bag, which he had lost.

He seemed very anxious about it, and examined the house throughout in search of it. He could not find it, and went to McDonald's hotel to see if it was there. He came back unsuccessful, and I went to Jones' with him, and he searched there, but failed to find it. When he gave up searching for it, I requested him to tell Ned I wanted to speak to him. I was near the door of Jones' kitchen then. He went into the hotel and brought Ned out, and I told him that Mr. Stanistreet possessed a loaded revolver from the railway department, and advised them for their safety to obtain it, as someone might get it and do them an injury. They thanked me, and I perceived that I had in a great measure obtained their confidence by telling them this.

About dusk I heard Ned Kelly saying to Mrs. Jones (they were standing between the hotel and the kitchen, which was a detached building) that he was going down to the police barracks to capture Bracken, and that he was going to take her daughter to call him out. Mrs. Jones asked him not to take her. Ned Kelly said that he did not intend to shoot Bracken, and that her daughter must go. I advanced to them, and said to Ned Kelly that I thought it would be better for them to take Dave Mortimer, my brother-in-law, to call Bracken out, because Bracken knew his voice well, and by hearing it would suspect nothing. Ned Kelly, after a pause, said that he would do so. He then went to Mrs. Jones' stables, and I followed him and asked him if he would allow me to take my party home when he went down to Bracken; and I assured him that he had no cause for fearing me, as I was with him heart and soul. He replied, "I know it, and can see it," and he acceded to my request. I went over to Mrs. Stanistreet and brought my wife and sister over to Mrs. Jones', and took them into the kitchen. Ned Kelly said that we must wait until he was ready to go. I found, on going back to Jones', that a log fire had been made on the Wangaratta side of the hotel yard, and that many of the prisoners of the gang were standing round it.

It was then dark. Other prisoners were in the hotel, and the outlaws encouraged them to amuse themselves by card-playing. I waited with my wife and sister in Jones' kitchen for, I believe, two or three hours before Ned Kelly directed me to put my horse in the buggy. He and Byrne then went into the room which they had reserved for their own use. I drove to the front of Jones' hotel and put my wife and sister and Alec. Reynolds, the son of the postmaster at Glenrowan, who was about seven years of age, into the buggy. Ned Kelly directed me to take the little boy with us. We were kept waiting in front of the hotel for about an hour. Ned Kelly then came to us on horseback and told me to drive on.

It was then, I believe, about ten o'clock. As we got into the road I found that we were accompanied by Ned Kelly, Byrne, and my brother-in-law, and R. Gibbins on foot, both of whom resided with Mr. Reynolds, the Glenrowan postmaster. On the road down, Ned Kelly said that he was going to fill the ruts with the carcases of the police. The outlaws had each a light-coloured overcoat on, and I was amazed at the bulky appearance which they presented. I had then no knowledge that the outlaws possessed iron armour. Each one carried a bundle in front of him, and in one hand a gun or rifle.

We reached the barracks, and were directed by Ned Kelly to halt about twenty yards distant from the front door of the building. Ned Kelly got off his horse and fastened him to a fence near, ordering my brother-in-law to do the same, and he did so. Kelly then ordered him to go to the barracks door and knock, which he did. Ned Kelly got behind an angle of the walls, and levelled his rifle, either at Dave Mortimer or at the door. No reply came to the knocking or calling, though they were often and loudly repeated at Ned Kelly's whispered command. When I saw Kelly level his rifle I told my party to get out of the buggy, which they did, and I advanced to my horse's head, for I thought Kelly might fire. I was then about seven or eight yards from Kelly. No result being produced by either knocking or calling, Ned Kelly left his position and advanced to Byrne, directing me, in an undertone, to call Mortimer away, which I did, and he came. Byrne, who had remained near us, and Ned Kelly then spoke to each other, and Kelly took Alec. Reynolds, the postmaster's son, and Mr. Reynolds, and passed with them into Reynolds' yard.

We neither saw nor heard anything, I think, for more than an hour, when Ned Kelly appeared, having Bracken, E. Reynolds, and Bracken's horse with him. Kelly stopped when he reached us, and ordered Bracken to mount the horse brought round, and Bracken did so. Ned Kelly put a halter on the horse, which he kept hold of, saying, "I can't trust you with a bridle, Bracken." Bracken said to Ned Kelly that had he not been ill in bed all day he (Kelly) would not have taken him easily, and that if the horse he was on was what it used to be, it would take more than Ned Kelly to keep him a prisoner. Ned Kelly and Byrne then mounted their horses, and I and my party got into the buggy.

It was then, I believe, between eleven and twelve o'clock. Ned Kelly then said I could go home and take my party with me. He directed me to "go quietly to bed, and not to dream too loud," and intimated that if I acted otherwise we would get shot, as one of them would be down at our place during the night to see that we were all right. I then left them and drove home, distant from the barracks one or two hundred yards, leaving the outlaws and their captives ready to start back to the railway station. As soon as we were out of hearing of the outlaws I announced to my wife and sister my intention to go to Benalla and give information as to the intentions and whereabouts of the outlaws. They both anxiously and earnestly opposed my purpose, saying that it was not at all likely that we should be allowed to come home unless some of the agents of the gang were watching; that I should not be able to reach Benalla, as I should be shot on the road by spies, and that, even if I succeeded, we should be hunted out and shot.

But at this point in Curnow's story I must make a break, in order that the sequence of events may not be disturbed; and to this end reference must be made to the movements of the police, who had been apprised of the re-appearance of the outlaws near Beechworth and the murder of Sherritt many hours before the events narrated by Curnow had taken place.

HOW THE SPECIAL TRAIN WAS SAVED.

The first news of Sherritt's murder appears to have been received in Melbourne on the Sunday afternoon by the Chief Secretary, who immediately communicated with Captain Standish, Chief Commissioner of Police, with whom he consulted. The result of that consultation was the decision to at once dispatch a special train with police to Beechworth—just what the outlaws expected would be done—previous experience having proved that if they allowed the Kellys to get a good start all the police in the country would not be able to come up with them, or even track them to their retreat. The Minister for Railways was informed of the decision arrived at, and within a short time a special train was placed at the disposal of the now restless authorities, the object being to get the black-trackers, who, as the reader will remember, had been withdrawn from the Kelly country, preparatory to returning to Queensland, back to Benalla, in order that they might accompany Superintendent Hare and the men under him to Beechworth. Word was sent to that officer that the special would arrive at Benalla shortly after midnight, and having gathered a company of police from the different stations Hare was prepared to join the special immediately upon its arrival, or run with it in another special containing his men, horses, ammunition, etc., to Beechworth—which station they expected to reach about four o'clock in the morning (Monday)—when men and horses would be unshipped and a start at once made for Sherritt's, where the black-trackers could pick up the tracks and follow the outlaws.

Before the special left the head station at Melbourne a party of five reporters connected with the city press had been told off for the journey in search of news. Owing to the engines being all cold when the call for the special was made a start was not effected until a quarter past ten; but once started, no time was lost on the road. At Essendon Inspector O'Connor and his five black-trackers were picked up, together with two ladies—Mrs. O'Connor and her sister—who seized the opportunity as a favourable one for an exciting run to Beechworth. It proved more exciting than the ladies anticipated or desired.

Benalla was reached at half past one o'clock, a delay having taken place on the road by the special running through a closed gate near Craigieburn.

Superintendent Hare was in waiting at the station with eight men and seventeen horses, and these having been "carriaged" for the hurried journey, a consultation was held as to the best mode of procedure—for rumours were already afloat that at some spot between that point and Beechworth the Kellys had been at work with dynamite, and had blown up portions of the line; and although all this appeared to be pure conjecture, both the railway officials and the police officers decided that every precaution should be taken to avoid falling into a trap. The moon was shining brightly at the time, and Superintendent Hare decided that one of the troopers should for the nonce be elevated to the position of advance guard; so arrangements were made for Constable Barry to be strapped to the brass rod which ran alongside the engine, and standing on the side-plate in front thus secured keep a constant lookout. But this plan was abandoned for a better. A spare engine on the station was utilised as a pilot, and was sent on in advance, the arrangement being made that it should keep at a distance of about a hundred and fifty yards in front of the train. Inspector O'Connor, Superintendent Hare, and the two ladies occupied one compartment, the five reporters another, and the police and trackers a third; and after a little delay a start was made, the intention being not to pull up until Wangaratta was reached, a station about twenty-three miles from Benalla, fourteen miles from Glenrowan, and about fifty miles from Beechworth.

The special had not gone more than about twelve miles, however, when the occupants, who were by this time settling down for the journey, were startled by a sudden stoppage.   In a moment they were all on the alert, making anxious inquiries as to the cause of the interruption. A shrill whistle from the pilot engine and the exposure of danger signals had caused the driver of the special to bring the train to a sudden stand, and no sooner had this been done than Superintendent Hare seized his rifle, clambered down from the carriage, and proceeded towards the pilot engine, which was also stationary on the line. On the way he met the guard, who was returning with a story both strange and startling. He said that as he was driving along he saw a red light on the line; pulling up to ascertain what it was, a man who said he was a schoolmaster had rushed forward and told him that Glenrowan was in the possession of the Kelly gang, who had torn up the line just beyond the station for the purpose of destroying the special when it came along. The man, he said, had refused to stop, and had disappeared into the forest as soon as he had delivered his sensational piece of information, saying that he must return to his wife, and could not even wait to see the superintendent. The news was soon imparted to the occupants of the special, who did not know how to accept it, as the man who had supplied it made off in a manner that was in itself suspicious. It was decided, however, to push on a little further, Glenrowan station being only about a mile distant, but to exercise the utmost care and keep even a more vigilant look-out. The five representatives of the press realised that they were on the border of sensational developments, and thinking that some stray bullets might find their way into their compartment if there was an engagement, they piled up the cushions of the carriage against the windows and extinguished the light. Calling three of his men, Superintendent Hare with them got on the pilot engine, and placed four other men on the engine of the special, both being coupled together, and half the men facing one side of the line and half the other side. In this way the train steamed slowly and almost noiselessly along, until they came to Glenrowan station, which they found in total darkness and without occupants.

Here again, however, I must make a break, in order that the remainder of Curnow's story may be given. His wife and sister, it will be remembered, stoutly opposed his purpose of giving warning to the police at Benalla—fourteen miles distant—on account of the risk to both themselves and him; but his mind was set upon the task, and this is his version of how he accomplished it :—

While the discussion was going on, and supper was being got ready, I quietly prepared everything, including the red llama scarf, candles, and matches, to go to Benalla, intending to keep as close to the railway line as I could, in case of the special coming before I could reach there. I declared to my wife that I did not intend to go by the road—that I meant to keep as close to the line as possible, in order to be safer. At last my sister gave way, but my wife worked herself into such an excited and hysterical state that she declared that she would not leave the house—that if I would go she would stay there, and she, the baby, and my sister would be murdered. I wanted to take them to my mother-in-law's farm, about one-third of a mile from my place, for safety while I was away. At length Mrs. Curnow consented to go to her mother's to obtain advice, and we were momentarily expecting the promised visit from one of the gang. I left the doors unlocked, and wrote a note, leaving it on the table, stating that we had gone to Mrs. Mortimer's to obtain medicine, as Mrs. Curnow was taken ill. My sister wore her red llama scarf at my request. When we got there Mrs. Curnow was exceedingly anxious to get home again, and would not stay there, and we went back. I succeeded in persuading Mrs. Curnow to go to bed, and my sister and I told her I had given up my project.

My sister engaged my wife's attention while I went out to harness my horse to go, for I could not rest, and felt that I must perform what was clearly my duty. I heard the train coming in the distance as I was harnessing my horse, and I immediately caught up the candle, scarf, and matches, and ran down the line to meet the train. I ran on until I got to where I could see straight before me some distance along the line, and where those in the train would be able to see the danger-signal. I then lit the candle and held it behind the red scarf.

As the guard's van got opposite me I caught sight of the guard, who shouted, "What's the matter?" I yelled, "The Kellys!" and the pilot engine then stopped a little past me, and the guard got down. I told the guard of the line being torn up just beyond the station, and of the Kelly gang lying in wait at the station for the special train of police. He said a special train was behind him, and he would go to the station and then pull up. I cried, "No, no; don't you do that, or you will get shot." He then said he would go back and stop the special, which was coming on. He asked me who I was, and I told him I was the school-teacher there, and requested him not to divulge who it was that stopped and warned him, as I was doing it at the risk of my life. He promised to keep my name secret. He asked me to jump in the van, but I declined, as my wife and sister were without protection. The pilot engine whistled several times while I was talking to the guard.

The pilot went back, and I hastened home and found Mrs. Curnow had been almost insane while I was stopping the train, and had been made worse by the whistling of the pilot engine. She would not leave the house after I had stopped the train, and we blew out the lights to seem to be in bed. My sister hid the red scarf and my wet clothes, and we were going to deny that it was I who had stopped the train, if one of the outlaws came down to us.

THE CONFLICT AT THE HOTEL AND CAPTURE OF NED KELLY.

As soon as the engine and special train had crept up to the station the order was given by the officer in charge, and the troopers, black-trackers, and press-men silently but swiftly took up their positions on the platform; but not a soul was to be seen—a circumstance which served to satisfy the police that there must be something in the schoolmaster's story. Observing a light in the stationmaster's house, about a hundred yards from the platform, Superintendent Hare told the men to keep a sharp lookout while he went over; and reaching the house he knocked at the window. Mrs. Stanistreet opened the door, but for a time was too hysterical to answer the question as to the whereabouts of her husband. At length, however, she gave Hare to understand that he had been taken over to Jones' hotel by Dan Kelly about ten minutes previously. Hare at once returned to the platform, and having told the men what Mrs. Stanistreet had said, he ordered the horses to be immediately taken from the train. But he had barely given the order when Constable Bracken rushed breathlessly up to the platform from the back and said that the bushrangers were over at the hotel, and unless the police went there immediately they would be gone, and further explaining that he had only just escaped from the hotel by a skilful piece of manœuvring. Seizing their arms and ammunition, and leaving the horses where they were, the whole of the party ran forward in the direction of the hotel, which by the path they followed was some two hundred yards distant. Hare was leading, and the men following as best they could, when their forward movement received a sudden check. They were within twenty paces of the hotel, which was in darkness, when they were greeted with a volley, evidently fired from the verandah full in their faces. Only one of the bullets, however, found its billet, and that was in Hare's left wrist, which it fairly shattered. It is not clear that the shot was intended for Hare, although it is natural that the outlaws from cover of the verandah should see the advantage of "winging" the leader; and, whether intended or not, it was very effectually done, for after returning the fire, in company with his men Hare had to retire from the field to the station, where one of the pressmen bound up his wounded wrist and stopped the hemorrhage. The attacking party were at a great disadvantage, for while they could not see the outlaws, who were under the verandah or near it, they were in the open, and in clear view, the moon not having yet gone down. The shot that struck the Superintendent was fired by Ned Kelly from about a yard in front of the verandah, and having fired he stepped back under the verandah, calling out to the police as they discharged their pieces, "Fire away, you beggars, you can't hurt us." For some minutes there was a rapid and continuous exchange of shots, and it was evident that the outlaws were using repeating rifles and revolvers. Before leaving to have his wounded arm bound up Superintendent Hare ordered his men to cease firing and surround the house, not getting too near or needlessly exposing themselves, for he noticed that the outlaws had gone inside, and from the shrieks of women and the cries of children proceeding from the hotel the police concluded that innocent persons were being injured by the bullets, which were penetrating the weatherboard walls of the building. Shortly after this the wounded Superintendent, who was becoming weak through loss of

xx

blood, placed Inspector O'Connor in charge of the police, and started on the return journey to Benalla on one of the engines to obtain surgical aid and to send more police.

Further particulars of this unique conflict may be given in the words of the special reporter of the Melbourne "Age," who was on the ground during the whole of the time.

A long and tedious interval followed, during which time Mr. Stanistreet, the station-master, suddenly left the hotel, where he had been kept prisoner with the other residents of Glenrowan. He walked boldly away, and had a narrow escape of being shot by the police, but he saved himself by proclaiming that he was the station-master. He reported that the gang were still in the house, and that the shots of the police had struck the daughter of Mrs. Jones, a girl fourteen years of age, on the head, whilst the son, a boy of nine years, was wounded on the hip. Very soon after this, painful, hysterical screams of terror were heard from Mrs. Jones and a Mrs. Reardon, both of whom were walking about the place, disregarding the danger to be feared from the volleys which the police, at short intervals, poured into the hotel. Mrs. Jones' grief occasionally took the form of vindictiveness towards the police, whom she called murderers. The police frequently called upon the women to come away, but they hesitated, and Mrs. Reardon and her son were afraid to accompany Mr. Stanistreet to the station. The poor woman was carrying a baby only a few months old in her arms, and she eventually ran to the station, where she received every kindness from the persons there assembled. She was then in a very terrified condition, and told the following story:—"My husband is a platelayer, employed on the railway, and we live about a mile from the station on the Benalla side. At three o'clock on Sunday morning we were all in bed. We were aroused by Ned Kelly, who knocked at the door and told my husband, when he opened it, to surrender. He advised us to dress, and I did so. They had also made a prisoner of Sullivan, another platelayer, and Kelly brought us to the station, where I was kept for some hours. Kelly took my husband and Sullivan down the line in order to tear up the line and destroy the train with the police. He was afterwards taken to the hotel. There are a lot of innocent people in there now, and they are frightened to come out, for fear the police will kill them. Amongst those who are in there are—James and Michael

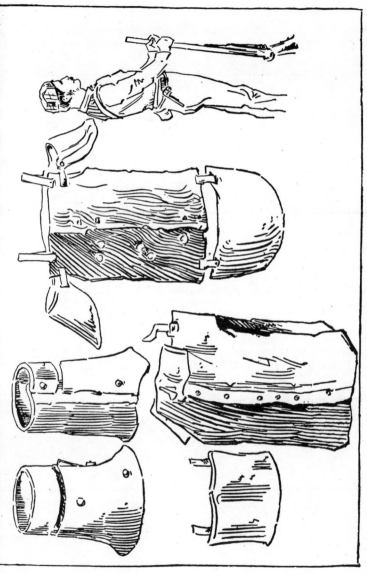

NED KELLY'S ARMOUR

Reardon, my husband and son; Catherine and William Reinson, John and Patrick Delaney (who are here coursing), W. S. Cooke (a labourer), Martin Cherry (a platelayer), John Larkins (a farmer), Edward Reynolds (the brother of the postmaster), Robert Gibbins, the brothers Meanliffe, and other strangers I do not know.

When the poor woman had completed her story, the firing of the police became very brisk, and it was replied to by the desperadoes in the hotel. Senior-constable Kelly at that juncture found a rifle stained with blood lying on the side of the hill, and this led to the supposition that one of the gang had been wounded, and had escaped through the forest towards Morgan's Look-out. Just then nine police with Superintendent Sadlier and Dr. Hutchinson came from Benalla; and almost immediately after seven policemen under Sergeant Steele arrived from Wangaratta. The alarm had been given there by Trooper Bracken, who caught a horse and rode the ten miles in a surprisingly short space of time. The conduct of Bracken and the promptitude of the Wangaratta police is to be highly commended. Just before their arrival a heavy volley was poured into the hotel by the police.

According to the statement of some of the prisoners, afterwards made, that volley proved fatal to Joe Byrne, who was standing close to young Delaney drinking a nobbler of whisky at the bar, when he was shot in the groin. He was then carried to the back of the building, where he gradually sank and died a painful death. This fact was unknown to the police.

The morning broke beautiful and clear. The police were disposed all round the hotel, when they were beset by a danger in the rear. Ned Kelly was the cause. It appears that he was the man who shot Mr. Hare, and he himself was wounded in the arm by the fire that was returned. He could not without danger get into the hotel, so he sprang upon his horse, and during the excitement which followed he got away towards Morgan's Look-out; but it was not the intention of the bold ruffian to desert his comrades, and he returned to fight his way to them. It was nearly eight o'clock when his tall figure was seen close behind the line of police. At first it was thought he was a blackfellow. He carried a grey coat over his arm, and walked coolly and slowly among the police. His head, chest, back, and sides were all protected with heavy plates of quarter-inch iron. When within easy distance of Senior-constable Kelly, who was watching him, he fired. The police then knew who he was, and Sergeant Steele Senior-constable Kelly, and Mr. Dowsett (a railway guard) fired on the ruffian. The contest became one which, from its remarkable nature, almost baffles description. Nine police joined in the conflict and fired point-blank at Kelly; but although, in consequence of the way in which he staggered, it was apparent that many of the shots hit him, yet he always recovered himself, and, tapping his breast, laughed derisively at his opponents, as he coolly returned the fire, fighting only with a revolver. It appeared as if he was a fiend with a charmed life.

For half an hour this strange contest was carried on, and then Sergeant Steele rapidly closed in on him, and when within only about ten yards of him fired two shots into his legs, which brought the outlaw down. He was only wounded, and appeared still determined to carry on the desperate conflict, but Steele bravely rushed him and seized the hand in which he held his revolver, the only weapon with which he was armed. He fired one shot after this, but without effect. When on the ground he roared with savage ferocity, cursing the police vehemently. He was stripped of his armour, and then became quite submissive, and was borne to the railway station by Sergeant Steele, Constable Dwyer, and two representatives of the Melbourne press.

. . . . At the railway station Kelly appeared to be very weak from loss of blood, and some brandy was given him. He was examined in the guard's van by Dr. Nicholson and Dr. Hutchinson, who found that he was suffering from two bullet wounds in the left arm, a bullet in the right foot near the right toe, and two wounds in the right leg, those inflicted by Sergeant Steele.

The outlaw was quite composed, and in answer to inquiries he made the following statement:—"What I intended to do, and in fact was just about doing, was to go down with some of my mates and meet the special train, and rake it with shot. The train, however, came before I expected, and I had to return to the hotel. I thought the train would go on, and on that account I had the rails pulled up, so that these —— black-trackers might be settled. It does not much matter what brought me to Glenrowan. I do not know, or I do not say. It does not seem much any way. If I liked, I could have got away last night. I got into the bush with my grey mare, and laid there all night. I had a good chance, but I wanted to see the thing end. When the police fired the first round I got wounded in the foot. It was the left one. Shortly afterwards I was shot through the left arm. It was in the front of the house where I received these injuries. I don't care what people say about Sergeant Kennedy's death. I have made my statement as to it, and if they don't believe me I can't help it. At all events, I am satisfied Scanlan was not shot kneeling. That is not true, as he never got off his horse. At the commencement of the affair this morning I fired three or four shots from the front of Jones' hotel, but I do not know who I was firing at. I only fired when I saw flashes. I then cleared for the bush, but remained there near the hotel all night. Two constables passèd close by me talking, and I could have shot them before they had time to shout if I liked. I could have shot several constables at one time. I was a good distance away, but I came back again. I have got a charge of duck-shot in my leg. Why don't the police use bullets instead of duck-shot? One of the policemen that was firing at me was a splendid shot; I don't know his name. Perhaps I would have done better if I had cleared away on my grey mare. It was just like blows from a man's fist receiving the bullets on my armour. I wanted to fire into the carriages, only the police started on us too quickly. I knew the police would come, and I expected them."

The policeman whom Ned Kelly described as "a splendid shot," was Constable James Arthur, and this is the account he gave of the encounter :—

I was one of the party of police which arrived at Glenrowan with the special train, and was just behind Superintendent Hare when he was shot; after that Hare asked Sergeant Kelly to place the men. He did so, and took me round to the north-western side of the hotel. We crawled under what shelter we could find. I paused behind a tree, about one hundred yards from the hotel. There was a bush close to the tree. I kneeled down to get a good look at the hotel, and in doing so I put my hand on a revolving rifle, which was covered with blood. A skull cap was close beside it. I was startled, and could not speak to draw attention. Sergeant Kelly picked it up, and formed the opinion that one of the outlaws had passed that way just previously, and hearing a sort of ringing noise listened, but could not see or hear anything. I have no doubt Ned Kelly was near. He told me afterwards he was. He said he could have shot both me and Kelly. I moved from that place to a log within eighty yards of the house, into which I commenced to fire. Sergeant Kelly left me there, and a bullet from the hut tore up the ground underneath my stomach. I consequently determined to go to another part of the log. It was very cold, and I filled my pipe to have a smoke. Just at daybreak I was in the act of lighting my pipe, when I heard Ned Kelly coming behind me. His extraordinary appearance so startled me that I let the pipe drop out of my mouth, and gazed at the strange object for a minute. not knowing but that it was a madman who had conceived the idea of storming the hotel with a nail-can on his head. I then said to him, "Go back you d——— fool, you will get shot." The figure replied, "I could shoot you sonny," and at that moment fired his revolver at me, but missed. He evidently was crippled, and did not take proper aim. We were then only between twenty and thirty yards apart. I levelled my Martini rifle, and fired at his helmet, thinking I would knock it off. It only staggered him slightly. An opening in the helmet looked like a huge mouth, and I fired at that and hit him again. He still came on. I fired a third shot at his body, and heard it hum off him. I was completely astonished, and could not understand what the object I was firing at was. The men around me appeared astonished too. Someone said, "He is a madman!" Dowsett, the railway guard, said, "He is the devil!" Sergeant Kelly exclaimed "Look out, boys, he is the bunyip!" At once I sought shelter, and tried to get round at the back. I did so because I found it was no use firing at him in front. Before I could succeed in doing so Sergeant Steele ran up from behind and shot him. When I shot at him first Sergeant Steele thought I had made a mistake, and called to me to stop firing. After he had been captured, Kelly shook his fist at me and swore.

Concerning the proceedings before and during the siege of the hotel, further particulars are obtained from a very succinct account given by Mr. Mortimer, Curnow's brother-in-law. After describing how Constable Bracken was arrested by Ned Kelly, he says:—

Byrne was with Kelly, and Curnow asked Ned if he would allow him to go home with his wife. Kelly replied "Oh, yes, you may go home and have a sleep, but mind you don't dream too loud." Having given this warning to him, he was permitted to go home. I do not know how he heard that the line had been torn up, but suppose he heard it at the hotel, and after he obtained his liberty he determined to warn the train of the danger. Reynolds, Bracken, and myself were taken back to the hotel. We all then heard that the line had been torn up. The whole of the members of the gang were very jolly, and Ned told us that he had come there to settle the black-trackers, and that he would be on the spot when the train run over the culvert, and would shoot all who were not killed. We knew that we could do nothing, and therefore did not take any steps to warn those on the train of their danger. Every member of the gang was then sober. They showed us their armour, and seemed to think the police could do them no harm. At half-past two on Monday morning, Ned Kelly said something to the effect that he did not think the special train was coming, and I then asked him if we could go home. He said "yes," and I thanked him. We could all then have gone, with perhaps the exception of Bracken, but we foolishly stopped listening to the remarks of Kelly. Just then, Dan Kelly, who had been standing outside, rushed in and said "Ned, here comes the ——— train." Our opportunity of escape was gone. Ned Kelly rushed out and commenced to examine his firearms. He spoke to one of the gang, and then left on horseback. Byrne locked the doors, and I believe that Bracken then succeeded in stealing the key. Ned Kelly returned in a few minutes, but remained outside. He asked some of the others to come out with him, but none of them did so. Just then we heard the train stopped at the station, and it became apparent that the gang expected that they would have to fight. Almost immediately the firing commenced, and we dropped on the floor. The bullets whizzed through the weatherboards in all directions, Our feelings at that time were indescribable. The poor women and children were screaming with terror, and every man in the house was saying his prayers. Poor little Johnny Jones was shot almost at once, and I put my fingers in my ears so as not to hear his screams of agony, and the lamentations of his mother and Mrs. Reardon, who had a baby in her arms. We could do nothing, and the bullets continued to whistle through the building. I do not think the police were right in acting as they did. We were frightened of them, and not of the bushrangers. It was Joe Byrne who cursed and swore at the police. He seemed perfectly reckless of his life. But the three of them got into an inside room into which the bullets seldom penetrated. We frequently called to the police to stop firing, but we dared not go to the door, and I suppose they did not hear us. Miss Jones was slightly wounded by a bullet, and when Mrs. Jones and Mrs. Reardon with the children ran out, Reardon and his son attempted to follow, but as soon as the police saw the figures one of the men fired. Young Reardon was hit by a bullet in the shoulder, and he and his father ran back into the house. One of the men carried young Jones away, and succeeded in passing the police without being fired on. Dan Kelly told us that we had better remain in the house, because the police would shoot us if we attempted to leave. Someone said to him, "You had better go out and surrender," and he replied, "We will never surrender, but most likely we will leave directly." I think they intended to do so, but shortly after five o'clock in the morning, Byrne was shot. He had just walked into the bar, and was drinking a glass of whisky, when a ball struck him in the groin. I heard him fall, and saw the blood spurting from him. I think he died very soon. This seemed to dishearten

Dan Kelly and Hart. They had been calling for Ned all night, and now renewed their calls for him. We had not seen the leader of the gang since the firing commenced, and did not know where he had gone to. Dan and Hart went into the inside room, and I heard one say to the other, "What shall we do?" I did not hear the reply; but Reardon said he thought they intended to commit suicide. We prayed for daylight, thinking that we might then escape, but even when morning broke, we dared not venture out. It must have been at this time that poor Martin Sherry was shot. He was sitting on the floor of the kitchen at the time. There were two other men with him, but they were protected by bags of oats, behind which they were sitting. During the morning, Dan Kelly told them that Ned Kelly had been shot. After that one of our company held a white handkerchief out of the door, and we all ran out. Poor Sherry could not move, and he was left behind. He was a decent, honest man.

In answer to the remark of one of the police that he must have wanted to kill the people in the train, Kelly replied, "Yes, of course I did. God help them, they would have got shot all the same. Would they not have tried to kill me?" This account accurately describes what took place up to the capture of Ned Kelly, but Sergeant Steele, in the story told by him, enters more into detail. He says:—

I arrived from Wangaratta with five men about 5 a.m. (Monday). We were at once challenged by the police, and answered "Wangaratta police." My men were then distributed around the hut, and I got to the tree near the back door of the hut (hotel). There was no firing then. A woman and child came to the back door screaming, and I told the woman if she ran in quick she would not be molested. A man then came to the door, and I told him to throw up his arms or I would fire on him. He was only about twenty-five yards distant. The man stooped and ran towards the stable, and I fired. He then turned and ran back to the house, and I fired again. I am certain I hit him with the second shot, as he screamed and fell against the door. There was then some hot firing, and the bullets whistled all round me. The firing was kept up for some time, and some of the men behind me called out. It was then breaking day. I looked round and saw a man stalking down. I thought he was a black-fellow, and called on the others to be careful. I then saw him present a revolver and fire at the police. I could see the bullets hitting him and staggering him for a moment, with no further effect. I therefore thought he had armour on, and determined to have a close shot at him. I ran towards him, and when within ten yards of him he saw me and turned round to fire at me. I then fired at his legs and he staggered, but he still tried to aim at me. I then fired the second barrel on his legs. We were then in the open. He fell, and cried, "I'm done, I'm done." I ran up to him then, and he again tried to shoot me, but I caught the revolver and pushed it down. I was behind him, and he could not turn on me quick enough to shoot me. Whilst I held the revolver away from me he fired the revolver. Senior-constable Kelly then came up and assisted me to secure him; so did O'Dwyer, and a host of others at once followed. We only found one revolver on him, and a bag of ammunition. We divested him of his armour. I was strained after the scuffle which ensued.

Senior-constable Kelly stated that he and Constable Arthur crawled towards the house during the earlier hours of the morning, and took a position behind a tree about fifty yards from the back door, where they kept watch and fired upon anyone they saw attempting to leave the hut. They saw four horses tied up at the back door ready saddled for use, and these they at once shot to prevent the escape of the outlaws. When Ned Kelly bore down upon them and began firing, the police at once gave all their attention to him, and at one time no less than ten rifles were pelting their bullets at his impenetrable breast. After he was captured the senior-constable asked him where the murdered Sergeant Kennedy's watch was, but he refused to say, declaring that he did not like to tell about it.

After his capture, the leader of the gang abandoned himself to the circumstances, and became very quiet, conversing with one and another of his captors in a calm matter-of-fact way. It was soon found that he was utterly disabled, having been shot in the left leg, left foot, and twice in the region of the groin, but no bullet had penetrated his armour, although it bore many indentations. Having had his wounds dressed by Doctor Nicholson, he was left at the station in charge of half-a-dozen constables, and there for once in his life went through the experience which the great men and mighty of the earth invariably have to undergo when visiting places where news-hunting reporters ply their calling—he was "interviewed." Every word that fell from his lips was looked upon as precious, and was hurriedly transferred to notebooks, to be worked up into a connected story for the different newspapers, which would have lost some of their best reporters had his designs upon the special train succeeded. While the constables kept guard and the reporters scribbled over the captured outlaw's couch, the officers returned to their positions near the hotel to superintend the attack upon the building, which was still proceeding, having learned from Ned Kelly that all his mates were still in the place with the crowd of men, women, and children whom they had taken there on the previous evening.

PROCEEDINGS WITHIN THE HOTEL.

It is necessary at this stage that the reader should know something of what transpired in the hotel after Constable Bracken had been taken prisoner and plucky Curnow had gone home with his women-folk; and I cannot do better than quote from the narrative given by one of the unfortunate prisoners who was compelled to share the dangers of injury or sudden death from the pelting bullets of the police during the long hours of the siege. Here is his story:—

About half-past one or two o'clock on Monday morning, the word went round that the Kellys were going to clear out, they having got sick of waiting for the train; at the same time they thought that perhaps the police had got word of their being there, and were going to surprise them from a different direction. The announcement that they were going away was received on all sides with evident satisfaction, as despite the rather novel experience, and the fun that we were most undoubtedly having, many, in fact, I may say all, were longing for a good sound sleep and a rest. Upon making enquiries from Ned Kelly as to whether the report was true or not, he said, "Yes, my boy" (he always addressed me familiarly), "we are off directly, and when we are gone you can clear out as soon as you like." I felt this rather comforting at any rate, and made arrangements to go home at once. When all was in readiness to go, and all waiting for them to clear out, Ned Kelly came out of the room where they had stacked all their accoutrements, and called out, "Everybody come into the dining-room; I have something to say, and want everybody to hear it." We all crushed in after him, wondering what it might be that he was going to say. After a few preliminaries, such as mounting a chair and getting off again, he proceeded:

"First, I wish to tell you all that if I should hear of any one of you present here to-night telling the police of any of our doings or sayings, or showing the way we left, or in fact telling anything whatever about us, I shall make it my duty to visit them some day and have a settling with them, and I can promise you that it will not be such a settling as I had this day with young Delaney there. I let him off, but, by God, I'll not let any more off the same way; so you know what to expect from me if any of you should let out any of our plans that you have heard here. I am not a bit afraid of the police, and know that if they alone hunted me I would never be taken; but what I am really afraid of is those d—— Queensland black-trackers; those boys I honestly fear, for I know what they can do; they can track me over bare stones, and a white man stands no chance with them at all; it was mainly to kill those —— that I tore up those rails down there, and in fact what brought me here. I knew very well that when they heard that we were down at Beechworth, they would pack those incarnate devils after us, and I was prepared to meet them, but only half way; I can't make out what has delayed that train, and think they must have taken a different route, but again I don't see how they are to get there, especially as they are not accustomed to the country. No, I think they have got information of our being here, and are leaving it till they are positive. Well, anyhow, let them come when they like; we are ready for them even now. I suppose some of you people would like to know what I have been doing lately, and how I have managed to escape capture so long. Well, I don't mind telling you a little. It can't do any harm, and it will pass away a few minutes. A lot of people imagine that after robbing the Euroa bank, and before sticking up the Jerilderie, that we were out of funds, and had to stick up the Jerilderie bank to supply ourselves. Nothing of the sort. I had no more intention of robbing the Jerilderie bank a fortnight before than I have now of flying. What brought us to Jerilderie was this. I was after that infernal scoundrel Sullivan that turned Queen's evidence in New Zealand. I heard that he came up the north-eastern, and was told of his being at Rutherglen. I followed him there, but he was too quick for me, and had gone on to Uralla. Up to Uralla we went, and found that he had gone to Wagga, and there we lost sight of him. We thought he had gone up Hay way from there, and consequently made for there, but abandoned the chase, and when coming home through Jerilderie it struck us to stick up the bank, which we did, as you all know. I don't know how much money we took away from either Jerilderie or Euroa, but a considerable deal more than they said in the papers. Anyhow, we lost sight of Sullivan, and I would sooner have met him than have robbed a dozen banks. I consider him to be one of the greatest villains unhung, and moreover the first time I come across him the Lord pity him. I won't shoot the hound—it is too good for such as he—but I will hang, draw, and quarter him—kill him by inches. I have not given him up yet, and will hunt the —— till I die. I will give £500 to the man who tells me where he is. I don't want to have him brought to me, only to be told where he is. I would follow him to England if I knew he was there. After coming down from Jerilderie I took a trip to Melbourne and bought some firearms—these revolvers and some Winchester rifles, besides as much ammunition as we wanted——"

Kelly's narrative was broken off rather short, as at this moment the shrill whistle of a train was distinctly heard a short distance from where we were. "By God!" exclaimed Kelly, "that b—— Curnow has deceived us!" and at once jumping down from his seat he hurried outside, and there mounting his horse he rode down to where the train was stopped, returning in a few minutes. He said, "Yes, Curnow has stopped the train and told the police, and they are now coming up here, so we must be ready. Dan," addressing his brother, "you keep your eye on these folk whilst we get ready, and then you can fix yourself up afterwards."

So saying, he led the others into their arsenal—if you can

call it such—and there they immediately put their armour on, and generally got themselves in readiness for the fray. We could hear the knocking of the armour and the smothered curses when a thing would not fit to their satisfaction. In a comparatively short space of time they emerged from the room clad in their sombre armour. This was the first time that I had seen the men in their "full dress," and the thought inwardly struck me that the police would stand a very poor show indeed when opposed to these desperate men, clad as they were in what seemed complete armour.

Whilst Dan Kelly was "doing his toilet" Ned gave us a bit of advice—viz., he ordered all the lights to be put out, the fire to be extinguished, and generally to make the place look as natural as possible; and he also told us that there would be some heavy firing, and the best thing we could do was to lie down as close to the floor as possible, and on no account try to escape, as by so doing we ran the double risk of being taken for one of the gang by the police, and for one of the police by some of the gang.

We heard the train slowly steam into the station, the officers giving orders, and the noise made by the horses getting out of the trucks, and then we could distinctly hear the police walk down the line to Mr. Stanistreet's house and ask some questions. Mrs. Stanistreet immediately told them that the Kellys were up in Jones' hotel, and had half the town with them, and then closed the door in their faces.

The excitement now waxed intense as we heard the police outside, in front of the hotel. After a delay of a few moments, one of the police called out to the Kellys—who were by this time arranged in a row on the verandah—to surrender in the Queen's name. "Surrender, be d——d!" they called out, rattling the points of their revolvers on their iron breasts, "you can shoot at us for six months and never hurt us."

The firing now began, but whether it was the police who began first or the Kellys I am not quite sure, as they seemed to begin together. Almost as soon as the firing began, we heard one of the Kellys exclaim, "My God, I'm shot." It turned out to be Ned, who was shot both in the elbow and in the foot; but the firing did not seem to abate at all, both sides keeping up a brisk cannonade, meanwhile all us poor unfortunates lying down full on our faces and expecting every minute to be the last, when the firing abated, which it did at intervals. At this time Constable Bracken effected his escape from the house and found the police, and it was well that he did so, as both Dan Kelly and Joe Byrne came in immediately after and made repeated inquiries as to where he was. Their object was, no doubt, to shoot him, as they both seemed to be in a terrible rage when they were convinced that he had escaped. I made an attempt to get away, thinking, and no doubt rightly, that it was a little safer a bit farther away, when I was met at the door by Joe Byrne, who asked me where I was going. I told him that I wanted to get away from the house. "Well," he said, "you can go if you like, but if you take my advice you will stop where you are; the place is surrounded with police, and ten to one they will take you for one of us and shoot you. Stop inside and you will be all right." Accordingly I went back again, though rather reluctantly, and had scarcely got inside when the firing began. Creeping on my hands and knees, I joined the others, and laid very low—very low indeed. There were about thirty or thirty-five in the room, not one of whom ever expected to get out alive. The position I occupied was just inside the parlour door against a couch, and in a good position should any chance arise of getting out. The bulk of those in the room were praying, and some few were sleeping, especially the young fellow who went asleep almost as soon as the firing commenced, and did not awaken till we were all leaving the place. However, again some of the more daring of those present got up and had a look outside, but only to be frightened back again by the shots which were being fired continually into the house by the police outside.

Young Reardon, who was lying next to me, feeling rather stiff from lying so long in one position, got up to turn round, and while doing so received a shot in his shoulder; he fell back moaning that he was killed, and calling on his father to come and see where the wound was. With the aid of a few matches we examined the wound; it seemed to be a revolver bullet that had struck him, the hole being a very small one. Of course we could do nothing for the poor fellow, and consequently he had to endure the pain. Almost immediately after young Reardon was shot, Mrs. Jones came running frantically into the room, crying and exclaiming that her son Jack was shot and was dying. She asked if there was a man in the room who would help her to carry him to bed. For a time nobody seemed to be anxious to run the risk of being shot to carry the boy to his bed. When Martin Cherry (who was afterwards shot dead himself) said to me, "Come on, lad, we'll carry him in." Accordingly Martin and myself followed Mrs. Jones to where her boy was, and taking him up we carried him to the back part of the house and laid him on the bed. The wound was a frightful one, and even to our unpractised eyes it was easily seen that he could not long survive it; the bullet went in his left hip, and travelling in an upward direction came out in his right side through the ribs. After doing all we could for the poor lad, we again retired to our place of safety—if it could be called such. The firing now seemed to be more intense: as a matter of fact more police had in the meantime come to the scene of action, and of course every new arrival, as soon as he got into position, fired as many shots as he possibly could into the unfortunate building, with the hope of killing the bushrangers; one of the shots struck the clock on the mantelpiece and started it striking. It struck, I suppose, about forty before I began to count them, and then I counted sixty odd, when another shot shattered it and laid the fragments on the floor. I am not at all superstitious as a rule, but this I will say, that I looked upon that clock striking as a sort of a death knell. One of those in the room, thinking the fire-place a safe retreat, accordingly got up it, but upon seeing one of the bricks displaced by a Martini-Henry bullet, changed his mind, and once more joined the crowd upon the floor.

There were numerous suggestions from different people in the room as to a means of escape, some suggesting that we should all make a rush to the door, and, holding up onr hands, call out to the police for protection. This seemed to savour of too much danger to the majority, and was abandoned. One daring individual suggested that we should borrow some arms from the Kellys and retaliate on the police. This again did not meet with much favour; and I question very much if the individual referred to was game enough to attempt it, should anyone be ready to join him. I forget the time exactly, but think it was about six o'clock in the morning, that Joe Byrne came into the room and asked how we were getting on. Several appealed to him to get them away, but he said, "Stop where you are; you are a great deal better off than we are." He then went into the bar for the purpose, I think, of having a drink. Almost immediately I heard a dull thud, and turning around saw him lying at full length on the floor. He was the first of the gang to fall. The wound he received must have proved fatal in a few minutes after receiving it. He was lying about four feet from where I was situated, and his presence there did not in any way tend to reassure me as to our own individual safety.

About an hour after Byrne paid the penalty of his crimes, someone in the room heard the police calling out to us, and on listening attentively we heard someone outside calling out that all civilians would be allowed ten minutes to get out. When it was explained to everybody that we were allowed a time to get away, some of them were so much terrified that they would not agree to it, saying that we were almost sure to be killed if we attempted to leave the place.

"Well," I said, "We may as well be shot outside as in, and I for one am going," and so saying I got up, and rushing to the door, which I opened, made at once for a covered spot

which I knew of in front of the hotel. The example being
set, the rest soon followed, and on making their appearance
were called upon by the police to hold up their hands, and
when they had got a short distance away from the hotel they
were told to lie down on the ground and hold up their hands.
In the meantime I had separated from the rest, and continuing
my run, jumped into the drain inside the railway inclosure.
As it happened I had jumped fairly into the midst of Inspector
O'Connor's detachment of black-trackers, who, immediately
on seeing me, closed around and, presenting their revolvers
to my head, called upon me to surrender. I explained, as
well as I could under the circumstances, that I was not a
bushranger, and seeing O'Connor, appealed to him.   He
released me from his men, and, instead of letting me go to
some place of safety, made me go back the way I had come
and join the rest, who by this time were lying on the ground,
and being examined by the police. Accordingly I passed in
front of the hotel again, and joined my comrades.

We were examined one by one by the police, and then
allowed to take our own course. Naturally I made for the
railway station, where there seemed to be a crowd, and was
at once seized upon by reporters, who wanted to know what
had passed inside. After satisfying these, I asked for something to eat, as it must be remembered that we had fasted
for nearly twenty-four hours. The police were pretty well
provided in the line of refreshments, and after satisfying the
inner man I went round to the back part of the station buildings to see Ned Kelly, whom I had heard was captured before
we had got out of the house. Coming into the room I saw
him lying on his back on a stretcher, guarded by about six
troopers. He seemed to be covered with blood, and looked
very downhearted. I stood looking at him for a time, and
was about to turn away, when he turned round and, looking
me full in the face, said, "Well, I'm done for now, old man;
my race is run," and, falling back, seemed to go in a sort of
faint. I left the room then, and, mingling with the crowd,
waited the advent of further excitement. We had not to wait
long, as the police, directly all the civilians had left the
premises, commenced firing from all points into the hotel,
with the hope of shooting the two surviving bushrangers.
Byrne they knew was dead, for we told them that after getting
out. Some idea of the amount of shooting that now took
place may be gained when you consider that about forty-five
or fifty police, each armed with a breech-loading rifle, were
firing as quickly as they could into all parts of the house.
Whilst the civilians were in the hotel the police had orders
to fire high, but now the order was to fire where you liked,
and there is no mistake about it they did fire where they liked.

For a short time a few answering shots were heard from the building, but these soon relapsed, and for a long time before the place was set on fire no shots were heard from the inside.

The prisoners of the outlaws must have spent a terrible time in the hotel during the firing, and the marvel is that they were not, everyone of them, riddled by the bullets that poured through the windows and boarded walls of the place. It was a terrible risk they ran, and not a little obloquy was cast upon the police for what many persons considered reckless firing—endangering the lives of thirty persons in order to shoot three. For some of their subsequent proceedings also the police were soundly rated by the Melbourne press, as they were considered both injudicious and unnecessary.

HOW HART AND DAN KELLY FELL.

Up to this point two of the outlaws have been accounted for—Ned Kelly lying bound at the railway station, and Byrne lying dead in the hotel. During the morning, and before the terror-stricken men and women had escaped from the hotel, more police arrived from the districts surrounding, most of the residents of the district living within sound of the firing having also gathered at the spot to witness the extraordinary conflict. Amongst these were not a few of the outlaws' relatives and friends including one notorious sympathiser named Wild Wright, and one of the sisters of the Kellys—Mrs. Skillian, who was dressed in a dark riding habit trimmed with scarlet, and wearing a jaunty hat adorned with a conspicuous white feather.

Amongst those who left the hotel were two youths named McAuliffe, and when the police were

examining the small crowd one by one, preparatory
to giving them permission to leave, these two were
taken into custody on suspicion of being Kelly sympathisers. They were handcuffed and sent up to the
railway station for safe keeping. Young Reardon,
who was severely wounded in the shoulder while in
the hotel by a bullet fired from one of the rifles in the
hands of the attacking party, was also sent up to the
station for treatment by the doctors there.

Meanwhile a close watch was being kept upon
the hotel, as it was feared that the two outlaws who
were still alive might make a rush and get away; and
a constant fire was kept up by the police, some of
whom took up sheltered positions quite close to the
building. For a time the fire was returned by the
outlaws, but shortly after midday that firing ceased,
and the attacking party thought that the outlaws had
decided to keep quiet until darkness set in and then
endeavour to make their escape. How to bring
matters to a climax appeared to be a problem which
the officers in command of the police had some difficulty in solving. They were afraid to rush the place,
having good reason to believe that lives would be
sacrificed in the assault, and to continue firing as they
had been was simply a waste of ammunition. At last
an inspiration came to the authorities in Melbourne,
and they decided to make use of heavier metal than
ordinary rifle bullets. They would blow the house
down, using one of the heavy pieces of ordnance in
Melbourne for that purpose. Accordingly a third
special was started from Melbourne for Glenrowan,
having on board a detachment of artillery under

Colonel Anderson, and a 12-pounder field-piece and ammunition sufficient to blow a hole through the wall of a fortified city. Further than this, the Colonial Secretary also advised by telegram that a wooden bullet-proof shield should be constructed to be fitted on a dray or waggon, under cover of which the attacking party might approach sufficiently near the building to ensure its destruction by the broadside that should be poured into it. And still further did the Chief Secretary go, so determined was he to do the thing effectually. Fearing that darkness might set in before the cannon could be brought to bear upon the wooden tenement, he communicated with Mr. Ellery, Government Astronomer of the colony, asking his advice as to the practicability of sending to the seat of war an electric-light apparatus to preserve the continuity of the besiegers' work; but that gentleman discountenanced the project, explaining that even if the apparatus were placed on the ground it would take quite twenty-four hours to get into fair working order. Then Mr. Ramsay fell back upon a more primitive method, and by wire suggested to the men in command on the ground that huge bonfires should be lighted round the hotel when night set in, the light from which would serve a double purpose— preventing the escape of the outlaws and showing clearly to the gunner the object at which he should aim. It is creditable to the great mind that could plan the details of a destructive attack so cleverly that he could think of the possibility of other lives being sacrificed in the blowing-down process, and issue orders that before shooting the

destructive bolt care should be taken to ascertain that
the only occupants of the building were members of
the gang.

But as it turned out, none of these carefully
planned and elaborately offensive movements were
needed. Before the 12-pounder had reached Benalla
the Glenrowan citadel had been effectually stormed,
and the uncaptured outlaws—or all that remained of
them—were in the hands of the police. How the
storming was accomplished may be briefly told.

While the instruments in the telegraph offices
were clicking out their messages to and from headquarters, the officers in charge of the attacking party
had decided upon a plan of their own for dislodging
the outlaws. They would set fire to the building and
burn it over the outlaws' heads, so that they would
either have to run from their shelter and be shot or
captured, or remain under the roof and be roasted.
They remained and were roasted.

There were about two hundred people at the railway station when this plan was conceived, some of
them having been passengers by the ordinary midday
through train from Melbourne, who had elected to
make a break in the journey at Glenrowan when they
discovered the startling developments that were there
taking place. Amongst these arrivals was Rev. M.
Gibney, Roman Catholic priest, of Perth, West Australia, who had been travelling through Victoria.
Having heard on the road that the Kelly gang were
at Glenrowan and that a desperate fight was going on
between the outlaws and the police, he left the train
when it reached the station, thinking that he might be

of use in his clerical capacity. When he learned that Ned Kelly was at the station dangerously wounded, he proceeded at once to the room where the outlaw was lying and spoke to him in private. He says he found the wounded man very penitent, and when he asked him to say "Lord Jesus, have mercy on me," he repeated the words most reverently and added "It is not to-day I began to say that." Believing him at the time to be in a dying state, Father Gibney heard his confession and then anointed him; after which he proceeded to watch the storming party at work. He was with the police when Mrs. Skillian arrived on the scene, and he earnestly requested her to go to the hotel and persuade her brother and Hart to surrender; but she replied that although she would like to see her brother before he died, she would sooner see him burned in the house than ask him to surrender. Shortly after this the police made arrangements for burning down the hotel.

Senior-constable Johnson, having been authorised by Superintendent Sadlier to fire the house, visited one of the houses near and obtained a bundle of straw and a bottle of kerosene. He then pretended to the people about the railway station that he was going to feed the horses in the railway paddock. He accordingly went down in that direction, entered the bush, and made a detour round to the other side or end of the hotel. In his peregrination, and when passing round the other side of the rise beyond the hotel, he came across four men fully armed with guns and revolvers. He recognised none of them. Certainly they were not policemen, and the conclusion arrived at was that they were sympathisers waiting for an opportunity to assist the gang. Johnson saw at once that they were not friends, so he put the evasive question to them "Did you see two horses (a

SKETCH PLAN OF GLENROWAN

1. McDonald's Hotel.
2. Half-a-mile from this spot the rails were torn up.
3. Railway Station.
4. Station-master's House.
5. Platelayers' Tents.
6. Trench (Lieut. O'Connor and black tracker's post).
7. Positions taken up by the police.
8. Jones' Hotel.
9. Outhouse.
10. Paddock where horses were shot.
11. Road to Bracken's Station.
12. Spot where Mr. Hare was shot.
13. Tree where Ned Kelly was captured.

grey and a brown) pass here recently?" They replied in a surly manner that they had not, and he passed on down to the hotel. Rapidly approaching the building he placed the straw against the weatherboards, threw on the kerosene, and applied a lighted match, his companions meanwhile keeping up a heavy fire upon the place from the front and rear, in order to divert the attention of the outlaws from Johnson's proceedings.

The fire speedily gained a hold upon the building, and in a very short time the flames were playing right up to the roof. But still the outlaws made no sign, and the police and spectators began to ask each other wonderingly: "Are they dead? or, have they escaped? or, do they mean to stay there till they're roasted?" And at this moment a startling cry was raised—"Old Martin Cherry is still in the house!" Such was the case. In the rush from the hotel none of the other prisoners had given a thought to him in their anxiety to escape; and after that no opportunity had presented itself for him to leave the hotel, even if he had been able, for during the firing earlier in the day he had been badly wounded. The reader may imagine the feeling of horror that ran through the crowd at the thought that the helpless old man must die in the flames with the outlaws whose death the police were bent on compassing.

As the fire rapidly spread, and it was seen that the whole building would soon be enveloped in flames, the excitement among the crowd increased. Kate Kelly now came upon the scene and joined her sister, wailing in accents of deepest grief, "Oh, my poor, poor brother!" Then Mrs. Skillian rushed forward, declaring that she would see Dan before he died, and was rapidly making her way to the burning building when the police ordered her back. And at this juncture Father Gibney stepped forward and expressed his determination of saving Cherry if the old man was still alive. Holding the crucifix aloft, and amid the cheers of the crowd, the brave priest walked rapidly up to the door of the burning building, and was soon lost to view amidst the dense smoke. A moment later the whole structure appeared to burst into a blaze, masses of flame rushing out from the sides and the roof simultaneously. A shout of horror went up from the crowd, and a simultaneous movement was made towards the burning pile. Several policemen and others ran to the rear of the house, and rushed into the building through the back door; and shortly afterwards they emerged with Father Gibney in their midst, bearing in their arms the old man Cherry, who was in a dying condition, and the body of Joe Byrne.

By this time very little doubt remained concerning the fate of Dan Kelly and Hart. That portion of the hotel in which they were was burning most fiercely, and it was concluded that they must be dead. The fact was made plain when some of the rescue party affirmed that they had seen the forms of the two outlaws prostrate in the burning room, but had not been able to get to them. There was nothing for it, therefore, but to stand and wait until the fire had burnt itself out. Then a sickening sight presented itself. From the smouldering embers were raked out the two charred skeletons of Dan Kelly and Steve Hart. How they had died could not be ascertained, and the spectators were left to conjecture whether they had been shot down by the police during one of the heavy fusilades or been suffocated by the smoke and heat, or whether each had shot the other or himself. The mystery has not been and never in this world will be cleared up. The bodies presented a horrible spectacle—nothing but the trunk and skull being left, and these almost burnt to a cinder. Their armour was found lying by their side, and although there was nothing about the remains to lead to their identification, the presence of the armour and other circumstances rendered doubt as to the identity of the dead men impossible. And the fact of the armour having been removed before death lends colour to the supposition that in their last spirit of desperation they took off the iron, so as to allow their own shots to take effect.

As to Byrne's body, it was found in the entrance to the bar-room, which was on the east side of the house, and there was time to remove it from the building, but not before the right side was slightly scorched. The body likewise presented a dreadful appearance. It looked as if it had been ill-nourished. The thin face was black with smoke, and the arms were bent at right angles at the elbows, the stiffened joints below the elbows standing erect. The body was quite stiff, and its appearance and the position in which it was found, corroborated the statement that Byrne died early in the morning. He had a ring on his right hand, which had belonged to Constable Scanlan, who was murdered by the gang in the Wombat Ranges. The body was dressed in a blue sac coat, tweed striped trousers, crimean shirt, and very ill-fitting boots. Like Ned Kelly, Byrne wore a bushy beard.

Poor old Cherry, who had been too severely wounded to leave the house when the others did, was found by Father Gibney in an outer room at the rear of the building, and was dying when carried out. He was promptly removed to a short distance from the burning hotel, and laid on the ground, when Father Gibney administered to him the last sacrament. Cherry was insensible, and barely alive. He had evidently suffered much during the day, and death released him. He was born at Limerick, Ireland, and was sixty years old, was unmarried, was an old resident in the district, and was employed as a plate-layer, and resided about a mile from Glenrowan.

While the house was burning, some explosions were heard inside. These were alarming at first, but it was soon ascertained that they were cartridges bursting, and no damage was done by them. All that was left standing of the hotel were two brick chimneys, the lamp post, and the signboard, and these served for many days afterwards as forcible reminders to every traveller on the railway that the place they were passing had been the scene of a conflict unique in the history of Australia. The black ashes were covered in part by the sheets of corrugated iron that had formed the roof. The iron was pierced by innumerable bullet and slug holes, and on the chimneys also were a number of bullet marks, showing how fierce and constant the firing of the attacking party had been. The wrecks of two iron bedsteads, a sewing machine, and a few tin cans, some of which bore shot marks, were the only recognisable objects in the debris.

After the house had been burned, Ned Kelly's three sisters and Tom Wright were allowed an interview with him at the station. Tom Wright, as well as the sisters, kissed the wounded man, and a brief conversation ensued, Ned Kelly having to a certain extent recovered from the exhaustion consequent on his wounds; at times his eyes were quite bright, and, although he was of course excessively weak, his remarkably powerful physique enabled him to talk rather freely. During the interview he stated:—"I was at last surrounded by the police, and only had a revolver, with which I fired four shots; but it was no good. I had half a mind to shoot myself. I loaded my rifle, but could not hold it after I was wounded. I had plenty of ammunition, but it was no good to me. I got shot in the arm, and told Byrne and Dan so. I could have got off, but when I saw them all pounding away I told Dan I would see it over and wait until morning.

"What on earth induced you to go to the hotel?" inquired a spectator.

"We could not do it anywhere else," replied Kelly, eyeing the spectators, who were strangers to him, suspiciously. "I would," he continued, "have fought them in the train, or else upset it, if I had the chance. I did not care a —— who was in it, but I knew on Sunday morning there would be no usual passengers. I first tackled the line, and could not pull it up, and then came to Glenrowan Station."

"Since the Jerilderie affair," remarked a spectator, "we thought you had gone to Queensland."

"It would not do for everyone to think the same

way," was Kelly's reply. "If I were once right again," he continued, "I would go to the barracks and shoot everyone of the —— traps, and not give one a chance."

Mrs. Skillian to her brother: "It's a wonder you did not keep behind a tree?"

Ned Kelly: "I had a chance at several policemen during the night, but declined to fire. My arm was broken the first fire. I got away into the bush and found my mare, and could have rushed away to beggary, but wanted to see the thing out, and remained in the bush."

A sad scene ensued when Wild Wright led Mrs. Skillian to the horrible object which was all that remained of her brother Dan. She bent over it, raised a dirge-like cry, and wept bitterly. Dick Hart applied for the body of his brother, but was told he could not have it until after the post-mortem examination.

Subsequently the charred remains of the two outlaws were taken to MacDonnell's hotel, and here Dick Hart, the brother of Steve, openly dared the police (who were not present) to interfere in any way with the funerals, declaring that if they wanted the bodies back they would have to fight for them. Later on they were removed to Mrs. Skillian's hut at Greta, and their arrival caused great excitement in the town among the numerous friends and relatives of the Kelly family residing in the locality. They were laid out on a table in the hut, which was soon crowded. So great was the rush that Mrs. Skillian lost her temper, and, seizing a gun, hustled the crowd out, and then allowed them to view the remains in couples. Many of the male sympathisers were armed, and, whilst in a drunken state, professed to be anxious for a brush with the police. One of the relatives of the Kellys held up his hand over the remains and swore to Kate Kelly that he would be revenged for the slaughter of the gang. His name was subsequently given to the police. Lest any disturbance should take place in the district whilst the sympathisers were in this state of intoxication and excitement, Senior-constable Kelly and four troopers were sent on again to Glenrowan, and remained there some time; but beyond a little bluster, nothing occurred to warrant direct interference. The police were quite satisfied with what had been done in the direction of breaking up the gang; and having killed three of the principals and secured the fourth, ready for the hangman's rope if he should recover from his wounds, they were disposed to pass over much that the gang's sympathisers might say and do. No inquest was held upon these bodies, the police considering that it was wiser not to interfere until the excitement had cooled down.

An inquest was held upon Byrne's body, but the proceedings were conducted so quietly that no one knew of the affair until it was over, and there were only two or three persons in the court house, where the inquiry was held. The inquiry was of a purely formal character, and a verdict of justifiable homicide was returned.

Old Cherry's body was interred quietly at Benalla on the following Tuesday, as also was Byrne's body, the police undertaking the interment of the latter, much against the wish of Byrne's friends, who applied for the remains to be handed over to them, but met with a refusal, the reason of which was not clearly stated. During the forenoon the body of Byrne was brought out of the lock-up, where it lay, and slung up in an erect position on the outside of the door, the object being to have it photographed by an enterprising artist from Melbourne. The features were composed in a natural way, and were easily recognised. The face was small, with retreating forehead, blue eyes, the upper lip covered with a downy moustache, and a bushy beard covering his chin, whilst his hair had been recently cut. His figure was that of a tall, lithe young fellow. The spectacle, however, was very repulsive. The hands were clenched and covered with blood, whilst blood also covered his clothes. The police soon had the body removed from the public gaze. The officers, policemen, trackers, and civilians who were there at the barracks, and who were present at the encounter, were also photographed in a group.

During the day Detective Ward proceeded to Glenrowan, and on making some inquiries, discovered five of the horses of the gang stabled at Macdonnell's Railway Hotel, which stood on the east side or the line opposite the scene of the fight. They had evidently been fasting ever since they had been stabled there, which of course was on the arrival of the gang two days before. Why Mr. Macdonnell did not give voluntary information to the police concerning the horses was not explained. The horses were all brought to Benalla, and two of them were identified as having been stolen within the previous fortnight from

Mr. Ryan's farm on the Major Plains. One of the two was ridden by Joe Byrne when he committed the murder of Sherritt, at the Woolshed, near Beechworth, on the Saturday. A third was recognised as a pack-horse belonging to Mr. Fitzsimmons, of Benalla, and was stolen from his farm, near Greta, about twelve days before. Ned Kelly's grey mare was also caught, and brought on to Benalla. On one of the horses was found one of the Government saddles taken from the police horses on the occasion of the Mansfield murders. It may be here mentioned that the gang brought the pack-horses with them for the purpose of carrying their armour.

All the members of the gang were comfortably clad and wore boots which were evidently made to order. Ned Kelly had riding-boots, which showed well how he prided himself on having neat feet. When the doctor was dressing his wounds the boots had to be cut off, and it was found that he wore no socks. The gang all had the appearance of being well fed, and Byrne stated to one of their prisoners that they had always lived well, but that the want of sleep, which they had often to endure, was very trying.

NED KELLY'S TRIAL AND CONVICTION.

Wounded so badly as he was, most of those who saw Ned Kelly concluded that he would not live to go to trial; but he was a man of remarkably strong physique, and by skilful nursing his health was again built up, in order that the law might have its full exercise in his formal trial, conviction, and execution.

On the evening of his capture he was carefully removed to Benalla, where the authorities had better

zz

means of guarding him and attending to his wants; and as it was thought desirable to get him away as quickly as possible from the locality where relatives and sympathisers abounded, lest those friends and sympathisers might make an attempt to rescue him from the police, arrangements were made to remove him to Melbourne without delay. On the Tuesday morning, June 29, therefore, at about eight o'clock, a spring cart emerged from the local police barracks, and was driven down the street at a slow pace. It was accompanied by eight armed policemen on foot, and the curiosity of the townspeople was naturally excited as to what the vehicle contained. A peep over the side showed that inside, on a stretcher; lay the wounded outlaw. The police were conveying him to the railway station, and were all fully armed. On the arrival of the train, Kelly was carried carefully to the guard's van, and laid on the floor. Miss Lloyd, cousin of the outlaw, was the only relative present, and as the train left she cried without restraint. It was understood that he was to be conveyed to the hospital of the Melbourne Gaol. Just before Ned Kelly was taken away from Benalla, Senior-constable Kelly had a short interview with him, in his cell. The senior-constable said, "Look here, Ned, now that it is all over, I want to ask you one question before you go, and that is— Did you shoot Constable Fitzpatrick, at Greta, when he went to arrest your brother?" The prisoner replied, "Yes, I did; I shot him in the wrist, and the statements which have been made that Fitzpatrick inflicted the wound himself are quite false." This, it will be seen, bore out the statements made by Fitzpatrick, and subsequently by Kelly's sister. It will be remembered that the shooting of Fitzpatrick was the original cause of Ned and Dan Kelly taking to the bush. The senior-constable also talked with the outlaw about the police murders. He told him that Mrs. Kennedy had telegraphed to know whether he had got a letter for her from her murdered husband. Ned Kelly replied that he had got no letter from Sergeant Kennedy, and that Kennedy never uttered a word after he was brought down, except "God forgive you." "I shot him," continued the outlaw. "He kept firing all the time, running from tree to tree, and tried to kill Byrne until his ammunition was done."

After an affecting parting with his sisters at Benalla, Kelly left by the ordinary train for Melbourne. On the journey to Melbourne he maintained a very reticent and sullen demeanour, answering any questions which were put to him very gruffly. At each station on the road there was a great rush of people anxious to obtain a glimpse of him, and on being asked by Senior-constable Walsh if he had any objection to their crowding round the van and looking in, he replied that he had none. He seemed much refreshed by his sleep on the previous night. Dr. Ryan was very attentive, and many times during the journey attended to his wounds and administered stimulants to him. As soon as it became known that the notorious outlaw would arrive by the ordinary train from Benalla, a crowd gathered; but the police cleared the platform and yards, and the people congregated in the street, climbing on all stationary vehicles and to the windows of the houses opposite the station, in the hope of being able to obtain a good view of what was expected to occur. They were all disappointed, however, for it had been decided previously that he should not be taken from the train at that place. About fifty persons only had gathered at the North Melbourne station, and at two o'clock the ordinary train from the north-east steamed in. There were two brake-vans attached to it, the wounded outlaw being in the last one, lying on a pile of mattresses, and surrounded by about a dozen armed policemen. The well-guarded prisoner looked terribly emaciated, his spare countenance being rendered more wan by the terrible bruises with which it was covered—the effects of the bullets which struck the helmet he wore when he had the fight with the police. His utter helplessness was apparent at a glance, and as he lay on the floor of the van there was something horribly pitiful in his appearance. The crowd quickly surrounded the van, but the police soon cleared a passage. A stretcher was handed in, and the outlaw was placed upon it. Mattresses were then placed on a four-wheeled vehicle which stood outside the reserve, and he was carried on the shoulders of the policemen thither. Very little time was lost in placing him comfortably in the trap, but there was ample opportunity for the people to gratify their morbid curiosity; and the lower portion of the assembly did so, the while giving expressions to exclamations of pity. Then instructions were given to drive on, and the vehicle, followed by several others, proceeded up to Victoria-street, and thence to Melbourne gaol; and along all the line the city folk rushed to the doors as the escort passed, hoping to catch sight of the man whose deeds of daring and of blood had sent more than one thrill of horror through the community. Near the gaol an immense crowd of people was gathered, and an attempt was made to raise a cheer, but it was a very feeble one. No stoppage was made, and the large gates having been thrown open for the purpose, the cavalcade passed in and the gates were again closed. Precautions had been taken to guard against a rush by sympathisers and friends of the outlaw, a strong body of police being in attendance, but nothing of that kind was attempted. Within the gaol Kelly was received by the governor of the institution, Mr. Castieau; some warders and prisoners removed him from the cab to the hospital, where he was at once placed upon a water bed, which had been prepared for his reception. Dr. Shields, the medical officer of the gaol, was immediately communicated with, and on his arrival he took charge of the case. The Rev. P. J. Aylward was also permitted to see Kelly, and that gentleman kindly undertook to acquaint Mrs. Kelly, the mother of the bushranger, of the fate of Ned and his brother. He had not far to go to find her, for she was still in gaol, the sentence passed upon her for the part she had taken in the assault upon Constable Fitzpatrick in 1878 not having expired.

As a matter of fact, Mrs. Kelly had already been informed of the result of the Glenrowan attack, and had then stated that she was not at all surprised, as on the Saturday night she had dreamed that there had been a collision between the police and the gang, and that the "Bobbies" had been victorious. When she heard that "her boy Ned" was in the gaol hospital she manifested the greatest anxiety to see him. It was not deemed wise to allow the interview for a couple of days, but as soon as Ned Kelly had gained a little strength the request of Mrs. Kelly was complied with, and the meeting between mother and son took place, the governor of the gaol being present during the interview. Mrs. Kelly was allowed to remain with her son for nearly half an hour, and was very reluctant to leave him, until she was promised that another opportunity of seeing him would be afforded to her after he had been restored to a better state of health.

The imprisoned outlaw continued to improve, but several weeks elapsed before he was sufficiently recovered to be brought before the police court. He gave his guardians very little trouble, and in the matter of good behaviour under discipline he was a model prisoner. At last Dr. Shields, the visiting surgeon at the gaol, who had been in constant attendance upon him, announced that he was quite fit to undergo the ordeal of preliminary trial, and arrangements were at once made for his removal to Beechworth, that place having doubtless been chosen for the initial proceedings on account of its contiguity to the scene where the outrage with which he was to be charged occurred.

To Beechworth, therefore, he was taken by train, the guard's van having been made comfortable for him, he being still unable to walk, in consequence of the wound in his foot and groin. The journey was accomplished in safety, and so secretly that only the few people who were on the platform at the Beechworth Station on other business became aware of the fact that such a distinguished traveller was on board. Before the case had been called on at the court, however, the public had been made aware of the proceedings about to take place, and shortly after the doors were opened the court was crowded, the galleries being filled with ladies. Kelly was conveyed to the court house secretly in a cab at eight o'clock a.m., and was kept in one of the rooms until the court opened at eleven o'clock, when he was carried into the dock and placed on a chair in full view of the crowd assembled.

The charge preferred was the murder of Constables Lonerigan and Scanlan at Stringy Bark Creek, on 26th October, 1878. Three legal gentlemen appeared for the Crown—Messrs. Smith, Chomley, and Garner—and one for the defence—Mr. D. Gaunson. An effort was made by the latter to obtain a remand for a week, but the Bench refused to grant the application, as they did also an application for Kelly's relations to see the prisoner.

During the trial it was elicited that for a short time there was a fifth man in the gang, but that he was tried and it was found he would not do, and after being allowed to go was kept under strict surveillance. It also transpired that the armour worn by the outlaws was made near Greta. As previously stated, this armour was of a most substantial character. It was made of iron a quarter of an inch thick, and consisted of a long breast-plate, shoulder-plates, back-guard, and helmet. The helmet resembled a nail-can without a crown, and with a long slit at the elevation of the eyes for the wearer to look through. All the articles were believed to have been made by two men, one living near Greta and the other near Oxley. The iron was procured by the larceny of plough-shares, and larcenies of this kind having been rather frequent just previous to that time in the Kelly district, the police had begun to suspect that the gang were again preparing for action, although they could not understand what they and their friends could want with this part of the most commonly used implement of agriculture. Ned Kelly's armour alone weighed ninety-seven pounds—a not by any means inconsiderable weight for an ordinary man to carry. After it was taken off him five bullet marks were found in the helmet, nine on the back-plate, and one on the shoulder-plate; but these marks may not have been made by the police, for it was elicited during the trial that after the armour was made it was tested by firing ball at it from a distance of twenty yards.

Frequent and urgent appeals were made by the relatives and friends of the prisoner to be allowed to interview him, but those appeals, for reasons which must be manifest to every reader, were refused. The probability that some relative or sympathiser would attempt to provide him with a means of "cheating the gallows," if opportunity offered, induced the authorities to take every precaution; and no person was allowed to approach the dock where he was seated, lest some deadly weapon or poison phial should be handed to him. Dick Hart, who attended the court, and the prisoner were observed to frequently exchange nods and smiles, and the prisoner was noticed on several occasions to "throw kisses" to a young woman

in the gallery, who seized sly opportunities of respond-
ing to the silent act of endearment. A number of
ladies had been accommodated with seats near the
Bench, and these, with a curiosity natural to the sex,
stared rather frequently at the prisoner, the latter in
turn staring back at them until they were compelled
to turn their glances in another direction, when Kelly
quietly smiled to himself and looked away from them.

A committal followed as a matter of course, and
two months thereafter Ned Kelly was again prominently before the public in the Melbourne Criminal
Court being tried for the Mansfield murders. Judge
Barry presided, and the court was crowded with spectators. Mr. Bindon appeared for the prisoner, who
had evidently recovered his health, but who appeared
very listless, and only occasionally displayed interest
in the proceedings. At the commencement of the
trial his counsel applied for a postponement, but the
judge refused the application. The evidence taken
was very voluminous, McIntyre again being the chief
witness; and his evidence was most damning, remaining unshaken under remarkably keen cross-examination. The jury were not long in arriving at the verdict
which the reader has already anticipated—guilty of
wilful murder.

Ned Kelly heard the verdict without emotion, and
when asked if he had anything to say why sentence of
death should not be pronounced against him he very
coolly addressed the court in the following terms:
"Well, it is rather too late for me to speak now. I
thought of speaking this morning and all day, but
there was little use. There is little use blaming any-

one now. Nobody knew about my case except myself,
and I wish I had insisted on being allowed to examine
the witnesses myself. If I had examined them I am
confident I would have thrown a different light on the
case. It is not that I fear death; I fear it as little as
to drink a cup of tea. On the evidence that has been
given no juryman could have given any other verdict;
that is my opinion. But, as I say, if I had examined
the witnesses, I would have shown matters in a different light, because no man understood the case as
I do myself. I do not blame anybody, neither Mr.
Bindon nor Mr. Gaunson (who at an earlier stage had
conducted the defence); but Mr. Bindon knew nothing
about my case. I lay blame on myself that I did not
get up yesterday and examine the witnesses; but I
thought that if I did so it would look like bravado and
flashness."

The Judge then proceeded to pronounce sentence
of death; and the following interrupted deliverance
was made by him:—

His Honour: "Edward Kelly, the verdict pronounced by
the jury is one which you must have fully expected."

The prisoner: "Yes, under the circumstances."

His Honour: "No circumstances that I can conceive
could have altered the result of your trial."

The prisoner: "Perhaps not from what you now conceive,
but if you had heard me examine the witnesses it would have
been different."

His Honour: "I will give you credit for all the skill you
appear to desire to assume.

The prisoner: "No, I don't wish to assume anything.
There is no flashness or bravado about me.   It is not that
I want to save my life, but because I know I should have been
capable of clearing myself of the charge, and I could have
saved my life in spite of all against me."

His Honour: "The facts are so numerous and so con-
vincing, not only as regards the original offence with which
you are charged, but with respect to a long series of trans-

actions, covering a period of eighteen months, that no rational person would hesitate to arrive at any other conclusion but that the verdict of the jury is irresistible, and that it is right. I have no desire whatever to inflict upon you any personal remarks. It is not becoming that I should endeavour to aggravate the sufferings with which your mind must be sincerely agitated."

The prisoner: "No; I don't think that. My mind is as easy as the mind of any man in this world, as I am prepared to show before God and man."

His Honour: "It is blasphemous for you to say that. You appear to revel in the idea of having put men to death."

The prisoner: "More men than I have put men to death, but I am the last man in the world that would take a man's life. Two years ago—even if my own life was at stake—and I am confident, if I thought a man would shoot me—I would give him a chance of keeping his life, and would part rather with my own; but if I knew that through him innocent persons' lives were at stake, I certainly would have to shoot him if he forced me to do so; but I would want to know that he was really going to take innocent life."

His Honour: "Your statement involves a cruelly wicked charge of perjury against a phalanx of witnesses."

The prisoner: "I dare say; but a day will come, at a bigger court than this, when we shall see which is right and which is wrong. No matter how long a man lives he is bound to come to judgment somewhere, and as well here as anywhere. It will be different the next time there is a Kelly trial, for they are not all killed. It would have been for the good of the Crown had I examined the witnesses, and I would have stopped a lot of the reward, I can assure you, and I don't know but I won't do it yet if allowed."

His Honour: "An offence of this kind is of no ordinary character. Murders had been discovered which had been committed under circumstances of great atrocity. They proceeded from motives other than those which actuated you. They had their origin in many sources. Some have been committed from a sordid desire to take from others the property they had acquired; some from jealousy, some from a desire of revenge; but yours is a more aggravated crime, and one of larger proportions; for, with a party of men, you took arms against society, organised as it is for mutual protection and for respect of law."

The prisoner: "That is how the evidence came out here. It appeared that I deliberately took up arms of my own accord, and induced the other three men to join me for the purpose of doing nothing but shooting down the police."

His Honour: "In new communities, where the bonds of

society are not so well linked together as in older countries, there is unfortunately a class which disregards the evil consequences of crime. Foolish, inconsiderate, ill-conducted, and unprincipled youths unfortunately abound, and unless they are made to consider the consequences of crime, they are led to imitate notorious felons whom they regard as self-made heroes. It is right, therefore, that they should be asked to consider and reflect upon what the life of a felon is. A felon who has cut himself off from all, and who declines all the affections, charities, and obligations of society, is as helpless, and as degraded as a wild beast of the field; he has nowhere to lay his head; he has no one to prepare for him the comforts of life; he suspects his friends and he dreads his enemies. He is in constant alarm lest his pursuers should reach him, and his only hope is that he might lose his life in what he considers a glorious struggle for existence. That is the life of an outlaw or felon, and it would be well for those young men who are so foolish as to consider that it is brave of a man to sacrifice the lives of his fellow creatures in carrying out his own wild ideas, to see that it is a life to be avoided by every possible means, and to reflect that the unfortunate termination of a felon's life is a miserable death. New South Wales joined with Victoria in providing ample inducement to persons to assist in having you and your companions apprehended; but by some spell, which I cannot understand—a spell which exists in all lawless communities, more or less, and which may be attributed either to a sympathy for the outlaws, or a dread of the consequences which would result from the performances of their duty—no persons were found who would be tempted by the reward or love of country, or the love of order, to give you up. The love of obedience to the law has been set aside, for reasons difficult to explain, and there is something extremely wrong in a country where a lawless band of men are able to live for eighteen months disturbing society. You are self-accused. The statement was made voluntarily by yourself that you and your companions committed attacks on two banks, and appropriated therefrom large sums of money amounting to several thousands of pounds. Further, I cannot conceal from myself the fact that an expenditure of £50,000 has been rendered necessary in consequence of acts with which you and your party have been connected. We have had samples of felons, such as Bradley and O'Connor, Clarkes, Gardiner, Melville, Morgan, Scott, and Smith, all of whom have come to ignominious deaths. Still the effect expected from their punishment has not been produced. This is much to be deplored. When such examples as these are so often repeated, society must be re-organised, or it must soon be seriously affected. Your unfortunate and miserable companions have died a death which probably you might rather envy, but you are not offered the opportunity."

The prisoner: "I don't think there is much proof they did die the death."

His Honour: "In your case the law will be carried out by its officers. The gentlemen of the jury have done their duty, and my duty will be to forward to the proper quarter the notes of your trial, and to lay before the Executive all the circumstances connected with your trial that may be required. I can hold out to you no hope, and I do not see that I can entertain the slightest reason for saying that you can expect anything. I desire to spare you any more pain, and I absolve myself from saying anything willingly in any of my utterances that may have unnecessarily increased the agitation of your mind. I have now to pronounce your sentence." His Honour then sentenced the prisoner to death in the ordinary form, ending with the usual words "May the Lord have mercy on your soul."

The court was then cleared, and the prisoner was removed to the Melbourne gaol. Everything was very quiet, and nothing approaching to any scene occurred, although some of Kelly's relatives were in court at the time. In common with the other spectators they accepted the verdict and the sentence quite as a matter of course.

AGITATION FOR REPRIEVE.

Of late years it has been an unusual thing for a criminal to go to the gallows in any English-speaking community without an effort being made to obtain a reprieve, and the greater the criminal generally the stronger the effort made on his behalf. In the case of Ned Kelly, before the day for his execution had been fixed, an agitation in this direction was commenced in Melbourne, the brothers Gaunson, one of whom, at least, was well known in legal and political circles, being the centre around which the agitators gathered, and from which the appeals for the reprieve of this king of robber-murderers issued. Public meetings were held, and deputations were formed to wait upon prominent members of the Government, while petitions many yards long were prepared and signed and presented. The following extracts from Melbourne newspapers of the day will give the reader a good idea of the extent of the movement among a certain class of the population :—

The agitation for the reprieve of Edward Kelly was continued yesterday by William Gaunson. The proposed procession of ladies to Government House was not a success; but during the morning about two hundred persons of both sexes turned out from the back slums of the city, and assembled at the Town Hall. They had the impudence to enter the building, but Sub-inspector Larmer, with some constables, soon appeared on the scene, and turned them out. William Gaunson, with Mrs. Skillian, Kate Kelly, James Kelly, and Wild Wright eventually arrived and set out for Government House, with the unwashed-looking mob at their heels. At Princes' Bridge, Sub-inspector Larmer endeavoured to check the crowd, but not willing to use violence, he was obliged to let them pass. He, however, proceeded in front to the Domain gates, and had them closed. In the meantime Mr. Gaunson and his Kelly friends got into cabs. When the crowd reached the Domain gates they were refused admission; but, after a little discussion, the cabs and their occupants were admitted, and, drawing right up to Government House, the occupants, through Mr. Gaunson, requested an interview with the Governor. Captain Le Patourel, his Excellency's Private Secretary, received Mr. Gaunson, and told him that the Governor would positively receive no deputation that day. He intimated, however, that the petitions which were spoken of could be sent to his Excellency at the Treasury up to two o'clock, the hour appointed for the meeting of the Executive. The self-elected deputation then returned to town, and were followed by the crowd. Jim Kelly and Wild Wright, who returned on foot, were evidently objects of veneration to the mob, for they were accompanied by a large number of them through the streets to the Robert Burns Hotel, in Lonsdale-street West. Their loafing-looking retinue were not, however, satisfied with gazing at them in the streets, but they also besieged the hotel, crushing through the passages and into the rooms, in order to feast still further their morbid curiosity; and yet these people were just the kind of persons who would rush, if they had the chance, to see Ned Kelly hung, and who would gloat over the event in the afternoon. William Gaunson attended at the Treasury with Mrs. Skillian and Kate Kelly, to await the decision of the Executive Council, as if it had not been given a week ago. Over one thousand idle persons collected at the same time opposite the building. Mr. Gaunson and the Kelly sisters were admitted to a retiring-room, and the former handed Captain Le Patourel the petitions he had been getting signed for presentation to the Governor, stating that they contained 34,434 signatures. An examination of the petitions showed that they were signed principally in pencil, and by illiterate people, whilst whole pages were evidently written by one person. The Executive, of course, determined to adhere to their decision—that the convict shall be executed on Thursday morning. This having been communicated to the prisoner's relatives, they left, and returned to the Robert Burns Hotel. They were accompanied, as before, by a crowd, and during the whole afternoon and evening the hotel was rushed. Immediately after their return Jim Kelly addressed the crowd from the door, and told them that it was not all over yet, a remark that was loudly cheered. The three Kellys, Wild Wright, and Mrs. Jones (the keeper of the Glenrowan Hotel which was destroyed) are all living at the Robert Burns Hotel. On Thursday last, when the sisters visited their brother in gaol, they stated that they were going home on Saturday, and were told that they could see the condemned man again before they left. Since then, however, the Gaunsons have started the present agitation, and the consequence is that the sisters remain in town, but do not seek another interview with their brother. Another mass meeting is to be held to-morrow night on the Supreme Court Reserve, and petitions are being sent by William Gaunson all over the colony for signature. The object of this meeting is to carry a resolution in favour of a reprieve, and to present it to the Chief Secretary.

All efforts made were unavailing, however, and the day having been fixed for the execution by the Executive, the dread sentence of the law was carried out within the precincts of the gaol in which the wounded outlaw had been nursed back to life.

THE EXECUTION.

On the day preceding that upon which it had been decided the public hangman should perform his duty, the gaoler visited Ned Kelly in his cell and informed him that he must prepare for the worst, as there was not the slightest hope of a reprieve. The outlaw himself had made frequent written appeals for clemency, protesting that he had never intended to shed blood, but had been compelled to do so in his own defence; and knowing what his relatives and friends had been doing in his behalf outside, he entertained sanguine hopes of reprieve. Every hope was abandoned, however, before the fatal morning dawned, and he made an appearance of being resigned to the inevitable.

After sentence of death had been pronounced, additional precautions were taken by the gaol authorities to ensure the safe custody of the condemned man. He was placed in one of the cells of the old wing, and irons were rivetted upon his legs, leather pads being placed round his ankles to prevent chafing. The cell had two doors—an outer one of solid iron and an inner one of iron bars. The outer door was always kept open, a lamp was kept burning overhead, and a warder was continually outside watching the prisoner. During the day he was allowed to walk in the adjoining yard for exercise, and on these occasions two warders had him under surveillance. He continued to maintain his indifferent demeanour for a day or two, professing to look forward to his execution without fear, but he was then evidently buoyed up with the hope of reprieve. When he could get anyone to speak to, he indulged in "brag," recounting his exploits and boasting of what he could have done when he was at liberty if he had pleased. Latterly, however, his talkativeness ceased, and he became morose and silent. Within the last few days of his life he dictated a number of letters for the Chief Secretary, in most of which he simply repeated his well-known garbled version of his career, and the spurious reasons he assigned for his crimes. He never, however, expressed any sorrow for his crimes; on the contrary, he always attempted to justify them. In his last communication he made a request that his body might be handed over to his friends —an application that was necessarily in vain. At his own request his portrait was taken for circulation among his friends.

The mother and sisters paid him a farewell visit on the evening of the last day of his imprisonment, but not in company. The old lady, who was still an inmate of the gaol, was brought to his cell, and her last words to him were, "Mind you die like a Kelly, Ned!"

He was hanged the next morning at ten o'clock: the formal inquest was held a couple of hours afterwards, and the body was then coffined ready for burial by the authorities on the following day. An immense crowd of persons had congregated outside the gaol, but there was no disturbance.

A few of the more dangerous sympathisers with the Kelly gang were prosecuted under the Felons' Apprehension Act; but the great end of police effort —the destruction of the gang—having been compassed, the authorities did not trouble very much to bring to account the men and women who, while the outlaws were at large, acted as their "scouts," emissaries, and providers. Mrs. Jones, the licensee of the house at Glenrowan which formed the last temporary shelter of the murderous quartette, was prosecuted, in company with one or two others, for harbouring; but the case was not pressed so severely as it would have been had the charge been preferred before Ned Kelly and his companions had been brought to their account. And the fate of the gang was a far more powerful deterrent of lawlessness in the district than any amount of police activity would have been. Within a week from the execution, the colony, as far as bushranging was concerned, was at peace. That peace had certainly been purchased at great cost. Under proper administration in the police force, it should have been won more easily and at far less cost to the State. But although expressions of disfavour were heard in the Victorian Parliament when a return was submitted showing that the capture of the outlaws had involved an expenditure of about £40,000—not counting the "pay" of those engaged in the search, and which amounted to an additional £75,000—there was really very little complaining among the people from whose treasury the cheques had been drawn; for they saw that the necessity for capturing the ruffians who were working such terrible mischief in the community could not be weakened in the slightest degree by any monetary consideration. The preservation of the morality of the community, the protection of the people's lives and property, and the vindication of the law, were matters of so high importance that they could not be weighed in golden scales. Nevertheless, the fact remained that had the police force of Victoria, in its higher grades particularly, been more efficient, there would have been less expenditure of public money and, what is of far more importance, less sacrifice of human life.

THE BLACK-TRACKERS AND THEIR WORK.

A brief reference to the Queensland black-trackers, who were feared so greatly by the Kellys, and their work in this connection, will doubtless prove interesting to the reader. They were called "native troopers" in official circles, and they had been engaged by the Victorian Government for the purpose of tracking the bushrangers to their haunts. They were six in number, and were placed, as I have already stated, under the direction of Sub-Inspector Stanhope O'Connor, of the Queensland Native Mounted Police. Their names were:—Hero, Johnny, Jimmy, Jack, Barney, and Sambo, the latter being a corporal in the corps to which he was attached. Each man was armed with a Snider and a revolver, and wore a blue uniform with red facings. They were members of various tribes located in the south and north of Queensland respectively, and were enlisted for five years when they were quite young by Mr. O'Connor. The oldest was only 24 years of age, and the youngest about 18, and some of them had been in the force seven or eight years, during which they had seen some very active service, and over and over again demonstrated their capabilities as trackers. They were, indeed, the best of the kind that could be selected, and had fequently followed horse-stealers and cattle-duffers to their haunts. Their bravery was undoubted, for it was proved by conflicts with Chinese rioters in the north of Queensland, and with mobs of predatory and murderous aboriginals, when these were attacked in their strongholds. It might seem an easy thing for troopers armed with rifles to attack and defeat a mob of aboriginals, but the spears of the blacks of tropical Queensland, with the aid of wommeras, were most terrible weapons, and carried almost certain death with them at a hundred yards. It required no small amount of courage to face a shower of them, or to chase through long grass or thick scrub those who were capable of hurling them with almost scientific precision.

The pay the troopers received was £3 a month each, with uniform and quarters, but out of the money they had to contribute something towards the cost of their rations. Those who were engaged in the Kelly campaign received £3 a month, and had everything necessary provided for them. These men could follow fresh tracks of men, horses, or cattle at a gallop, but unfortunately in Victoria their powers of discernment were not very frequently tested in the requisite direction. Notwithstanding this, their eagerness for pursuit remained unabated, and on one occasion they were instrumental in bringing two marauders to justice. They were dreadfully sea-sick on the voyage to Sydney, and during his journey to Victoria, Corporal Sambo contracted congestion of the lungs, from which he died. This poor fellow was kindly attended to by one of the police of Victoria, with whom he was a great favourite, and was buried at Benalla. It speaks well for all of them that no complaints were made against any of them in Victoria, but that, on the contrary, they were described as a credit to any force. They seemed to be favourites with everyone who knew them, except the Kellys.

After reaching Sydney, the troopers proceeded direct by way of Wagga Wagga to Benalla, where their headquarters were established. Captain Standish met them on their arrival there, and two days after Mr. O'Connor had been sworn in as a sub-inspector of the Victorian police, they were set to work, as the place in which they were located was in the midst of the Kelly district and populated with Kelly sympathisers. It was thought on their arrival that the gang were moving about in the district, and what were confidently affirmed to be their tracks were followed for four days, when they ran into a hut in the King River Ranges. Rain then fell and obliterated the tracks, and the troopers returned to Benalla in consequence. Whether the tracks were those of the gang was not proved. The troopers were placed on numerous other tracks, which, however, all turned out to be those of ordinary travellers. Every mark that had a suspicion of the Kellys about it was scrutinised with the deepest interest, but it could not be stated with confidence that the men were ever in pursuit of the outlaws. If they were, they were set to work too late —when the tracks had become too weatherworn to be read distinctly. Unfortunately for the cause of justice they could not move out of their quarters without creating a sensation. Their movements were at once telegraphed to the Kellys, who were quickly off to the fastnesses. The value of their aid was promptly recognised by the Victorian authorities, and on one occasion they had a slice of luck which compensated them for many disappointments. It transpired in connection with the Lancefield bank robbery. The troopers proceeded by special train to Kilmore, and then rode to Lancefield. Here it was stated that the two robbers had gone to a public house and bought some provisions. Their tracks were quickly picked up, and followed along highways and byways and through paddocks to where the robbers had made a meal, and then on until it was ascertained that the men had hired a spring-cart and been driven to Sandhurst. A telegram explaining this was sent to that town, and the robbers, on arrival, found themselves in the hands of expectant police, who took care of them until they were tried and convicted. The troopers returned to headquarters, and were again subjected to false alarms. In one instance they travelled to a spot where it was said that the Kelly gang were taking down the telegraph wires, but they found only a company of reapers, whose reaping machine had got foul of a telegraph pole.

Ned Kelly and his associates made no secret of the fact that they were in constant dread of the trackers, whom they designated "—— black devils," and yet for some reason that has never been satisfactorily explained, Sub-Inspector O'Connor and his charges were in Melbourne and on their way home when the news of Sherritt's murder reached headquarters. Mr. O'Connor, however, was at once requested to proceed to Beechworth and thence to Sherritt's house, with the view of picking up tracks, and he obeyed, with the result already known. It was intended to make Beechworth the temporary headquarters of the troopers, and it was to that town the special train so fortunately stopped by Mr. Curnow was proceeding.

This accounts for the presence of Mrs. O'Connor and another lady in the train, and consequently their presence at the annihilation of the gang. The ladies intended staying at Beechworth until the labours of the trackers were completed; but the services of the latter were no longer required, the tragedy at Mrs. Jones' public house at once putting an end to the career of the Kellys, and opening the way for the return of the trackers to their headquarters in Queensland.

When the reward money of £8,000 was divided, each of the trackers received £50, and Sub-Inspector O'Connor £237 15s.

THE END OF GANG BUSHRANGING.

With the Kellys there died gang bushranging in Victoria. Isolated cases of bushranging there have been since, it is true; but a "run" of a week, or a month at most, has invariably brought the solitary "ranger" to the last of his exploits.

To say that Ned Kelly was the "Last of the Bushrangers" is not literally correct; yet in the sense that he was the leader of the last gang, that term may be fittingly applied to him. Australia has outgrown its days of bushranging such as that followed by the characters imperfectly sketched in this story; although, like countries of larger experience and greater age, it is still troubled with criminals of other types. With these, however, I have nothing here to do; and in bringing this history of Australian bushranging to a close, I am assured the reader will join with me in an expression of thankfulness that this particular phase of criminality, together with the conditions that gave it birth and promoted its growth, has disappeared, never more to be revived in this "sunny Southern land."

THE END